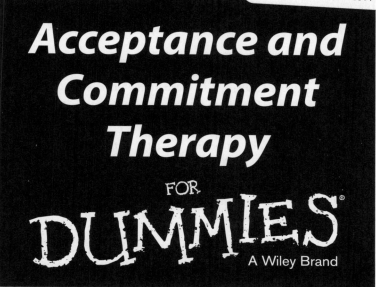

Acceptance and Commitment Therapy

FOR DUMMIES

A Wiley Brand

by Dr Freddy Jackson Brown & Dr Duncan Gillard

Foreword by Steven C. Hayes, PhD
Foundation Professor of Psychology, University of Nevada
and Co-Developer of ACT

FOR DUMMIES

A Wiley Brand

Acceptance and Commitment Therapy **For Dummies**®

Published by: **John Wiley & Sons, Ltd., The Atrium, Southern Gate, Chichester,** www.wiley.com

This edition first published 2016

© 2016 by John Wiley & Sons, Ltd., Chichester, West Sussex

Registered Office

John Wiley & Sons, Ltd., The Atrium, Southern Gate, Chichester, West Sussex, PO19 8SQ, United Kingdom

For details of our global editorial offices, for customer services and for information about how to apply for permission to reuse the copyright material in this book, please see our website at www.wiley.com.

For general information on our other products and services, please contact our Customer Care Department within the U.S. at 877-762-2974, outside the U.S. at 317-572-3993, or fax 317-572-4002. For technical support, please visit www.wiley.com/techsupport.

Wiley publishes in a variety of print and electronic formats and by print-on-demand. Some material included with standard print versions of this book may not be included in e-books or in print-on-demand. If this book refers to media such as a CD or DVD that is not included in the version you purchased, you may download this material at http://booksupport.wiley.com. For more information about Wiley products, visit www.wiley.com.

A catalogue record for this book is available from the British Library.

Library of Congress Control Number: 2015960021

ISBN 978-1-119-10628-9 (pbk); ISBN 978-1-119- 10629-6 (ebk); ISBN 978-1-119- 10630-2 (ebk)

Printed and Bound in Great Britain by TJ International, Padstow, Cornwall.

10 9 8 7 6 5 4 3 2 1

Contents at a Glance

Table of Contents

Foreword

Successful businesses across the world apply this simple principle: focus more on the few things that do a lot, rather than the many things that do a little.

This is such a book.

If you look at the table of contents for this book you will see that after a handful or two of short chapters it bangs through a pretty incredible list of important topics: love, anxiety, depression, anger, pain, addiction, work and even psychosis. And every one of those later chapters shows how psychological flexibility applies.

Is that even possible?

It turns out that it is. ACT is about the few core things in psychology that make an important difference in lots and lots of different areas. Last time I counted there were over 125 controlled studies (and hundreds more of lesser kinds) showing that the small set of skills that ACT targets makes a difference virtually everywhere that human minds go.

This is an *ACT For Dummies* book, but you could also call it an *ACT for When You Are Too Smart for You Own Good* book. Minds do not know when to stop! They are figuring it all out even when what they need to do is just be quiet and let people learn new ways of being and doing. There is a conflict between how your analytical mind works and how learning by direct experience works. Our analytical minds are great for doing taxes – but they are awful at getting over past hurts. Your minds are great in the role of a tool and lousy when put in the role of being the boss or dictator. What ACT does is to teach you *how* to put your mind on a leash – so you can use it when you want rather than it using you when it wants.

This book will help. There is nothing dumb about that!

Steven C Hayes, PhD

Foundation Professor of Psychology, University of Nevada

Co-developer of ACT

Introduction

· ·

*A*cceptance and Commitment Therapy (said as one word, 'ACT') is an evidence-based psychological intervention that uses acceptance and mindfulness techniques alongside behaviour change strategies to help you live life according to what really matters to you. Based on recent break-throughs in understanding how language works, ACT offers a genuinely original perspective on the human condition and the challenge everyone faces in living a life with meaning and purpose.

ACT is all about doing the things that really matter to you and not letting your mind get in the way. Often, without you realising it, your mind — what goes on in your head — can push you around and interfere with your daily life. You're so connected with your thoughts that you don't always notice what they do and, importantly, what they stop you doing. But your mind is really just a tool and, like all tools, is good at solving certain problems and pretty hopeless at addressing others. ACT shows you how to use your mind for what it's good at and then to set it aside when your thoughts are less helpful.

To help you get on with the life you want to be living, ACT uses a range of exercises to enable you to become more open, aware and active:

- ✔ *Openness* involves stepping forward into life and accepting all that comes with it.
- ✔ *Awareness* means increasing your connection with the world around you rather than living in your head.
- ✔ Being *active* is about doing the things that truly matter to you.

This is an exciting time for ACT. Every month, new research articles and books explore how it can be applied in different settings and to a host of human problems. In fact, so many new applications are being developed that there's insufficient space in this book to cover them all. Rather, we provide a general introduction to ACT with the aim of helping you understand the central principles, ideas and practices that underpin the model. Contrary to popular belief, doing the things that really matter to you can be quite difficult. And the reason for that, according to ACT, is human language. While language enables you to do amazing things, it also allows you to ruminate on the past and worry about the future. And when you become overly entangled in your thoughts you stop living the life you want to be living — and instead your life is dictated by your anger, fears, worries and doubts. This insight isn't particularly new, but where ACT differs to other approaches is in how it responds to these events. Rather than tackling this negativity head on, ACT shows you new ways to relate to your thoughts, feelings and emotions so that they have less impact on your day-to-day life.

About This Book

If you want to know more about ACT and how to apply it to your own life, then this book's for you. In broad terms, we:

- ✔ Describe how the ACT model builds your psychological flexibility by helping you become more open, aware and active.

- ✔ Explain the scientific processes and concepts upon which ACT is based and how these relate to your everyday life.

- ✔ Provide exercises and activities to help you understand ACT and create positive change in your life.

- ✔ Offer an explanation of the new theory of language, Relational Frame Theory (RFT), which underpins ACT.

- ✔ Relate ACT to real-life challenges, such as weight problems and anger management, as well as more complex mental health difficulties, like anxiety and depression.

Developing new ways to relate to your own thoughts, feelings and memories (collectively, your 'mind') takes practice and can't be achieved through the understanding that results from reading alone. Understanding how to relate to your thoughts differently isn't enough; you actually need to practise the necessary skills directly to be able to do it. It's rather like learning to swim — no amount of reading or knowledge about swimming will ever be a substitute for getting into the water and learning how to swim directly. The exercises in this book aim to help you 'learn to swim in your mental world'. While these experiential exercises aren't always easy to do, they're central to ACT and we recommend that you try as many as possible.

While reading the whole book will give you the fullest picture of what ACT involves, it's not necessary for it to be useful to you. It's better to think of this book as a general reference guide about ACT rather than a manual that needs to be read sequentially. That said, we do recommend that you read the chapters in Part I sequentially because we wrote it that way to take you through the key features of the ACT model. Reading those chapters in the order in which they're written, while not absolutely necessary, enables you to find out about ACT in a systematic way, without any gaps. The chapters in the rest of the book can be read in whatever order you fancy.

Of course, the downside of ensuring that each chapter has enough information in it to make sense on its own is that some repetition of ideas exists. We've endeavoured to keep this to a minimum but you will note some recurrence of key points. On the upside, it means you'll have multiple opportunities to make sense of the core principles, ideas and exercises.

Throughout the book you'll find sidebars that provide additional detail that's interesting but not necessary to understanding the main text. You can read them if you choose.

Foolish Assumptions

We've assumed some things about you and why you're reading this book:

- ✔ You have little or no prior knowledge about ACT or the ideas that underpin it.

- ✔ You're a layperson who wants to know more about how ACT works and how to apply the ideas to your own life, or you're a professional therapist who wants to broaden your knowledge.

- ✔ You're motivated to try all the exercises because you understand that to benefit from ACT you have to directly engage with it.

Finally, a comment on the technical language we use from time to time. While we try to avoid being overly technical, sometimes 'therapy speak' is necessary because an understanding of the subject matter isn't fully possible without it. When you come across technical terms and explanations, we advise you to stick with them but not worry about understanding them all in one go. It's often better to skim read the text a couple of times to get the general picture and thus not get bogged down and frustrated. Because the chapters often repeat or build on ACT concepts, you gradually come to understand the technical details.

Icons Used in This Book

For Dummies books use icons to alert you to important details in the text. We use the following:

We use this icon to signal a new term you may not have encountered before, or at least not in the way we use it.

This icon draws your attention to a key point or something that's useful to bear in mind for the future.

This icon highlights practical advice and guidance that can help you understand how to apply an ACT principle or work through an exercise.

This icon points out practical exercises and activities.

Beyond the Book

In addition to the material in the print or e-book you're reading right now, this product also comes with some access-anywhere goodies on the web. Check out the free Cheat Sheet at www.dummies.com/cheatsheet/acceptance andcommitmenttherapy for helpful tips and pointers to help you understand ACT and how to apply it to your life. You can also find extra articles at www.dummies.com/extras/acceptanceandcommitmenttherapy.

Where to Go from Here

A good place to start is Chapter 1! It sets out some of the basic ideas that we expand on in more detail in subsequent chapters. After that, you can read the rest of the chapters in Part I as we recommend, or check out the contents and jump into whichever chapter you feel is relevant to you at the time.

Part I
Getting Started with Acceptance and Commitment Therapy

Find more about ACT and many other topics at www.dummies.com.

In this part . . .

✔ Discover the basic ACT model and how it applies to
your life.

✔ Learn more about the nature and origins of human suffering
from an ACT perspective.

✔ Explore how to use ACT techniques to engage in a fuller and
more meaningful life.

✔ Use mindfulness to enhance your wellbeing.

Chapter 1

Introducing ACT

In This Chapter

▶ Recognising what matters to you

▶ Working on your psychological flexibility

▶ Taking an active approach to your own life

*A*cceptance and Commitment Therapy (ACT) is a genuinely new way of understanding the human condition. Informed by the scientific understanding of language, it offers a radically different perspective on human cognition and emotion and why human beings can struggle to be happy.

ACT is an evidence-based Cognitive Behavioural Therapy (CBT) that uses acceptance and mindfulness techniques alongside behaviour change strategies to help you live in line with what really matters to you. While the 'T' in ACT stands for *therapy*, ACT goes beyond that: it provides a framework for a deeper understanding of what it is to be human and, more specifically, how to live your life with purpose, openness, vitality and fun!

ACT has never been needed more. In spite of being materially wealthy, many people in Western societies struggle to find a sense of meaning, happiness and fulfilment in their everyday lives. Psychological distress and mental health problems result. ACT was developed (and is continuing to be developed) in response to these challenges.

This chapter explains how your linguistic ability to evaluate parts of your own experience as negative, and therefore something to be avoided, can get in the way of doing the things that matter to you. ACT shows you how to respond more flexibly to your experiences so that, rather than battling against yourself, you can live in line with what truly matters to you.

Doing What Matters

Put simply, ACT aims to help people identify their values and then to live consistently and openly with them. This is important because when you live in line with your values you're more likely to feel that your life has meaning and direction. And conversely, when you don't do what matters, you can feel frustrated, unfulfilled and dissatisfied, even anxious and depressed.

You may think that doing the things you feel are important would be pretty easy — unfortunately, that's not the case. Human beings are well-practised at delaying, avoiding, stopping or simply not starting things that really matter to them. For example, even though the following things may be important to you, you may:

- Not contact family or friends on a regular basis
- Give up on diets
- Abandon exercise programmes
- Remain in the same job even though you're fed up with it
- Avoid asking people on dates
- Not clean the house

Take a moment to think about your own life. When did you last avoid, delay or stop doing something that really mattered to you? You can probably think of numerous examples. It's a curious fact that doing what matters to you isn't always easy or straightforward. But why is this? According to ACT, experiential avoidance is the answer.

Experiential avoidance means being unwilling to experience unwanted thoughts, feelings or bodily sensations and engaging in counterproductive behaviour to avoid them (check out the nearby sidebar, 'Experiential avoidance and rejection', for an example).

Figure 1-1 shows how human beings, like all animals, generally approach things that lead to positive experiences and avoid those that lead to negative ones. Behaving in this way makes complete sense in evolutionary terms, because it means you're more likely to avoid dangerous situations and embrace people and experiences that are good for you.

Experiential avoidance and rejection

Recent research into the relationship between experiential avoidance and interpersonal problems found that the sample of 159 university students demonstrated a strong association between experiential avoidance and social traits such as coldness, social evasion and hostility. The researchers concluded that, in an effort to hide their anxiety, individuals behaved in cold and impersonal ways or attempted to avoid social interactions altogether. In effect, their fear of rejection encouraged them to act in ways that increased the likelihood of rejection. In terms of relationships, US President Franklin D Roosevelt appears to have been correct in his assertion that, 'The only thing we have to fear is fear itself'.

Figure 1-1: Turning your back on negative experiences and seeking out the positive.

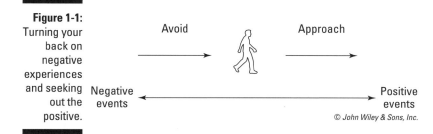

© John Wiley & Sons, Inc.

For human beings, however, the situation is more complex. Because language enables people to evaluate their thoughts and feelings as good or bad, it's easy for people to move towards or away from their own experiences — even when doing so isn't in their best interests. If you evaluate part of your experience as 'bad', you'll be inclined to stop doing the things that led to it even if doing so also stops you doing what you really want. Consider walking up a mountain. Before you start out you may have doubts about whether you can do it and, during the hike, you'll inevitably experience some physical discomfort as you go higher. If you're not prepared to experience these negative thoughts and feelings, you won't experience what it's like to walk in the mountains.

Figure 1-2 shows this situation pictorially — unwillingness to experience negative thoughts and feelings causes you to turn around and move away from the things that matter to you. While doing so may solve the immediate problem — you reduce the impact of negative thoughts and feelings — unfortunately, it also creates another problem: you're now no longer moving in a valued life direction. Experiential avoidance is occurring!

Turning the tables on avoidance

Nic, a university lecturer and ACT researcher, has turned experiential avoidance on its head. He realised that avoidance was getting in the way of his ability to learn new skills, meet new people and connect with life. And because meeting people and learning new skills were important to him, he took a somewhat radical step. Now every time he notices any resistance to doing something, rather than letting this feeling dictate his actions, he automatically steps forward and does it. This approach doesn't always make life easy for him, but by refusing to allow his life to be dominated by avoidance, he's behaving in ways that are consistent with his values of openness, learning, exploration and fun. And he sleeps all the better for it!

Figure 1-2:
Avoiding negative experiences can mean you miss out on the good things life has to offer.

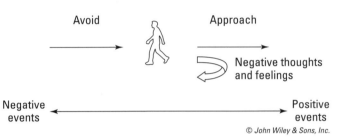

© John Wiley & Sons, Inc.

As well as interfering with everyday life, experiential avoidance can be a major contributor to mental health problems. Avoiding daily doubts, reservations or sources of emotional discomfort is one thing, but some people who experience highly disturbing thoughts and memories go to even greater extremes in order to evade them, such as disassociation or drug and alcohol misuse. When this happens, their solution becomes their problem.

Increasing Your Psychological Flexibility

You can counteract your inclination to avoid parts of your own experience by becoming more psychologically flexible.

Psychological flexibility is your ability to be open to all your experiences — good and bad — while simultaneously doing the things that are consistent with your values. With a strong sense of psychological flexibility, negative thoughts and feelings are no longer barriers to doing the things that you want to be doing.

ACT focuses on six core processes associated with psychological flexibility. Although they're set out as distinct processes, lots of overlap exists between them. And, while they can be applied individually, ACT is really about all six processes functioning together as one.

The six core processes are:

- ✔ **Values:** Deciding what you want your life to be about and the on-going actions that take your life in those directions

- ✔ **Committed action:** Doing those things that bring your values to life

- ✔ **Acceptance:** Noticing, accepting and embracing all your experiences, especially the unwanted or negative ones

- ✔ **Defusion:** Noticing your thoughts and thinking processes, without being inside them or trying to alter or control them

- ✔ **Contact with the present moment:** Being fully aware of your experiences as they're occurring here and now

- ✔ **Self as context:** Getting in touch with your deep sense of self — the 'you' who sits just behind your eyes, who observes and experiences, and yet is distinct from your own thoughts, feelings and memories

  We return to these six core processes in Chapter 3 so that you can really understand how they work and link together. Here, it's important to understand that ACT aims to enhance your psychological flexibility so that you can get on with doing what matters.

Living a Life that's True to Your Values

In ACT, the things you really care about, deep down inside, and want your life to stand for are called your values. They're not specific items or goals that you can hold or achieve; rather, they're statements that reflect how you want to behave in life on an ongoing basis. For example, 'being a loving partner', 'being healthy' or 'reducing my impact on the environment' are values as they describe how you want to behave towards other people, yourself or the world in general. You can think of values as the directions you want your life to be going in as they guide your behaviour to reflect what's important for you.

Even though being true to your values leads to a greater sense of purpose and contentment in life, doing so isn't always easy. It can involve doing things that you may not actually want to do at that particular moment — for example, communicating calmly with your children when you're very angry or making a cup of tea for your partner when you feel upset with him. Doing these things in the service of your values of being a good parent and a loving partner means that you're being true to what you hold most dear.

Accepting Life

Many traditional therapeutic approaches focus on changing or altering unwanted or troublesome thoughts and feelings. ACT is different in that it works to change how you *relate* to these events rather than to change them directly. The aim is to become more open to, and accepting of, your thoughts and feelings instead of battling against them.

ACT takes this approach because research carried out over the last 20 years or so indicates that people have much less control over their thoughts and feelings than they often think they do. For example, while you can choose to think about different things, such as a red car or a polar bear, you can't sustain these thoughts for anything other than short periods before your attention moves on to something else. And if you try your best not to think about something, then the opposite happens and you end thinking about it all the more. These findings (and what does your own experience tell you?) mean that your efforts to control, minimise or avoid your thoughts can only ever have marginal success. Chapters 7 and 11 explain in more detail how your thoughts work.

A similar situation exists with your emotions. What you feel depends on what's happened to you, and this means that you can't change how you feel at any one point in time without first changing your past. Of course, that's impossible, and so attempts to manage or change your feelings in the present won't be successful.

The aim of ACT is to help people live open and fulfilling lives, which is difficult to do if they're spending lots of their time trying to change, control or avoid things that can't be easily changed, controlled or avoided. For this reason, acceptance is so important. When faced with things you can't change, your best option is usually to accept them. This challenge is nicely summed up by Reinhold Niebuhr's *Serenity Prayer*:

Grant me the serenity to accept the things

I cannot change,

The courage to change the things I can,

And the wisdom to know the difference.

Acceptance provides an alternative to experiential avoidance as a way to engage with life. In practising acceptance you create the space to do the things that really matter to you rather than waste your time and energy on trying to control the uncontrollable. This doesn't mean that everything you do will be successful. Some things you do will work out and others won't, but at least you're now doing the things that are important to you rather than trying to control or avoid the things you don't like. At the end of each day you can then rest your head on the pillow and fall asleep knowing you've lived according to your values.

And something else happens when you practise acceptance: life becomes less scary and less focused on the negatives. It transpires that your unpleasant thoughts and feelings aren't as bad as you think they are. Sure, they're not very nice, but they aren't something you need to unduly worry about much of the time. And they certainly aren't things to which you need to devote significant energy trying to avoid or control.

Defusing from Your Thoughts

Human language can occur in the public domain (speech and writing) and the private domain (thoughts and cognitions). While human language is an essential part of modern life and helps you with all kinds of challenges and problems, when you become too attached to its literal content it can also lead to difficulties.

When you believe that your thoughts reflect the world accurately (as it 'really' is), they can have a greater influence over how you behave. Allowing your thoughts (and language in general) to direct your actions is problematic for a number of reasons. For a start, your thoughts are usually negative and often wrong. And even when they're accurate, your thoughts aren't always useful to you in terms of living in line with your values. Consider a young woman who wants to quit smoking. She might have the thought, 'A cigarette right now would relax me'. And such a thought may be accurate; having a cigarette may indeed allow her to relax. However, being 'fused' with (believing it literally) and acting on that thought would move the young woman no closer to her value of healthy living.

Defusion is the process by which you gain some distance from your thoughts, cognitions and language by reducing their believability. It involves becoming aware of your thoughts (and your thinking processes) and not being stuck inside them. ACT uses lots of different experiential techniques to help you discover how to become less attached to the literal content of your thoughts.

When you see your thoughts as just bits of private language in your head, you reduce their influence on your behaviour and this enables you to act in line with your values.

Recognising that ACT Is an Experiential Learning Process

ACT is an experiential learning process. Most chapters in this book contain exercises for you to complete and learn from. While we can describe what ACT involves (such as its six core process and psychological flexibility; check out Chapter 3), doing so won't tell you what these processes feel like or, more importantly, what they *do*. For that, a direct experiential process is necessary. You can only learn how to swim (and what swimming is like) by getting in the pool — and ACT is the same.

The good news is that, while the exercises take some effort, they're often also fun.

Think of ACT as an acronym for three basic steps:

1. **Accept your thoughts, feelings and bodily sensations.** Because you can't really avoid or control how you think and what you feel, you're better off accepting these experiences.

2. **Choose your life values.** Spending your time trying to manage or avoid the things you don't want isn't a positive way to exist; instead, put your energy into identifying what matters to you — your values — and defining how you want to live.

3. *Take action.* Start doing the things that matter to you. Begin with small steps and gradually build bigger and bigger patterns of behaviour that are informed by your values. If you want to become fitter, for example, begin with a gentle walk or short jog. Soon you'll be able to run farther and faster and eventually you may run a marathon!

Accepting those things in life that you can't change is the challenge everyone faces. It isn't easy, but it's often your best option nonetheless. Next, you need to decide what's important to you and how you want to live your life, so that you can focus on what matters. This can be tricky too, but the prize is everything — it's a life filled with purpose, vitality, meaning and fun.

Chapter 2

Understanding that a Little Unhappiness Is Normal

*E*very day people struggle to live meaningful and positive lives. Rather than feeling energised and upbeat, people often report feeling anxious, stressed or depressed. What's going on? Why do people find it so hard to be happy or to do the things that matter to them? According to recent break-throughs in psychological science, the root cause of our suffering is human language and how we respond to it.

Your language is what enables you to remember sad events from the past or worry about things that may happen in the future. These events in them-selves, though unpleasant, aren't necessarily problematic. But it's when you try to control or avoid them that you can get into trouble and embark on a road that takes you away from doing the things that really matter to you and leads to yet more psychological suffering.

This chapter looks at how your language enables you to evaluate your own experiences as well as events in the external world. We introduce the assumption of healthy normality and how it encourages you to try to avoid or control those parts of your experience that you evaluate negatively. This chapter also begins to describe how ACT offers an alternative way forward, in which you connect with your values and what really matters to you in life rather than try to avoid or control your negative thoughts and feelings.

Linking Language and Human Suffering

Language is at the heart of humanity's greatest achievements, from science, engineering and architecture to literature, music and art. In many ways, language is the defining feature of human beings and it sets us apart from the other animals on this planet.

Language enables you to:

- Think
- Remember
- Dream and aspire
- Plan and arrange
- Co-operate and organise

But language also has a darker side, which makes it possible for you to:

- Worry
- Experience regret
- Ruminate
- Fret and feel fearful
- Remember past difficulties and trauma

Some of these more negative mental processes can be useful, of course. Worrying about things can help you to understand what's happening and then to do something about it. But sometimes your thoughts and feelings can come to dominate your experience to such an extent that they interfere with your ability to get on with your life.

Struggling with your thoughts and emotions

Even when life is good, you can still worry and feel anxious or sad. Other animals aren't like humans in this regard. Give a dog a good meal, some exercise and a warm place to sleep and it will be quite content — every day! Of course, animals can be anxious or distressed, but only when they're in negative or adverse circumstances. In contrast, human beings can experience negative thoughts and feel lost, scared and alone at any time. And it's language that enables this to happen. If the events you think about are negative, you'll experience negative feelings no matter what your immediate circumstances.

Non-human animals don't have this problem because they don't have the same language ability. How human language functions is at the heart of ACT. ACT is based on a new theory of language called *Relational Frame Theory* (*RFT*). This theory provides a contextual account of language that has wide-ranging implications for psychological wellbeing and, indeed, almost all walks of human life.

Although RFT is central to ACT, an understanding of it isn't necessary here. You don't need to know how an engine works in order to drive a car, and neither is knowledge of RFT a requirement before engaging in ACT (if you do want to know more, check out Chapter 11, which covers RFT in detail).

Differentiating between public and private language

It is useful to be aware that language occurs in two distinct domains — public and private. *Public language* refers to any shared form of symbolic communication and includes:

- ✔ Spoken words
- ✔ Written words
- ✔ Signing
- ✔ Semaphore and Morse code
- ✔ Poetry

Private language refers to your mental processes, or what you experience 'inside your head', and includes:

- ✔ Thinking
- ✔ Planning
- ✔ Remembering
- ✔ Judging
- ✔ Evaluating
- ✔ Criticising

Although public and private language look and feel quite different, the same core processes underpin them. Essentially, language enables you to link different stimuli together into arbitrary relations (here we use *stimuli* as a general term for different objects, events or processes). For instance, the word 'dog' is an arbitrary collection of letters (themselves arbitrary marks) and there's nothing dog-like about them (as Figure 2-1 demonstrates). The relationship between 'dog' and an actual dog is merely an arbitrary social convention and this relationship forms the basis of what's termed language.

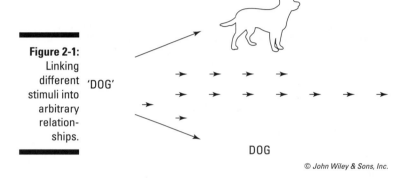

Figure 2-1: Linking different stimuli into arbitrary relationships.

© John Wiley & Sons, Inc.

Language enables you to link all sorts of things together, which can be really useful. But how you relate to language can cause problems, and it's these problems that ACT seeks to address. The rest of this chapter looks at how you relate to language in more detail and, in particular, how your capacity to evaluate the world can cause you difficulties.

Evaluating Yourself

As a human being you're very good at scanning the world around you and evaluating it for opportunities and dangers. This ability has clear adaptive and survival benefits and maximises your effectiveness in any given environment. It enables you to identify issues and then to quickly engage in problem-solving behaviours. In other words, when you see something you don't like you can avoid it or change it in some way. For example, if your washing machine breaks down you may feel a little upset and think, 'Now I've got to get rid of it and buy a new one'. This thought makes perfect sense if you don't want to wash your clothes by hand.

Problems can arise, however, when you apply this same strategy to the world inside your skin. That is, when you evaluate what you think and how you feel and then treat these thoughts and feelings in the same way as external events. Noticing a negative psychological experience, for example, you may think, 'I don't like this feeling or that memory; I'm going to get rid of it'. Responding to your thoughts and feelings in this way is a mistake because you simply don't have enough control over them to make doing so a successful strategy.

While you can evaluate both a broken washing machine and an unpleasant thought or feeling as being negative, you can't respond to them in the same way. Thoughts and feelings aren't like things in the external world, such as spiders, apples or dogs, for the important reason that they can't be as easily controlled or avoided. You can pick up spiders, eat apples and avoid going to a park popular with dogs, but the way language works means that you haven't got the same level of control over what you think and how you feel.

A simple fact of life is that from time to time you, like everyone else, will experience negative thoughts, feelings and physical sensations. The less willing you are to remain in contact with these events, the more likely you are to engage in counterproductive or even harmful attempts to avoid or change these experiences. ACT calls this behaviour *experiential avoidance* and sees it as the root of human suffering and mental health difficulties.

While it can seem a good option in the short term, experiential avoidance often just adds to your problems. For example, an anxious person may not leave the house so as to avoid uncomfortable feelings of anxiety, but as a result she can't go out to work, do the shopping or visit relatives. Similarly, a depressed person may think he's feeling too low to be good company and thus decline an invitation to a party. Declining enables him to avoid dealing with difficult thoughts or feelings in social situations, but he's also missing out on seeing friends. And if seeing friends is something he values and cares about, not seeing them will add to his sense of depression.

ACT argues that, by acknowledging and accepting your difficult thoughts and feelings, rather than seeking to change or avoid them, you can create the space to begin working towards valued life goals. In turn, doing so can reduce the unpleasant feelings (though not necessarily) and, more importantly, enable you to get on with living the life you want, defined by your values.

Experiential avoidance is an important concept in ACT and we explore it further in Chapter 9.

The following sections look at some assumptions you may hold about your thoughts and feelings, and examine how much control over them you actually have.

Wondering if thought control is possible

You may assume you can control your thoughts but, in fact, you have much less influence than you think. Try the exercise below to see how true this is.

Take a moment to think about an apple. Close your eyes and picture it — its colour, shape and smell. When the image is clear, focus your attention on it for the next 60 seconds and think about nothing else.

If you managed to think about the apple for the full 60 seconds, well done! However, notice how much effort it took to do so. Focusing your attention on even a simple, neutral thought like an apple isn't easy, and often you can't devote that much energy to a single thought.

The overwhelming majority of people report that they're unable to keep their attention on the apple for the duration of this exercise. Instead, their minds wander onto other topics and the image of the apple subsequently disappears. So much for being able to control your thoughts!

The simple truth is that your thoughts (and other mental processes, such as memory) are triggered by all sorts of events and stimuli (known as *situational cues*) over which you have little or no control. While you can focus on a single thought for a short period of time, your attention naturally shifts quickly on to something else and there's little you can do about it.

Trying to avoid the situational cues that influence your thoughts is unlikely to work, because too many of them exist and they can become linked to any event via arbitrary relationships. For instance, a traumatic event may come to be associated with a particular date or number. Each time that number appears in the environment, it can then provide the stimulus for remembering the original event.

Thought suppression increases thoughts!

The limited control you actually have over your thoughts has been well-established by researchers. Psychologists Richard McNally and Joseph Ricciardi, for example, demonstrated that suppressing negative thoughts works in the short term, but as soon as you stop actively trying to suppress these negative thoughts, they're three times more likely to return. Everyone can suppress thoughts and memories, but as soon as you drop your guard, up they pop!

The situation is the same for both emotions and physical sensations. Attempts to suppress the feeling of pain, for example, actually tend to increase it.

Dealing with feelings from the past

What you feel in your body depends on what's happened to you in the past. The implications of this knowledge are stark — unless you invent a time machine to change your past, you can't change how you're feeling right now. Unfortunately, Western culture often doesn't reflect this perspective. A parent, for example, may say to a small child 'cheer up' or 'don't worry' in her efforts to help the child feel better. While this approach is understandable, within these messages is the idea that the child can control how she feels, when actually that's not possible. This doesn't mean you're completely powerless in the face of your emotions, however. You can control how you behave when you feel different emotions, but not the emotion itself.

As how you feel depends on your history, giving yourself new 'happy' histories is the key to feeling better. How do you do so? By doing the things that matter to you. ACT calls the things that matter to you, your values (Chapters 3 and 4 look at values in detail). Values reflect the things that you want your life to represent and stand for. Identifying and understanding your values is critical in ACT because they provide your sense of direction for life. As such, your values define the meaning and purpose of your life and help to organise your behaviour over the longer term.

Accepting what you can't change

Some things in life you can't change and to avoid adding to your suffering it's best to just accept them. Doing so is much easier said than done, of course! This is because acceptance means opening up to unpleasant psychological experiences, such as disturbing thoughts, bad memories, difficult emotions or painful physical sensations. Accepting these experiences is difficult and nobody *wants* to do so; however, long term, acceptance transpires to be better than living in denial.

Unpleasant experiences such as pain, anxiety and sadness are part of life and, while they can be minimised to some extent, they can never be eradicated completely. However, these experiences, or the events that produced them, aren't at the root of human suffering. ACT argues that human suffering occurs when you embark on the ultimately futile task of trying to avoid or get rid of your own thoughts and feelings. When you try to control the uncontrollable, you only make your situation worse and waste valuable time and energy that can be better spent getting on with doing what you really care about.

Scottish psychotherapist and psychiatrist RD Laing noted, 'There is a great deal of pain in life and perhaps the only pain that can be avoided is the pain that comes from trying to avoid pain'. Replacing avoidance with acceptance won't get rid of the original pain, but at least you won't add to it.

Accepting difficult thoughts and feelings is a challenge that everyone faces. Fortunately, ACT provides a way of understanding what's going on in your head and, importantly, shows you how to address it.

Challenging the healthy normality assumption

A widespread assumption in Western societies is that human beings are by nature psychologically positive and happiness is typical. ACT calls this the *healthy normality* assumption. The healthy normality assumption is so deep and pervasive that it's rarely noticed, let alone challenged. And yet when it's pointed out, almost everyone knows that this assumption isn't correct. Happiness is not people's default emotion. Feeling uncertain, anxious or depressed is much more common. Of course, you sometimes feel happy or positive, but those periods are the exception rather than the rule. Experiencing negative thoughts and feelings is much more common.

From an ACT perspective, negative thoughts or feelings aren't necessarily problematic. While not very nice, they can be very useful. Consider stress. Stress is often seen as a bad thing, and, indeed, it can have serious physiological and psychological consequence. However, too little stress can also lead to negative outcomes, because you need a little bit of pressure to get things done. Feeling anxious before a job interview, for example, can keep you focused on what you want to say. If you're too relaxed, you may not concentrate fully on the task at hand.

The healthy normality assumption unfortunately encourages the belief that if you're not feeling happy or positive, there's something wrong with you. Psychological distress or discomfort comes to be seen as some kind of pathology or disorder, rather than part of people's normal experience.

This idea is further reinforced by the language you use. Terms such as 'mental illness' or 'mental health problems' are commonly used to describe the difficulties people face when dealing with negative psychological experiences. By definition, negative thoughts, feelings and memories aren't pleasant, and obviously people don't want to have them.

Don't shoot the messenger!

The human body evolved to feel pain because it's useful for survival. It provides important feedback from the environment and helps you to take care of yourself. But you can also become fearful of pain and behave in ways that avoid it. For example, you may develop an addiction to painkillers or restrict your movements in such a way that it leads to other physical problems. In this way, the fear and avoidance of pain compounds the original problem. Because the healthy normality assumption encourages you to see pain as bad, you're further inclined to avoid it.

It's no coincidence that misuse of painkillers is at an all-time high. The assumption of healthy normality encourages you to see the painful parts of your experience as the enemy within that needs to be avoided or defeated. But pain isn't the enemy. It's a messenger that you need to learn to live with and even embrace, rather than attempt to silence.

In these circumstances it's quite logical to conclude that if you can just get rid of these negative experiences, you'll feel better. On one level this conclusion is true, but notice what's happened here: the task of feeling better has become focused on getting rid of your negative psychological content — your negative thoughts and feelings. Thus begins a journey into experiential avoidance as you try to keep these experiences out of your life.

The healthy normality assumption encourages you to engage in experiential avoidance. It leads to the conclusion that your negative thoughts, feelings and memories are getting in the way of your happiness. You think that you'll feel better and be able to get on with your life when you're free of this negativity. Thoughts and feelings matter, of course, but from an ACT perspective, focusing on them as the problem is putting the cart before the horse. It's not that you'll be able to do the things you care about when you're thinking and feeling positively; rather, you'll feel and think more positively when you're doing the things you care about.

Your challenge is to get on with living a life with meaning, vitality and purpose, not to minimise or avoid negative experiences. And this is the real secret of living a positive life — do what matters.

Acknowledging that negative thoughts and feelings are normal

ACT replaces the healthy normality assumption (refer to the preceding section) with the proposition that negative thoughts and feelings are quite natural. Unpleasant yes, but not unusual.

This view of the human condition has a long tradition in most of the major religions. For example, Buddhism and Judeo-Christian religions place a heavy emphasis on the experience of human suffering and see it as central to everyday living. People may experience moments of happiness, comfort and peace, but these are fleeting against the backdrop of worry, stress and angst.

While it may not seem so immediately appealing, ACT argues that this position more accurately reflects most people's everyday experience — that at any given moment you're more likely to experience negative rather than positive thoughts and emotions. Negative psychological content isn't in itself the problem. On the contrary, your negative thoughts and feelings can be very useful as they help you to make sense of the world and remain safe. Worrying and evaluating can alert you to risky situations, while physical and emotional pain tells you that something's wrong. If you weren't worried about being hit by a car, you wouldn't take care when crossing the road. If you didn't worry about your child's health, you may not take her to the doctor when she's unwell. To understand more about the negativity of your psychological make-up, take a moment to consider your experiences over the last week and complete the following exercise.

- ✔ Take a moment to think about each of the following questions and then write down your answers.
- ✔ Today, have my thoughts been more negative (anxious, angry, unhappy) or positive (calm, easy-going, relaxing)?
- ✔ Over the past week, have I experienced more moments of happiness and contentment or stress and anxiety?
- ✔ When I was last outside, did I notice more of the things I like or more of the things I dislike?
- ✔ When I see people in the street, am I more inclined to evaluate them positively or negatively?
- ✔ In general, which do I notice first, people's flaws, faults and blemishes or their strengths and successes?

While responses vary from person to person, you generally find that most are negative.

Even when something wonderful is about to happen, such as getting married or moving house, people still report high levels of anxiety and stress. According to a recent survey, 20 per cent of the British public found getting married the most stressful thing they'd ever experienced. Only moving house, bereavement, divorce and redundancy scored higher. Evidently, even something that you really want to do can involve difficult emotional elements! And if you're not prepared to accept the stress, anxiety and difficult thoughts that accompany getting married, you could miss out on a very special day.

When you recognise and acknowledge that you're more inclined to see life's negatives than positives, you can be a little more relaxed when critical thoughts and uncomfortable feelings rear their heads. You can view these feelings as part of your normal psychological functioning rather than something that you need to do battle with. Having negative thoughts and feelings is just part of who you are. Understanding that doesn't stop these feelings from occurring (indeed, that's impossible), but it does reduce their influence over you and free up your time to do the things that really matter.

Chapter 3

Developing Psychological Flexibility

The primary goal of Acceptance and Commitment Therapy (ACT) is to help you live your life with openness, vitality and meaning. To do this, you need to increase your psychological flexibility. The original developers of ACT, Steve Hayes, Kirk Strosahl and Kelly Wilson, defined psychological flexibility as follows:

> *contacting the present moment fully as a conscious human being, as it is, not as what it says it is, and based on what the situation affords, changing or persisting in behavior in the service of chosen values.*

Psychological flexibility therefore means being open to and accepting of all your thoughts and feelings while simultaneously getting on with what you want to do in life. That may sound straightforward, but it turns out to be quite difficult!

This chapter introduces the concept of psychological flexibility and its various components. We describe the concepts of acceptance, defusion, contact with the present moment, self as context and committed action, which collectively inform the ACT take on psychological health and wellbeing.

Accepting Negative Thoughts and Feelings

While accepting positive thoughts, feelings and memories is easy, unsurprisingly accepting negative ones is much harder. Nobody wants to experience unpleasant thoughts and feelings, after all. The problem is that an unwillingness to experience negative thoughts, feelings or physical sensations can lead to counterproductive attempts to alter or avoid them.

ACT terms this avoidance behaviour *experiential avoidance* (see Chapter 9 for more details) and it can be hugely problematic, because it takes you down a fruitless path whereby you waste time and energy trying to control things that can't be controlled.

Every day you may experience a range of difficult psychological experiences that you'd rather not have, such as:

- ✔ Unkind or critical thoughts ('I'm a failure')
- ✔ Low self-esteem ('I'm stupid')
- ✔ Disturbing memories
- ✔ Negative feelings (sadness, anxiety, boredom)
- ✔ Physical pain

These psychological experiences are by definition unpleasant, and it's easy to see why you'd want to avoid, change or minimise them. The problem is that you have very little control over your thoughts and feelings for the following reasons:

- ✔ Your thoughts are linked to cues and events happening around you and over which you have little or no control, which means that regulating or controlling what you think is very difficult, if not impossible.
- ✔ How you feel or what you remember depends on what's happened to you previously, which means that you can no more change your emotions and memories than you can change your past.

Your efforts to control, minimise or get rid of unwanted thoughts, feelings, memories or sensations will thus only ever have limited, if any, success. Indeed, evidence suggests that efforts to reduce or avoid negative thoughts and feelings actually makes them worse (see the nearby sidebar, 'If you don't want it, you've got it').

If you don't want it, you've got it

It's a counterintuitive fact that the more you try to avoid your thoughts and feelings, the more you experience them. Psychologist Daniel Wegner and colleagues found that people who were instructed not to think about a 'white bear' for a period of five minutes reported more thoughts about that particular animal than people who hadn't tried to suppress thinking about it. Apparently, the more you don't want something in your life, the more that particular thing is likely to show up in your experience.

In addition to making them worse, another problem with attempting to control or change your thoughts and feelings is that it takes up precious time and energy that's better spent focusing on value-based living — that is, living a life shaped by doing things that are important to you. If instead you divert your time and energy into influencing your thoughts and feelings, your life can become narrower and more rigid and ultimately you can head into a negative downward spiral. Your efforts to change or avoid negative psychological experiences interferes with your ability to do the things that you really want to do. And doing less of what matters to you typically leads to more negative thoughts and feelings in the longer term.

Realising that pain is unavoidable

Even when you're doing things that you enjoy and care about, you still experience negative moments too. If you don't accept these negative experiences, you face a significant barrier to getting on with the life you want to be living.

For example, as part of a drive to be healthier you may decide to exercise more and start cycling to work. But cycling up hills or in the cold and wet will inevitably lead to some degree of physical discomfort. If you're not prepared to experience such discomfort, you'll be unlikely to get on your bike each morning — even though you may really want to be healthier!

Psychologically, flexibility is about being willing to experience the periodic discomfort (mental and physical) that comes with life. Doing so means that your life is then defined positively by your values and not negatively by attempts to avoid unpleasant thoughts, feelings and sensations. Weight loss provides a good example of using psychological flexibility to help you lead a life in accordance with your values.

Applying psychological flexibility to weight loss

A 2013 survey of dieters in the UK found that 10 per cent lasted a day, 40 per cent a week, 30 per cent a month and a mere 20 per cent made it to three months. Most of these said that the physical discomfort associated with dieting — hunger, fatigue and cravings — is what made them abandon their plan to lose weight. People also reported finding the social pressure to eat difficult to resist. These 'effects' of dieting are all negative experiences, and if you can't find a way to accept them dieting becomes impossible.

Emerging research is demonstrating just how critical acceptance is to value-based living. A 2014 US study divided students into two groups and taught one acceptance-based strategies (for example, acceptance of cravings) and the other group traditional weight loss strategies (counting calories, weighing daily and exercising). Following the intervention, the first group of students lost 1.57 kg each and managed to maintain that weight loss for up to a year; the control group — poor devils! — gained more than 1 kg each. In this case, a brief acceptance-based intervention was clearly more effective than traditional approaches.

One key to successful dieting (and indeed much more in life) is to find a way to live with and accept the difficult aspects of it. Focus on your goal of being slimmer rather than on how much you hate feeling hungry.

Introducing the Six Core Processes of ACT

ACT focuses on six core processes associated with psychological flexibility. Although they're set out as distinct processes, lots of overlap exists between them. And, while they can be applied individually, ACT is really about all six processes occurring together as one.

The six core processes are:

- ✔ **Values:** Recognising what matters most to you in life and what you want your life to be about.

- ✔ **Committed action:** Doing those things that bring your values to life.

- ✔ **Acceptance:** Noticing, accepting and embracing all your experiences, even the unwanted or negative ones.

- ✔ **Defusion:** Noticing your thoughts and thinking processes, without getting too caught up in them or trying to alter or control them.

> ✔ **Contact with the present moment:** Being fully aware of your experiences as they're occurring in the here and now.

> ✔ **Self as context:** Getting in touch with your deep sense of self — the 'you' who sits just behind your eyes, who observes and experiences and yet is distinct from your own thoughts, feelings and memories.

To remind you of the interconnectedness of these six processes, they're placed together in a *Hexaflex*, a term coined by Steven Hayes, Kirk Strosahl and Kelly Wilson in 1999 to describe the six points associated with psychological flexibility; see Figure 3-1.

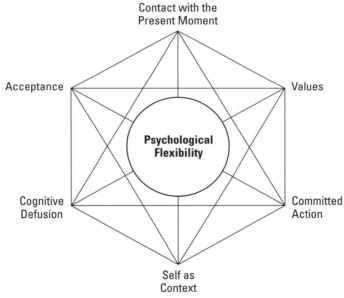

Figure 3-1:
The
Hexaflex.

© John Wiley & Sons, Inc.

At first sight the Hexaflex can appear quite complex and hard to understand. However, at its heart is a simple idea — to live your daily life with purpose and dignity according to what matters to you. The following sections look at each of the six core processes in more detail.

Values

Values are central to ACT because they represent what you want your life to be about and to stand for. They frame how you want to behave on an ongoing basis and give your life meaning and purpose.

ACT defines *values* as freely chosen verbal statements about what matters to you. Identifying your values is critical because they provide the motivation to deal with the difficult things in life. They're the reason you're prepared to struggle to overcome the challenges you experience as you strive to achieve your goals. As such, they dignify your life.

For instance, if you value being artistic and learning new skills, you may sign up to an evening pottery class. This class will mean the expenditure of time, money and energy and may occasionally lead to a range of negative thoughts and feelings. You may think, 'Can I do it?' or 'Do I have enough time?' and you may feel anxious or hesitant. However, the reason you're prepared to have these negative experiences is because you can then do the things that matter to you. From an ACT perspective, you're taking committed actions (that is, behaving) in the service of your values.

This is why values are so essential to life. They remind you of what's important and help you stay on course with committed actions. Identifying your values is an important early task in ACT. As soon as you know what you want your life to be about, you can then start moving in those directions.

Try out the short exercise below to help identify your values.

Imagine you're 80 years old and only have a few days or weeks left to live. You're sitting in a comfy chair, perhaps gazing out of a window, looking back on your life and what you've done with it. Now write down your answers to the following questions.

I wish I'd spent more time _____

_____

I wish I'd spent less time _____

_____

I wish I'd been more _____

_____

I wish I'd been less _____

_____

I spent too little time focused on _____

_____

I spent too much time worrying about _____

_____

I wish I could've been a little bit _____

_____

If I could live my life again, I would _____

_____

The one thing I regret is _____

_____

The one thing I would like to have done is _____

_____

By projecting yourself forward in time, you give yourself the opportunity to reflect on how you've lived your life until now and what's actually important to you. If this exercise reveals something you'd like to do or change in your life, now is the time to do something about it.

From an ACT perspective, your values are those personal qualities that you most want to be represented in your actions. If, for example, being a helpful person is important to you, this activity can help you recognise circumstances in which you haven't been helpful and can address in the future. You can establish what you have to do in order to embody this personal quality in your actions.

Your values give your life meaning and purpose, and make it worth living. Your challenge is to be clear about what your values are and then to behave consistently with them. And you do this by engaging in committed action.

Tomorrow and tomorrow and tomorrow

Procrastination — putting off until later what can be done right now — is a serious problem and accounts for vast amounts of wasted time. For the procrastinator, tomorrow is the busiest day of the week!

Research recently discovered that people who procrastinate tend to have lower levels of psychological flexibility. They're more avoidant of internal discomfort associated with work tasks and hence find other things to do instead. While this approach reduces their immediate level of discomfort, it also means they don't get any work done. Rather than berating such people for being weak-willed or easily distracted, ACT-based interventions focus on increasing their acceptance of discomfort in the service of doing what matters to them.

Committed action

The ultimate aim of ACT is to help you live your life in the real world — and this means *doing* things. It involves putting one foot in front of the other as you move in valued life directions. In many ways, all ACT processes exist to support committed action.

Committed action is the process whereby you build larger and larger patterns of activity that are linked to your values. Rather than allowing your life to be defined by the avoidance of pain or discomfort, committed action is how you step forward positively into the life you want to be living.

When you've clarified your values and where you want your life to be heading, the next step is to set goals that take you in that direction. ACT uses phrases such as 'value-based goals' to remind you that you're not picking any old goal, but something that's based on what really matters to you.

Setting value-based goals involves three stages:

1. **Choosing and clarifying the value you want to work on**

2. **Developing goals that represent this value**

3. **Taking action**

For example, if after completing the exercise in the preceding section you identify that you wish you'd spent more time with your family, the next step is to ask what you can do that represents this value. You could, for instance, come up with some goals that you can achieve this evening, such as reading a book to or playing a game with your children, or preparing a favourite meal for or really listening to your partner.

Have a go at the following exercise to help you set some value-based goals.

Follow these steps:

1. **Choose and clarify as precisely as you can the value you want to work on.**

   The value that I want to work on is _____

   _____

   For example: 'The value that I want to work on is being a good friend'.

2. **Develop goals that represent this value.**

   Unfortunately, not all goals are 'good' goals because some are complex, remote or simply unachievable. For this reason, set SMART goals, that is, those that are specific, measurable, achievable, realistic and time-framed.

The goal I want to achieve is _____

_____

For example: 'The goal I want to achieve is to call two friends this evening to see how they are'.

This goal is a SMART goal because it:

- Clearly specifies what to do

- Is measurable, as you'll know when you've achieved it

- Is attainable and can be achieved

- Is relevant to the chosen value — being a good friend

- Is time-framed — it specifies when it should be achieved by

3. Take action.

Pick up that phone!

The taking action step may appear easy, but it can be surprisingly difficult. The next section explains why doing the things you want to do can be hard and what you can do about it.

Acceptance

Acceptance involves being open to all your experiences and embracing them for what they are (and not what your mind may tell you they are). In essence, acceptance is the opposite of avoidance. Acceptance is a profound and complex psychological process, which is closely related to compassion and forgiveness.

Acceptance is important because it can free up your energy to do the things you really want to be doing. Struggling against things you can't change — such as trying to control or avoid certain thoughts and feelings — is pointless. You just don't have the necessary control over what you think and feel to make this a worthwhile strategy. In the face of this reality, you're better off accepting such thoughts and feelings for what they are, even when they're unpleasant.

Acceptance involves more than the ability to tolerate negative experiences, however. It means being completely open to them, almost welcoming them — not because you enjoy negativity but because any struggle with negativity is futile.

What follows is a short acceptance exercise; give it a go!

This exercise takes about five minutes and you need an ice cube (you can use anything frozen but an ice cube is easiest) and a hand towel (because your hands will get wet!).

Acceptance and human happiness

Happiness is something everyone strives for. Acceptance appears to be an important factor in attaining that goal, because happiness isn't merely the absence of bad stuff but also the presence of good stuff. Resisting or avoiding bad things may make sense (and can be a good thing in the right circumstances, such as when facing a hungry lion), but if you spend too much time and energy trying to control or avoid bad experiences, you'll have less time for engaging in the positive things that can make you happy. As the writer George Orwell said, 'Happiness can exist only in acceptance'.

Follow these steps:

1. **Place an ice cube in the palm of your hand and leave it there for about 60 seconds.** If you can, close your fingers and hold it tightly.

   After a short time, the cold of the ice cube will make your hand ache and you'll probably notice having thoughts such as, 'My hand feels numb' or 'That hurts'.

2. **Be aware of your physical discomfort and any negative thoughts you're having, but continue to hold the ice cube for as long as you can.**

This mildly painful exercise helps you to learn about and practise acceptance. It's a value-based action in that you freely choose to hold the ice cube because, in doing so, you discover how you experience and respond to discomfort.

This exercise is a microcosm of the challenges you face in your everyday life. At some point each day you'll probably experience negative events, difficulties and discomfort. These experiences are inevitable and attempts to avoid or resist them are doomed to failure. Instead, your best option when facing events or experiences that you can't change or control is to accept them for what they are. Doing so may not be pleasant but, like all things, they'll pass.

Acceptance is *not* submission or tolerance; rather, it's an openness to experiencing the moment, even if it's bad, so that you can move your life forward in ways that matter to you.

Defusion

Defusion is the opposite of fusion. *Fusion* is your commitment to, or belief in, the literal content of your thoughts. When you believe your thoughts to be literally true — you fuse with them — they can exert considerable influence over what you do. The problem with believing your thoughts is that they're often wrong or inaccurate! And even when they're accurate, they may not always be a useful guide to how to act. If you fuse with the thought 'I can't do it', you're more likely to give up or not even try in the first place. Even if that thought is currently accurate, believing that the thought is true can act as a barrier to learning how to do whatever 'it' is.

In contrast, *defusion* is the process by which you gain some distance from your thoughts and cognitions (including memories and mental images). It involves being aware of your thoughts (and thinking processes) and not being stuck inside them. It means looking *at* your thoughts rather than *from* your thoughts. Defusing from your thoughts is difficult because they're so immediate, intimate and persistent that they can slip into your awareness unnoticed and unchallenged. As a consequence, it's easy to relate to their content as an accurate reflection of how things really are, rather than just as a thought you're having. ACT seeks to undermine the arrogance of 'words' and see a thought as just a thought.

But what are thoughts? From an ACT perspective, thoughts are no more than a private language — words, images and memories that you experience inside your head (check out Chapter 11 for the technicalities). Thoughts may be useful, but they can also be wrong and unhelpful. The challenge is to work out when they serve a useful purpose and when they're just getting in the way of value-based living.

ACT uses a range of defusion techniques to help you notice your thoughts and thereby gain a little detachment from them. This sense of detachment reduces the believability of your thoughts — so you can make decisions based on your values and not on what happens to be going through your mind at any particular point in time.

Below is a short defusion exercise for you to try.

This is a particularly active exercise, and to get the best out of it you have to really go for it. Don't worry if you feel a bit self-conscious or silly — everyone does. Just notice these thoughts and do it anyway.

Find a quiet spot where you won't be disturbed for a few minutes and a clock that measures seconds. Now think about a glass of milk. Picture it in your mind — the white milk in a glass, shown in Figure 3-2. Now imagine picking up the glass and drinking from it. What does it taste like? Is it cold or warm? Swallow the milk and then picture holding the glass in front of you.

With that image fresh in your mind, start saying the word 'milk' out loud. Start slowly and then gradually build up your speed until you're saying the word quickly, over and over: 'milk, milk, milk, milk'. Increase your volume as you speed up. At times you'll stutter and stumble; don't worry, stick with it. Try to keep it up for 45 seconds.

Figure 3-2:
Picture a
glass of milk
in your
mind's eye.

© John Wiley & Sons, Inc.

When you finish, take a moment to reflect on the experience and ask yourself:

- How did it feel?
- What happened to my mental image of the glass of milk?
- Did I struggle to produce the sound 'milk'?
- What did the word 'milk' sound like?

When people do this exercise, they often report that they stop hearing the word 'milk' and instead feel they're just making funny-sounding noises. Although a bit of vocal distortion does occur, in fact you're still making the sound 'milk'. You no longer connect it with the notion of 'milk', however. You're still hearing the actual sound, 'milk', but it's been stripped of its symbolic meaning.

People also often report that the image too disappears. Again, this happens because repeating the word 'milk' decontextualises the image and thereby strips away its meaning.

You can use this process to strip away or change the meaning of any word or phrase. Because the meaning of a word is closely related to the context in which it occurs, when you change the context, you also change the meaning.

Changing the context in which a word or phrase occurs is the basis of defusion. As a result of changing the context of a word, you can come to see it as just a sound with meanings attached. And, importantly, these meanings can change. No longer are they fixed or exact descriptions of reality; rather, you come to see them as merely sounds people make to communicate with one another. When you notice this fact, words have less significance in your life. Language and words remain important and useful, but because you know that the meaning of words can change, so your commitment to their literal content wanes.

This changeability is particularly useful when you have negative or unhelpful thoughts, because rather than seeing them as factually accurate or literally true, you instead see them as just words or bits of language going through your head.

Contact with the present moment

Contact with the present moment means being fully aware of what you experience in the actual moment at which you're experiencing it. You may think that sounds quite straightforward, but it's surprisingly difficult. All too often you get caught up in your thoughts and overlook your immediate experiences.

Consider the very commonly reported example of driving somewhere and then having no memory of the details of the journey. Likewise, you can almost drift through life, in general, without really noticing it. You go on automatic pilot when you're so wrapped up in your thoughts that you don't notice what you're doing or what's going on in the wider world around you.

Why does this lack of contact matter? Being disconnected from the world around you can make value-based living more difficult because you aren't in touch with what really matters — your immediate world. Instead, you're away in your thoughts — planning, worrying, remembering, critiquing and so on. These mental processes aren't all bad, of course, but too much time spent on them can interfere with your capacity to do the things you actually want life to be about.

The present moment is all you have — don't miss out on it!

The secret of eternal life

Philosopher Ludwig Wittgenstein said that eternal life can only be found in the present moment. In a world where time never stands still, the only thing you can actually connect with is the present moment. And yet when you do so, you make contact with all of time. He wrote, 'Death is not an event in life: we do not live to experience death. If we take eternity to mean not infinite temporal duration but timelessness, then eternal life belongs to those who live in the present'.

ACT uses a range of techniques, such as mindfulness, to help you make contact with the present moment. The following mindful walking exercise is just one example from mindfulness that helps to connect you to the present moment.

You can do this mindfulness exercise almost anywhere, but finding somewhere quiet, where you won't be disturbed, is probably advisable for your first attempt.

In this exercise, you focus on the act of walking, noticing each sensation and movement as you place one foot in front of the other. While you can do this exercise in a small space, it's easier if you can find an area where you can move around freely in a circle without having to negotiate too many obstacles. You can do it inside or outside, with your shoes on or off, and it takes about ten minutes.

Follow these steps:

1. **Find a spot and stand still, with both feet flat on the ground.** Focus your attention on your breathing and notice the flow of air as you breathe in deeply through your nose and out through your mouth. Be aware of how your chest and shoulders rise and fall with each breath.

2. **Focus your attention on your feet.** Feel the weight of your body through your feet on the ground. Notice any sensations as you gently sway back and forth.

3. **Begin to walk forward, very slowly and deliberately.** Feel how movement flows through your body as you place one foot in front of the other. Be aware of the sensation of placing each foot on the ground. Notice how your arms and legs move as you walk forward.

4. **Look down at your feet as you continue to walk slowly and with full awareness.** From time to time your attention may wander — your mind may focus on other things, such as thoughts, sounds or other sensations. When this happens, be aware that your attention has drifted and, gently and without self-criticism, focus your attention back on your feet and each step that you take.

5. **Make contact with the present moment by mindfully and deliberately noticing each step you take.** Walking is something you've done for most of your life; it's so familiar you hardly notice it.

6. **Continue walking for ten minutes or so.** When you decide to finish, do so consciously and stand still for a moment. Thank your feet for the journey you've just completed and for all the journeys you've taken over the years.

Self as context

The self as context process is hard to explain because it's an experience rather than a concept. Like swimming, we could explain the process but you wouldn't really understand it until you get in the water.

Self as context (sometimes called the *observer self*) refers to your experience that exists beyond your immediate thoughts and feelings — it's your unique and ongoing perspective on life. Experientially, self as context is the sense of being 'I' or 'me' in the here and now.

Self as context is important because it enables you to be aware of your own experiences as they occur — be in contact with the present moment — without being directly involved with them. This awareness is useful because, from a self as context perspective, you can watch your thoughts and feelings come and go without feeling overly attached to them. This detachment enables you to notice that, while you experience your thoughts and feelings, you are actually more than those. You are a whole human being.

One metaphor that's often used in ACT to help understand the self as context is a chessboard stretching out infinitely in every direction, as shown in Figure 3-3. Imagine that all over the chessboard are black and white chess pieces, some of which are grouped together and others alone. What you see is a huge battlefield, with black and white chess pieces pitched against each other.

Figure 3-3: Visualise yourself as a chessboard.

Illustration by Joe Munro

Now imagine that your positive thoughts and feelings are the black pieces and your negative thoughts and feelings are the white pieces. They're battling against each other and you hope that the black pieces will win. You hope that your mind can be full of positive thoughts ('I'm a good person') rather than negative thoughts ('I'm stupid'). To achieve this outcome, you enter the fray and try to rid the board of the white pieces. You pick up the black pieces and attempt to smash or push the white pieces away. In the same way, each time you have a negative thought about yourself you counter it with a positive thought. You can imagine sending forward the black chess piece representing the thought 'I'm a really nice/good/loveable person' each time you experience a negative thought such as 'I'm stupid/ugly/hopeless'.

Although this strategy seems quite sensible — defeating one thought with another — unfortunately, no sooner have you destroyed one white chess piece than another pops up. It's almost as though getting rid of one bad thought merely creates space for another. The strategy doesn't actually clear the chessboard of the white pieces.

This strategy also has another, bigger problem too. By trying to get rid of your unwanted thoughts, you're declaring war on your own experiences. A large part of yourself is now your enemy. And here's the rub: you can never win this battle without also destroying part of who you are. What's more, living in a war zone is no fun. It's hard, it's nasty and it's never-ending. So what are your options? You can carry on with this war against yourself or you can try something different — and radical!

Instead of associating yourself with the pieces, you can be the chessboard itself — you're the space that *holds* the pieces. You're still in contact with all your thoughts and feelings as the pieces rest on the board, and they're still part of your experience — but you become an observer and have less interest in the outcome of the battle. You become the place where these events and experiences occur, without becoming directly involved.

This exercise allows you to discriminate yourself (as the chessboard) from your thoughts and feelings (the chess pieces). In the process, you can see how you are the context, the setting for cognitions and emotions, but are also more than this. And that's the root of self as context.

Chapter 4

Living a Life with Meaning

In This Chapter

▶ Establishing the values you want to live by

▶ Working through the Valued Living Questionnaire

▶ Living with a sense of dignity

An old psychotherapy joke goes like this, 'How many psychologists does it take to change a light bulb? One, but the light bulb has to want to change'. Admittedly it's not the funniest joke, but it does contain a grain of truth. You have to *want* to change for change to occur, and this comes down to what you care about in life. From an Acceptance and Commitment Therapy (ACT) perspective, the things you care most about are reflected in your values. Values aren't feelings, physical objects or a wish list of achievements — they're the personal qualities that you want to define yourself by. They are what you want your life to stand for and mean in a general sense and, as such, represent how you want to behave as you go through life. For instance, if kindness is important to you and something you care about, then it's a value that can guide how you behave towards other people and yourself.

When you know the personal qualities that you want to define your life, you can begin to live in line with them. If being a good mother or a loving partner is important to you, you can behave in ways that represent those values. In this way your values point you in the direction you want your life to be heading and they guide how you behave and act.

Values are like directions on a compass. They help set the course for your life. Without a compass it's very easy to get lost because you don't know which way to go. With a compass you can immediately orientate yourself and set off in the direction in which you want to be travelling.

This chapter looks at values in more detail and describes their four defining features. It provides exercises to help you identify your personal values so that you can begin the process of setting goals based upon them.

Letting Your Values Organise Your Life

Values are useful because they help organise your life. When you know what they are (even partially), you can begin taking steps in their direction. For example, you may value the environment and want to live more sustainably. With this knowledge you can start doing things that represent having a more balanced and positive relationship with the world around you; for example, you may start cycling to work rather than driving, growing your own lettuce instead of buying prepacked bags, recycling your household rubbish and so on.

To be guided by your values day-to-day, ACT recommends setting *value-based goals* and Chapter 5 covers this process in detail. Setting value-based goals ensures that you're doing the things that truly matter to you and this is the secret to living a life of purpose and meaning.

Describing the four core features of values

Values are:

- ✔ Freely chosen
- ✔ General ongoing actions
- ✔ Always present
- ✔ Prioritised, not justified

The following sections break these down in more detail.

Your heart's deepest desire

In JK Rowling's *Harry Potter and the Philosopher's Stone*, Harry discovers the Mirror of Erised, which shows the viewer her deepest, most heart-felt desire. From an ACT perspective that may seem to be a good thing, but wise old headmaster Albus Dumbledore tells Harry that the mirror has driven people to madness because it encourages them to dwell on their dreams and forget to get on with living.

Living in your fantasies isn't a good idea, and it's not what ACT means by identifying your deepest desires. Rather, ACT sees your values as the directions in which you want your life to be moving and the personal qualities you want to be defined by.

Values are freely chosen

In ACT, a critical feature of values is that they're *freely chosen*. They reflect your deepest, most personal desires and not what you think you *ought* to do. As social beings, people are highly sensitive to what others say and think, which can lead you to feel you *should* value certain things. But for values to really mean something, they have to represent what *you* truly care about. If they don't, they'll lack vitality and you'll struggle to find the motivation to complete the value-based goals you set yourself.

Values are general ongoing actions

Values are general ongoing actions, not goals, events or emotions. For instance, a value is the ongoing action of being loving, being helpful, listening or learning. In other words, they're things you do, not what you achieve or feel.

Thinking about life in terms of your values can be difficult in Western societies that are often highly goal-focused. From an early age you're encouraged to think in terms of goals, targets and outcomes as you move through life, rather than what they represent on a deeper level. In many ways this approach is very useful and helps you get things done, but its downside is that you can easily lose sight of the underlying values your goals represent.

Picture a compass to help you remember the distinction between *values* and *goals*. Values are the directions in which you want your life to be travelling and goals are the way-stations along the route. If your direction is westward, for example, your goals are the rivers you cross, the mountains you climb and the campfires you build along the way.

Values are directions of travel rather than specific places or destinations; as such, you can never 'complete' or reach a value. If your chosen direction in life is to head westward, you'll never get there (arriving at 'west' is impossible) because you can always go farther west. Likewise, if your value is to be kind and loving, there's always something more you can do to be kind and loving — even after a lifetime of kindness.

Life's a journey, not a destination

It may be a cliché, but when you die you won't be taking anything with you. Life's a journey and one day it will be over. Bear that in mind, work out your direction of travel and start putting one foot in front of another.

Here are a few more examples of values versus goals:

- **The value of being a loving partner and the goal of getting married.** Being loving is an ongoing act and can be realised in a number of ways, while getting married is a goal that represents one way of achieving this value.

- **The value of learning new skills and the goal of completing an evening class in carpentry.** You can always learn new things and carpentry is one of them.

- **The value of living more healthily and the goal of eating more nutritious food.** Eating one piece of fruit a day is just one goal that you can achieve that represents the value of living more healthily. Others include reducing the amount of salt you consume, exercising more and drinking less alcohol.

Values are always present

Your values are always with you. While they can be acted upon or ignored, they're always available. You can overlook or ignore a value for years, but at any moment you can choose to recognise it and bring it into your life.

In contrast, goals are the targets you strive for in the future. They're out in front of you until the moment they're achieved, at which point you can move on to the next goal. This means that while you can be in want of a goal, you can never be in want of a value. Your values are always in the here and now, always available; you simply need to decide what they are.

Values are prioritised, not justified

Because at any point in time you'll care about a variety of different things (family, work, health and so on), inevitably you'll also have a number and range of values. Like directions on a compass, you need to decide which values to focus on, because you're unable to travel in every direction at once. You therefore need to prioritise your values and set your goals in relation to those that are most important.

Your values represent your deepest desires about the kind of life you want to be living and as such they're highly personal and idiosyncratic. Trying to justify them therefore makes no sense. It's like asking someone to justify why she likes sunrises or apples or dogs. She just does. In contrast, you may need to justify goals that arise from your values. Goals are specific targets and actions that you set out to achieve and they can be 'good' and 'bad'. For instance, if one of your values is to be healthier, then going on a 10 km run every morning may not be the best option if it takes too much time or leaves you too exhausted for work. In these circumstances, running 4 km in the evening may be a better choice.

Recognising that emotions aren't values

When asked what they want in life, people commonly reply, 'to be happy'. This seems reasonable because obviously no one wants to be unhappy. Wanting to be happy, however, is not the same as stating a value. Although you may feel happy when you engage in valued living, values aren't the same as feelings. Being happy isn't an ongoing action; rather, it's the condition of your body that you feel. Values describe actions that you engage in to make your life reflect what really matters to you. They're what you choose to *do* as you live your life, not what you feel in your body.

As your most sincere and personal aspirations for how you want to behave in the world, your values enable you to persevere when things become difficult. This is an important quality of values as they help to organise your life over the longer term and to navigate more difficult times. In contrast, feelings aren't good guides to deciding what to do in life. Feelings inevitably ebb and flow with life and if you allow them to direct your actions, you'll struggle to stay on your chosen course for long. If your aim is to be happy, for example, you won't want to do things that can lead to any unhappiness. Unfortunately, even when you're doing things you enjoy or that are important to you, you'll still encounter difficulties and obstacles along the way that will bring up difficult emotions. Setting an emotion-based goal (to be happy, for example) will make it harder to accept any negative feelings that show up and this can stop you in your tracks or send your life down a path you don't really want to follow.

Living according to your values means doing the things that matter to you, often *in spite of* how you feel. Here are some examples:

- ✔ Going to a party with your partner (representing the value of being a loving partner), even when you're upset with her.

- ✔ Listening to a friend in need (representing the value of being a good friend), even when you feel disinterested.

- ✔ Going to the gym (representing the value of being healthy), even when you feel tired.

- ✔ Responding calmly to your child (representing the value of being a caring parent), even when you're angry with her.

Holding your values lightly

Although values are important, ACT recommends that you 'pursue your values vigorously, but hold them lightly'. Values specify what matters to you, but turning them into dogma to be slavishly pursued isn't helpful. Values are simply linguistic statements that describe what you want your life to be about. If you adhere to them too rigidly and elevate them above all else, you can miss their true worth. Your values are your guides, like personal lodestars; they're not instruction kits for life.

Your values will change over time, so review them on a regular basis to ensure that they still make sense to you and are leading you in the right direction.

Clarifying your values with the Valued Living Questionnaire

Knowing where to start is one of the difficulties you encounter as you try to identify your values — you probably care about so many different things. ACT provides a number of ways to help you identify your values, including the Valued Living Questionnaire in Table 4-1. You can use this questionnaire to narrow down the important areas in your life.

Table 4-1	The Valued Living Questionnaire	
Value Domain	*Importance (1 = not important, 10 = very important)1 = not important, 10 = very important)*	*Success in This Domain (1 = not at all, 10 = all of the time)*
Family (not including parenting)		
Parenting		
Friends		
Work		
Health		
Intimate relationships		
Leisure/fun		
Personal development		
Community		
Spirituality		

Developed by Kelly Wilson (one of the co-developers of ACT) and his colleagues, the Valued Living Questionnaire (Table 4-1) lists ten of the key domains of life. Take a moment to think about your life in relation to each of these value domains. On a scale of 1–10 (where 1 = not important and 10 = very important), rate these domains in order of significance to you. For instance, you may rate 'friends' as very important (9) at this point in time and 'leisure' as currently unimportant (3). Grading the domains in this way helps you prioritise where to spend your time. Apportioning your time appropriately can make a big difference to your life.

Now on a scale of 1–10 (where 1 = not at all and 10 = all of the time), rate how successful you are in these domains. How fully do you feel you are living a meaningful life in these domains? Are you living the life you want to be living with your friends, family, at work or in intimate relationships?

Completing this table helps you identify which areas of your life are important to you (at this point in time) and how successfully you're managing them. Identifying a difference in the scores between what you most value and how consistently you've observed those values recently is typical. After all, if you were living completely consistently with the things you value, your life would be pretty much on track and that's rarely the case for most of us, most of the time.

The opposite is also true. You feel less energised and connected with life when you're out of touch with your values. For instance, if you value contact with your family, but work commitments mean you're often away from home, you're unlikely to be feeling very positive about your current situation. Use the findings from Table 4-1 to prioritise the values you want to concentrate on right now.

Looking back from the future

Projecting yourself into the future and looking back at your life is a powerful way to consider how you're currently living and to identify the values you are or are not being directed by. The following exercise helps you focus on the things you wish you'd said and done — and because it occurs in your imagination, you can then address these things in the present!

Find a comfortable place to sit and focus on your breathing until you feel calm. Close your eyes and follow each breath in and then out again, noticing the temperature of the air as it flows in and out of your nostrils. Notice how your shoulders rise and fall with each breath. Keep breathing deeply and regularly.

Now try to imagine a funeral taking place. It's *your* funeral and everyone who has ever mattered to you is present. Look around and see your family, friends and anyone else who's been important to you. Even those who are no longer living themselves are there. All of them look exactly as they do today or as you remember them. Take a moment to picture the scene. Now imagine that you're there too, walking among everyone. They can't see you (you're a bit like a ghost) and you're free to move between them and listen to what they're saying about you.

Focus on four groups of people — your parents and members of your family, your partner and children, your friends and your colleagues — and instead of imagining what they may say, actually put the words in their mouths that you'd dearly like to hear. Be bold — remember, it's just an exercise! How would you like them to describe you and their relationship with you? What is it they miss about you? What did they like about you?

Notice what you feel as you listen to these people speak. Is it a positive or negative emotion?

When you finish listening to the different groups of people, imagine walking away from your funeral and take a moment to look back at everyone who's gathered there. These are the people you met during your life's journey. Then, when you're ready, open your eyes.

How did you get on? This exercise can be difficult and even quite upsetting, particularly if you imagine loved ones who are no longer with you. If that's the case, take a moment to compose yourself. Then, when you feel able, write down what you wanted people to say about you. What personal attributes did you want them to describe?

This exercise helps you to think about your behaviour in relation to others. If you value being kind to those you love, consider whether your actions demonstrate that. If they don't, do something about it.

Accepting your vulnerability in pursuit of your values

Living a rich and purposeful life means you'll inevitably encounter difficult and painful experiences. It simply isn't possible to connect fully with life and not experience some level of struggle and discomfort — the two go together.

In fact, a good rule of thumb is that the more you connect with the world and live a fulfilled and vital life, the more trials and difficulties you'll encounter. If you're not prepared to accept the troubles and discomforts that go with life, you won't be able to live it fully. That's the challenge you face — to find a way to live this life, right here, right now, while also experiencing the difficulties, anxieties and uncertainties that come with it.

Kelly Wilson points out that 'values and vulnerabilities are poured from the same vessel'. In other words, the things you feel anxious, worried or distressed about point you toward what really matters to you. For example, if you didn't care about having meaningful relationships with people, you wouldn't become anxious in social situations. The very fact that you do become tongue-tied at parties tells you that you do want people to connect with you; it's important to you.

The following exercise focuses on what your discomfort is signalling to you.

Think about three situations that have made you feel uncomfortable. Now follow these steps:

1. **Briefly describe each situation.** For example, being late for a meeting.

   a. _____

   b. _____

   c. _____

2. **Describe how you felt and what you thought in each situation.** For example, 'I felt awkward and wanted to apologise'.

   a. _____

   b. _____

   c. _____

3. **Note what value the sense of discomfort represents to you in each situation.** For example, 'I want to be polite and respectful'.

   a. _____

   b. _____

   c. _____

The idea behind this exercise is to explore why something matters to you and the value your discomfort represents. Spending a bit of time reflecting on when you felt uncomfortable about something you did or didn't do can help you identify the underlying value that's important to you.

Knowing that your values can change

Exercises such as the Valued Living Questionnaire (described in the earlier 'Clarifying your values with the Valued Living Questionnaire' section) help you identify the things that are most important to you at any particular moment in time. You may not be doing the things that represent your values but your values are nonetheless there, ever present, just waiting to be connected with.

Even though values are usually stable day to day, they can and do change over time. Different things matter to you at different times. For this reason, checking in with yourself occasionally to identify whether you're doing what really matters to you is helpful. But how do you know? How can you decide if a particular value really is important? From an ACT perspective, you can't determine whether a value is important simply by noticing how you're feeling at a single point in time. This is because pursuing a value-based goal will often involve experiencing difficult or painful experiences along the way. Consider going to the dentist for a filling. You may experience anxious thoughts beforehand or in the waiting room and also some physical pain during the procedure. But going to the dentist is still a valid goal based on your value of wanting to be in good health.

When evaluating your goals, the crucial question you need to ask is, 'Does this feel right at a deep-down, personal level?' Not necessarily good or pleasant, but *right* nonetheless. Answering it involves making a judgement about whether what you're doing expresses and represents your chosen values. If the answer is 'yes', you're connecting with your values and you can carry on with what you're doing.

Trying out values for size

Distinguishing between what you really want and what you think you *should* want can be difficult. However, the fact that it's hard to pinpoint your values needn't be a barrier. When this happens, one solution is to engage with a value for a while and see what happens. Not until you actually give something a go can you know if it's what you want. If you feel invigorated, satisfied or even excited about what you're doing, the value probably does really matter to you. If you don't, maybe you're going in the wrong direction and should stop and do something else.

The principle is a bit like trying on an item of clothing. A garment may look good on the hanger, but you won't know if it suits you until you try it on for size.

The following exercise puts this process into practice.

You can use this exercise each time you consider a new value. Follow these steps:

1. **Choose a value that you're willing to try out for a week or so.** The time period isn't set in stone, just make sure it's long enough to get a feel for it.

2. **Notice your reactions when you first select this value.** Do you feel enthusiastic about it or uncertain? Perhaps both. Just notice any thoughts and feelings you have and be aware of them as thoughts that have gone through your mind.

3. **Make a list of a few simple goals that you can set in relation to this value.** For example, for a health-related value, possible goals may be to eat two pieces of fresh fruit each day or to undertake a 15-minute walk five times a week.

4. **Choose a goal that you can commit to for the duration of your trial period.** Consider what you're doing for the next week or so and the feasibility of, for example, eating a particular type of food or having the time to walk regularly.

5. **Notice the judgements your mind makes about your goal.** Maybe that little interior voice is questioning the validity of your goal, your ability to commit to it or whether you'll enjoy it.

6. **Make a plan by writing down the actual behaviours you need to perform to achieve your chosen goal and decide when to get started.** The sooner, the better.

7. **Take action.** For example, eat that fruit salad or get walking! Be as natural as possible and don't tell anyone who's directly involved what you're doing — you're achieving this goal simply for you, not to impress or influence others.

8. **Record your thoughts and feelings in a daily diary.** Note observations about yourself and other people. Is your experience different each time you achieve the goal? Are your thoughts positive, negative or neutral?

9. **Commit to achieving your goal every day.** Be open to your experiences each and every time.

10. **Read through your diary and reflect on your observations.** What do they tell you?

This exercise enables you to experience directly what committing to a value feels like. If you gain a sense of vitality, purpose and fulfilment as a consequence of achieving a particular goal, this value clearly matters to you. If, in contrast, you feel ambivalent or lacklustre, then perhaps it isn't an important value at this point in time.

When deciding how important your values are, you may need to go beyond your immediate negative thoughts and feelings and make a judgement based on the deeper sense of meaning and purpose they give you. For example, maybe you've chosen to run the local marathon. The training requires lots of time, money and effort. And it hurts! You decide if the value is really important by checking whether that goal helps define your life as you want it and not whether you feel discomfort or have negative thoughts.

Living Your Life with Dignity

The aim of ACT is to help you identify your values (what matters to you) so that you can live consistently with them. Spending time and energy trying to avoid or get rid of the negatives things in life is all too easy, but that's no way to live! A life defined by what you don't want rather than what you desire ultimately leads to feeling unfulfilled and out of place.

Be under no illusions — living a life defined by your values isn't necessarily easy just because you want it. You'll still experience moments of difficulty, hardship, stress and angst as you go down your chosen path, but at least your trials and tribulations will have meaning. They'll be in the service of what matters to you and the life you want to live. In this way, your values dignify and give meaning to your pain.

Chapter 5

Moving Forward with Committed Action

*W*hen you've identified your values and what really matters to you, your next challenge is to make your life about those things. Acceptance and Commitment Therapy (ACT) calls doing so *committed action*. Chapter 4 describes values as the directions in which you want your life to be heading, rather like the points on a compass of your life journey. Continuing with this metaphor, if your values represent the direction in which you're headed, *committed actions* are the steps you take on that journey. Committed action involves gradually building larger and larger patterns of behaviour that are consistent with your values. It's the step-by-step process by which you widen and deepen your daily living so that you can engage more fully with life in ways that are meaningful for you.

Value-based committed action is ultimately what ACT aims to help you achieve. When you do the things that matter to you and behave in ways that are consistent with your values, you can make the most of life and live it to the full. And as an added bonus of living in line with your values, you usually feel more positive and content. It's pretty obvious why this is the case — do the things that matter to you and as much as is possible you'll be living the life you want to be living. But remember, this isn't about trying to feel happy. Your emotions will come and go as you engage in value-based actions, some good and some bad. But overall your sense of purpose, vitality and meaning will be greater when you behave in ways that reflect your deeply held values.

This chapter helps you understand that to achieve your goals you have to be willing to experience all that doing so entails. You discover that willingness is a choice you make in responding to the world. When you're willing to accept all that life brings you can move forward positively. In this chapter, we show you how to set effective short-, medium- and long-term value-based goals.

Being Willing Is the Key to Achieving Your Goals

Even when you're clear about the values that you want to be living by, engaging in committed action in their service can still be difficult. Part of the reason for this is that even when you do the things that really matter to you, you will still experience difficult and negative thoughts, feelings and bodily sensations. If you're unwilling to have these experiences, they will stop your efforts to engage in committed action in their tracks.

For this reason, ACT sees committed action and willingness as two sides of the same coin. You can't really commit to doing something if you're unwilling to experience any of the difficulties that show up along the way. To engage in committed action, you need to be willing to experience all that doing so brings.

Putting your values into action

Values are more than just idle dreams; they point you in the directions in which you want your life to be heading. By defining what you want your life to stand for, values also provide you with the motivation and drive to face the challenges you meet along the way. But for values to really mean anything, they have to be lived, they have to be acted upon. As Thomas Edison apparently said, 'Vision without execution is hallucination'.

Dealing with unpleasant or negative thoughts, feelings and bodily sensations is a challenge everyone faces. ACT pictures this challenge using the metaphor of walking through a swamp before climbing a mountain, shown in Figure 5-1.

Imagine that you see a beautiful mountain in the distance and you decide you want to climb it. You start out on your journey full of enthusiasm but pretty soon find yourself wading through a smelly, sticky, muddy swamp. The farther you go, the more the mud sticks to your clothes, and every step is hard going. You think to yourself, 'I didn't think it would be like this. Climbing the mountain was meant to be fun and I'm not sure I can do it'.

Figure 5-1:
If the direction of travel is important enough to you, taking one step at a time, even a swamp can be crossed.

Illustration by Joe Munro

At this point you have a choice. You can either carry on through the swamp until you reach your destination or you can give up, turn around and go home. If you do the latter you get out of the mud, but you also won't scale the mountain. To see the view from the top, you need to go through the swamp.

The swamp metaphor represents the dilemma you face in life. Difficult and negative experiences come along from time to time and you have a choice in how you respond to them. Your unwillingness to face these experiences and attempts to avoid them interfere with value-based living, and this is the source of yet further pain and suffering.

Defining willingness

In ACT the word *willingness* is often used as a more active synonym for the word 'acceptance'. Being willing is about choosing to be open to, and accepting of, all that you experience so that you can move your life forward in valued life directions. Willingness is not a feeling or urge; it is a choice to open up to everything in life, the good and the bad, including painful memories, emotions, thoughts or bodily sensations. Instead of struggling against the negative experiences you don't want, willingness means accepting them without defence or resistance.

The pain of physical effort

Intense physical effort hurts. You'll know that's true if you've sprinted over a short distance or run a marathon. Even climbing the stairs quickly can produce discomfort in your legs and make your heart beat faster. So why do you do it? People never say it's because they *want* to experience the pain that physical exertion produces. Rather, they describe what they're able to *do* while they feel the pain — it may be running a race, playing football, keeping fit or climbing a mountain. It's what your behaviour leads to that gives meaning to your pain and supports you in being willing to experience it.

While easy to say, most people find being willing to accept negative experiences profoundly difficult to do. The human body (like all biological systems) evolved to avoid, reduce or get away from pain or discomfort. Pain signified threat or damage, and minimising it had clear value in terms of survival. As a result, when you experience painful, distressing or unpleasant thoughts or feelings, your natural response is to want to get away from them. Being willing to have these feelings is thus no easy task!

Willingness is all or nothing

Willingness, like acceptance, has an 'all or nothing' quality to it. You're either willing or you're not. The 'all or nothing' nature of willingness can seem a little daunting at first, because being open to experiences that you may have spent a long time trying to avoid is hard. Fortunately, willingness is a skill that you can practise and gradually develop.

The reason willingness needs to be all or nothing is because if you're unwilling to experience something, even to a small degree, this resistance will cause you difficulties. If you're unwilling to experience anxiety, for example, then anxiety itself becomes something to be anxious about and this will add to your initial anxiety, making it greater still. In effect, you become anxious about your anxiety.

It's a similar story for low mood and depression. If you're unwilling to experience any negative mood states, each time one occurs it's something to be depressed about. In effect you can become depressed about your depression. An unwillingness to experience negative psychological events can lead you to become trapped in a downward cycle, as negative experiences become the basis for yet more negative experiences and so on. Faced with this situation, when even a small degree of resistance to feeling something negative becomes the basis for more feelings of negativity, ACT argues that your best option is to set your willingness high and be 100 per cent open to all your experiences.

ACT offers a metaphor for understanding this challenge: viewing unwilling-ness as like being stuck in a *ratchet*. A ratchet is a mechanical device that allows movement in one direction while preventing movement in the oppo-site direction — check out Figure 5-2. Unwillingness is like being in a ratchet because when you're unwilling to experience difficult thoughts or feelings, your life can only go in one direction. It's like a ratchet is engaged and negativity feeds more negativity, slowly squeezing all the goodness out of your life.

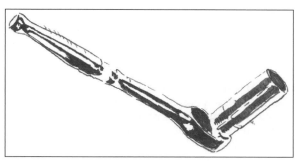

Figure 5-2:
A ratchet
moves only
one way.

Illustration by Joe Munro

The key point is that being willing to experience something negative doesn't reduce the discomfort you feel, but it does stop you adding to it. If you accept the painful, distressing or negative experiences that are an inevitable part of life, you won't feel any better — but neither will you feel worse.

Pain is inevitable, suffering is optional. Beat poet Allen Ginsberg understood the distinction between pain and suffering when he wrote, 'The suffering itself is not so bad, it's the resentment against suffering that is the real pain'.

Willingness is like jumping

ACT sees willingness like jumping. You either jump or you don't. As soon as you jump you're in mid-air, fully committed to whatever happens next.

Jumping from things can be a little scary, even dangerous. The trick is to pick a height that you can cope with, be it a ten-metre diving board or from the side of the pool. Choose a height that you can jump from successfully. While you need to commit to the jump 100 per cent, you can still control its height; that is, its difficulty.

Try the brief exercise below to experience willingness directly. It requires you to be still for just a few minutes. That may sound easy, but as soon as you start, perhaps even before, you may begin to experience thoughts and physical sensations. Some of these may be positive, some negative and some neutral. For instance, you may drift off into making plans for later in the day or wonder whether you're doing the exercise correctly. Or you may notice some mild physical discomfort, such as an urge to shift position or scratch an itch. Your task is to be willing to experience these thoughts and feelings. Notice your experiences and do nothing about them.

Find a quiet place, sit down and get comfortable. Place your feet on the ground, sit up straight and let your hands rest in your lap or by your sides. Take a moment to look around you and draw in a few deep breaths. When you're ready, close your eyes and bring your attention onto your breathing. Follow your breath in and then out. As you do so, notice how your chest rises and falls as you breathe in and out.

During the exercise your attention will wander from time to time as you drift off into your thoughts. If this occurs — and it almost certainly will — notice that it's happened and bring your attention back to your breathing and the moment you're in. If you notice you're struggling with something, such as an urge to move, just be aware of it and try to let it go. Be open to all your experiences.

Continue to sit still for five minutes, and simply notice what you experience. When you finish the exercise, take a moment to think about the following questions:

- ✔ What did you notice?
- ✔ What thoughts, sensations or feelings did you experience?
- ✔ Did you struggle with anything? If so, what happened next?
- ✔ Were you fully willing to experience what occurred?

This willingness exercise gives you an opportunity to practise making the choice to be open to all of your experiences. Interestingly, many people find even a simple exercise like this really quite hard to do. If that's the case for you, don't worry, because the more you practise being willing and open, the better you get at it. And this book offers you lots of practice!

Willingness is not wanting

Willingness is different to wanting. Being *willing* to have something in your life doesn't mean you *want* it in your life.

It's quite possible to not *want* a negative or painful experience, and yet still be *willing* to have it. Being willing isn't about wanting pain or distress in your life (you're not a masochist, after all!); rather, you choose to be willing to experience something because trying to avoid it isn't useful. For example, you can be willing to feel anxious on the first day of a new job so that you can get on with your career, not because you want to feel this way.

By proposing willingness and acceptance as the way forward, ACT isn't suggesting you submit or surrender to all of life's discomfort and hurt. If you can get rid of a painful experience, it often makes sense to do so. If you have a headache, drink a glass of water and get some fresh air; if you're feeling cold, put a coat on; if the music's too loud, turn it down. These are sensible things to do, but problems arise when you start trying to avoid and control things that aren't easily avoided or controlled, such as your own thoughts, feelings and bodily sensations.

ACT sees willingness as a pragmatic choice. You don't choose to be willing because you want to experience painful, disturbing or negative thoughts and feelings. Rather, you choose to be open to and accepting because resisting them doesn't work and comes at a cost — it stops you doing the things you want to do and it uses up precious time and energy that's better spent living in line with your values.

Setting Value-Based SMART Goals

When you've taken the choice to be willing to be open to all life's experiences, you're ready to start doing the things that matter. Committed action involves building larger and larger patterns of value-based behaviour, and you do so one step at a time by setting small and achievable goals.

In ACT you set your value-based goals in three stages:

1. **Choose and clarify the value you want to work on.**

2. **Develop SMART goals that represent this value.**

3. **Take action openly and without defence.**

Chapter 4 introduces tools such as the Valued Living Questionnaire that you can use to identify your values. When you've identified a particular value that you want to work on, the next step is to develop goals that reflect it.

Setting relevant value-based goals isn't as easy as it may seem because choosing overly ambitious targets that lack focus is all too easy. One way to ensure that you set goals that are likely to work is to make them SMART, which stands for Specific, Measurable, Achievable, Relevant and Time-framed:

- ✔ **Specific:** Goals that are specific and clearly state what you want to happen are most effective. It's a good idea to use verbs when specifying a goal as they tell you what you actually have to do. For instance, 'I will *cook* a healthy meal this evening'.

- ✔ **Measurable:** Goals that are measurable help you keep track of your progress. You need to set clearly observable criteria for success. For example, 'I will call my sister *every week*'.

- ✔ **Achievable:** Goals have to be achievable or they're worthless. It's fine to be ambitious, but over-stretching yourself will lead to failure. Think carefully about what you can achieve and then set a goal within that target. If you're successful you can then set another target that takes you further, but if you fail you have nothing to build on.

- ✔ **Relevant:** Goals need to represent your values and what's important to you. If they don't, you simply won't be motivated to complete them. Regularly checking whether the goal you're working on really matters to you will help keep you focused on achieving it.

- ✔ **Time-framed:** Specifying a time frame for achieving your goal is helpful. It keeps you focused and provides a sense of urgency. If your goal states, 'I'm going to start eating more healthily next month', you won't know when to start. A more useful goal is, 'I'm going to eat a salad *tomorrow night*'.

Establishing goals with different timescales

Think about your goals in terms of the immediate, short, medium and long term:

- ✔ **Immediate goal:** You can achieve this goal within the next 30 minutes. Immediate goals can be very powerful because they help you engage in value-based living instantly. You don't need to wait to start living the life you want. For instance, you can make a phone call to a loved one or choose a healthy option for lunch.

✔ **Short-term goal:** This is something you can do in the next few days and weeks. It may require some organisation, such as inviting friends over for a meal or submitting a job application.

✔ **Medium-term goal:** A few months are needed to reach your target here and some sub-goals may be necessary. For example, you may want to bake your own wedding cake to show your future wife how much you love her — but you need to learn the basics of cookery first.

✔ **Long-term goal:** This goal can take months or years to achieve. Maybe you want to visit South America or train to be a barrister. Long-term goals are nearly always made up of shorter-term goals and actions, but they're nonetheless useful for organising your behaviour over the longer term.

Offering three tips for setting effective goals

The following short sections describe three tips to help you set effective goals and to follow through and complete them.

Avoid 'dead man goals'

The preceding sections describe how to set simple goals to move your life forward positively. It's tempting, however, to set negative goals describing what not to do. American psychologist Ogden Lindsley advised against setting goals that could be achieved by a dead man. These are negatively-framed goals or goals that specify what *not* to do. For instance, a dead man could 'never smoke again' and 'never shout at the kids'.

Negatively framed goals that specify what not to do aren't particularly helpful, in the same way that asking someone for directions and being told where *not* to go doesn't lead you to your destination. Goals are most useful when they direct your behaviour towards positive actions that take you forward — in the direction of your values.

Make your goals public

Research demonstrates that telling someone else about your goal is helpful. When you make your commitments public, you're more likely to follow them through because human beings are social animals and want to be respected by their fellows.

Publicising your goals can feel like an extra burden, but that's the point. By telling other people about what you want to do, you raise the stakes and bring a social dimension to the commitment you've made.

The nice thing about this strategy is that if you aren't sure or you feel it will add too much pressure, you can decide not to tell anyone and to keep your goals to yourself. But if you think it will help you stick with your commitments, then tell someone, or even lots of people!

Get back on the horse

You probably won't follow through on all the commitments you make to yourself. No one does, of course. What matters is how you respond when you fail to keep a commitment. You can give up or try again.

Metaphorically, you've fallen off your horse. But as you sit on the floor nursing your bumps or bruises, notice that you have a choice. You can see the whole thing as a mistake and give up. Or you can pick yourself up, dust yourself down and start again. What do you usually do?

Maybe your goal was quite ambitious and its outcome was uncertain, but stopping at the first difficulty you encounter won't help. The one thing you can be sure of is that when you stop trying, change definitely won't occur.

When you engage in committed actions and put one foot in front of the other in pursuit of what really matters, you can be at peace and content with the life you're living.

Chapter 6

Overcoming Barriers to Living a Meaningful Life

In This Chapter

▶ Removing obstacles to living the life you want

▶ Utilising the power of defusion

▶ Using your failures to create successes

*E*ven when you really want something, doing what's needed to achieve it can still be difficult. Sometimes external factors genuinely beyond your control are the reason, but it's also the case that your 'mind' can put up psychological barriers (we look at the 'mind' in detail in Chapter 10). Understanding and then dealing with these barriers can help you stay on course to do what matters in life.

This chapter helps you to understand how to overcome barriers to engaging in actions that are consistent with your personally chosen values. You explore some of the typical ways in which fusion with unwanted thoughts and feelings can lead to behaving in a way that's inconsistent with the life you really want to lead. We also offer some defusion exercises for you to try, which help you disentangle yourself from such unwanted thoughts.

Overcoming Psychological Barriers to Change

One commonly offered explanation for why you fail to achieve your goals is that you just don't desire the outcome enough. According to this view, failures represent a lack of willpower or even laziness. If you can just be more focused or self-disciplined, you'll succeed.

Not everything is possible

'You can get it if you really want', sang Jimmy Cliff, 'but you must try, try and try, try and try, you'll succeed at last'. Although this message permeates Western culture, in reality there are some things you can't change, no matter how hard you try. For example, avoiding your thoughts, feelings and sensations in any meaningful way simply isn't possible.

While motivation is important, other psychological barriers can get in the way too. ACT identifies four primary psychological barriers that, if left unaddressed, are likely to undermine your capacity to achieve your goals; they can be summarised with the acronym *FEAR* (originally coined by Steve Hayes, Kirk Strosahl and Kelly Wilson):

- ✔ **F**usion with your thoughts
- ✔ **E**valuation of your experience
- ✔ **A**voidance of your experience
- ✔ **R**eason-giving for your behaviour

The following sections describe each barrier in detail.

Fusion with your thoughts

Fusion means becoming overly attached to and believing of the literal content of your thoughts (Chapter 3 deals with its opposite — defusion — and we also talk about defusion in the later section, 'Replacing FEAR with DARE'). When you fuse with your thoughts, you look at the world *from* those thoughts. It's as though you're inside your thoughts and can't separate from them. Your thoughts define you.

Fusion isn't wholly bad, as language works largely because of its literal content. That is, by listening to the content of what other people say, you can then respond to it accordingly. If a parent says, 'It's raining outside so put your coat on', the child can respond effectively to the situation (that is, put her coat on and stay dry) because she listens to literal content.

Fusion and panic attacks

A person experiencing a panic attack may think she's actually having a heart attack. If she fuses with this scary thought she may respond to the situation as though her life is actually threatened. In turn, her body releases adrenalin, which makes her heart beat faster, and her breathing quickens, further reinforcing the belief that she's having a heart attack. Fusing with your thoughts in this way can affect the way you behave — and not always positively.

Problems arise, however, when you become overly fused with your thoughts because they aren't always accurate. And even when they are, they're not always useful. Fusing with thoughts such as 'I can't do it' or 'I'm too ugly' means that you're more likely to behave as though they're true. You may not enrol on a photography course because you believe you're not intelligent enough or avoid going on a date if you're upset when you look in the mirror. Going against what you believe to be 'the truth' is hard.

ACT encourages you to have a more flexible relationship with your thoughts and your cognitive processes in general. Being psychologically flexible (Chapter 3 covers this concept) enables you to respond to the literal content of your thoughts and cognitions when doing so is useful, but also to see them for what they are — just words, images and bits of language going through your head (see Figure 6-1). This process is called defusion (see the 'Defusing from your thoughts' section later in this chapter for more details).

Evaluation of your experience

Evaluation is a primary psychological process and you do it all the time. Like everyone else, you're constantly making judgements about everything that's going on around you. That's fine, except for the fact that a great many of your evaluations are negative. No one's exactly sure why this is the case, but one explanation is that the evolutionary past has primed humans (like all animals) to be highly sensitive to potential threats and this biases you to notice life's negatives before life's positives. Being aware of possible threats and risks helps you to take evasive action and survive to live another day. While historically you may have scanned the environment for predators, today your attention may be drawn to a slippery floor, a wobbly ladder or social threats and tensions.

Figure 6-1:
Defusion from your thoughts means not taking them too seriously and recognising them for what they are — just mental events that bubble up and usually, just as quickly, fade away.

Illustration by Joe Munro

Evaluating risks in the environment, as survival dictates, is one thing, but problems arise when you start to evaluate yourself. When you evaluate parts of your own experience (that is, your thoughts, feelings and bodily sensations) as negative, you can come to see them as something to be avoided in much the same way as you'd try to avoid negative events outside your body (running away from a predator, for example). This approach may seem a good idea initially, but avoiding what's happening inside your own body turns out to be very difficult, and your efforts to do so are often wasted or, worse, counterproductive.

Avoidance of your experience

Experiential avoidance describes your behaviour when you're unwilling to remain in contact with difficult thoughts, feelings and bodily sensations and instead engage in what are ultimately counterproductive efforts to try to minimise or get rid of them.

Experiential avoidance occurs in part because you try to control your internal private emotions and thoughts in the same way as you attempt to manipulate external events. When you experience external negative events, you can take action to make things better. If your shoe rubs, you can remove it or stop walking; if your baby is crying, you can feed her or put her to bed. In short, you can take action that's consistent with your values (the value of being a loving, caring parent, for example). Basically, when you don't like something in the external world, you 'change it or leave it'.

However, this strategy doesn't work with your thoughts and feelings. The more you try to control, avoid or minimise them, the more dominant they become. You simply don't have the same level of control over your internal private thoughts and emotions as you do over events in the external world. While you can choose to think certain thoughts for a short while, most of the time your thoughts (and related cognitions, such as memories or mental images) are linked to external stimuli via a range of arbitrary relationships over which you have little or no control. As a result, your thoughts can be triggered by events happening around you in unpredictable and various ways. For example, if you experience agoraphobia (the fear of open or public places) you may feel anxious and afraid in busy or crowded situations. But you may also become anxious in relation to things associated with crowds, such as shops, football matches or even the mention of the words 'people' and 'outside'. Avoiding all associations with things you don't like is very difficult to achieve. The only way you can do so is to limit your contact with the world to a small range of predictable events (people with agoraphobia often confine themselves to a single room for years on end).

While you can't fully control the thoughts you have, you may think that you can change them or blank out the ones you don't like. Unfortunately, you can't. Research has demonstrated time and again that the more you try to suppress or control unwanted thoughts, the more you experience them. The very act of trying to control something means that you're focusing on it and it thereby becomes a part of your life.

The situation is much the same for your emotions, though for a different reason. Your emotions are what you feel in your body and depend on what's happened to you. You can't try to change how you feel right now because you can't change your past. Your only option is to do things now that create a new history that will enable you to respond more psychologically flexibly to difficult emotions in the future.

Reason-giving for your behaviour

Human beings are very good at providing reasons for why they behave as they do. Indeed, we ask children, from a very young age, to explain their own behaviour so we're well-practised by the time we get to adulthood. Although not in itself a problem, the need to provide explanations encourages you to refer to the thoughts, feelings, physical sensations and memories that occur as you behave as *causes* of your behaviour. And this leads to a related problem — because the two often co-occur, it's easy to assume that good behaviour is caused by positive emotions and cognitions and bad behaviour by negative emotions and cognitions.

A child may say, 'I'm too scared to go to school', for example. How she feels is presented as the cause of her refusal to attend school. Similarly statements such as, 'I hit him because I was angry' and 'I bought her flowers because I love her', refer to emotions as the cause of those actions. These statements can appear to explain the causes for your behaviour, but actually they're just words. So deep in Western culture is the idea that thought and feelings cause human behaviour that at first sight it can seem ridiculous to question it, but that's exactly what ACT asks you to do.

From an ACT perspective, 'reasons are not causes'. Whether you think them to yourself or say them out loud, reasons are just words — bits of language. What you think and say are important, but they don't cause what you do. If you don't believe us, try these:

- ✔ Say out loud or think to yourself, 'Touch my nose', but then do nothing.
- ✔ Say out loud or think to yourself, 'Don't say green', and then say 'green' out loud.

No doubt you managed to do the opposite of what you thought or said. How is this possible if your thoughts and statements control what you do?

Even when your reasons refer to your emotions, they're still not causal. Explanations such as 'I ran because I was scared' or 'I was so happy, I jumped for joy' are often acceptable in everyday discourse, but quickly fall apart under closer inspection.

Have you ever been in any of these situations:

- ✔ Feeling sad but smiling and pretending to be okay? And vice versa?
- ✔ Being angry but holding your tongue?
- ✔ Feeling sleepy but staying awake?
- ✔ Being hungry but not eating? And vice versa?

Everyone's experienced feeling one way and behaving in another. But if your feelings control your behaviour, this shouldn't be possible. How you feel is important, but the evidence indicates that your emotions don't cause your behaviour.

Try acting, dear boy

Legend has it that when Dustin Hoffman was filming *Marathon Man* he stayed awake for three nights in order to be able to play his part as realistically as possible. When he next arrived on set looking duly terrible, his co-star, Laurence Olivier, asked him what was wrong. After hearing Hoffman's explanation, Olivier paused for a moment, before saying, 'Try acting, dear boy . . . it's much easier.'

So what's going on? According to ACT, the explanation is that you behave and feel in certain ways because of something that's happened and it's to those events that you must look for the causes of your behaviour. Because your feelings typically co-occur with, or even precede, your actions, it's easy to conclude that they're causal. However, your experience tells you differently. You can behave in ways that differ from what you're thinking or how you're feeling. Indeed, the entire acting profession is based on that premise (check out the nearby sidebar, 'Try acting, dear boy').

In reality, the causes you ascribe to your behaviour are often little more than excuses for why you did or didn't do something. And you probably already know that!

Replacing FEAR with DARE

When you engage in FEAR (refer to the earlier section, 'Overcoming Psychological Barriers to Change'), it can be difficult to connect with what really matters and your life can drift away from your values.

ACT responds to FEAR with *DARE*:

- ✔ **D**efusion
- ✔ **A**cceptance
- ✔ **R**econnect with values
- ✔ **E**ngage and take action

This acronym was originally coined by the ACT writer Russ Harris and is explored in more detail in the following sections.

Defusing from your thoughts

Because cognitive fusion can be so problematic, dealing with fusion is one of the primary aims of ACT. Instead of fusing with the literal content of your thoughts, ACT helps you to notice that you're having those thoughts. Discriminating the process of thinking from the thoughts you're having gives you a little distance from their content and allows you to decide whether they're useful or not.

Defusion means:

- Noticing thoughts rather than becoming caught up in them
- Letting thoughts come and go rather than holding onto them
- Looking *at* thoughts rather than seeing the world *from* thoughts
- Changing how you relate to your thoughts

When you defuse you're able to notice that thoughts are just thoughts — merely words or images in your mind. When you do so, you're more able to step back from their content and choose how you want to behave.

Unhooking yourself from your thoughts is difficult for two related reasons. First, human language works because of its literal content, so it makes sense to focus on it. Your response to the literal content of statements such as 'be careful', 'it's hot' or 'turn right at the traffic lights', for example, enables you to behave effectively in these circumstances. Second, culturally you're not actively taught to discriminate your own thinking. As you grow up your parents and educators tend to focus more on what you think or say, because it's the literal content of language that makes it so useful.

By the time you reach adulthood, you've had extensive training in responding to the literal content of language, while simultaneously *not* being taught to notice or be aware of the processes that produce language; that is, your thinking. This focus on the literal makes unhooking from your thoughts and noticing the process that's giving rise to them very difficult. Fortunately, a range of activities exist that can help.

Defusion is a skill that improves with practice. The more defusion exercises you do, the more skilled you become at defusing from your thoughts. The less you fuse with your thoughts, the more able you are to choose whether or not to respond to them and to make judgements regarding how useful those thoughts are in helping you achieve your goals.

The following defusion exercise helps you to practise letting go of your thoughts.

This exercise involves watching your thoughts come and go. Follow these steps:

1. **Find a place where you won't be disturbed and get into a comfortable position.** You may want to close your eyes or focus them on a fixed spot.

2. **Imagine that you're sitting beside a gently flowing stream with leaves floating along the surface of the water.** Take a moment to really place yourself in that image.

3. **As each new thought emerges in your mind, place it on a leaf and watch it float away down the river.** Do so with every thought, whether it's positive, negative or neutral.

4. **If you don't have any thoughts for a while, just watch the stream as it flows by.** Eventually a thought or image will come into your mind and, when it does, gently place it on a leaf and watch it float away.

5. **If your mind says 'I can't do this' or 'this is stupid', merely notice these thoughts and place them on leaves to float away.**

6. **If a thought doesn't float away on a leaf, just be aware that it's hanging around.** Look at it and notice it.

7. **If some more difficult thoughts or images show up, acknowledge them and, once again, place them on leaves and allow them to float away.**

8. **If your mind wanders off — a very normal occurrence — gently bring your attention back to the exercise and continue placing your thoughts on leaves.**

Continue with this exercise for 5–10 minutes.

How easy did you find this exercise? Did you find yourself more able to notice thoughts as they showed up, and how was this different to the way in which you usually experience your thoughts? People often report that allowing thoughts to show up and simply fade away feels very different to their usual experience of becoming lost in or ensnared by their thoughts. Remember: they're just thoughts, nothing more.

Letting go of your thoughts isn't easy — but you will get better at it over time!

Being able to defuse from your thoughts means that you can accept them, which is essential if you're to face all that life offers.

Chocolate versus defusion

Psychologists at Swansea University studied 135 students who wanted to reduce their chocolate consumption. They divided the students into three groups and taught each group a different technique to help them eat less chocolate: defusion, acceptance or relaxation. The students were then given a bag of 14 chocolates and told to record each time they ate one over the next 5 days. The results showed that students using defusion ate less chocolate. Why? Because people often reach for chocolates automatically in response to thoughts such as, 'I need something sweet'. The defusion process helped the students notice the thought they were having, which then interrupted the automatic process. They realised they were just having a thought and not being issued a command that they had to obey.

Accepting life

Acceptance is the alternative to experiential avoidance. *Acceptance* means opening up to life's experiences, fully and without defence. Engaging with all that life has to offer, the good and the bad, is a conscious act.

Acceptance isn't easy, but the rewards are significant because it enables you to connect more fully with life. By being willing to remain in contact with what are at times difficult, painful or unwanted experiences, you're able to do the things that matter to you. And this means that you can live your life in relation to what you want (your values) rather than what you don't want (the bad stuff).

Acceptance is a central skill in ACT (the clue's in the name!) and is present across all six core ACT processes (Chapter 3 covers these processes in detail). For instance, defusion, committed action and self as context all require that you're willing to be in contact with negative thoughts, feelings and bodily sensations.

Mindfulness also involves acceptance and provides you with the opportunity to practise it. *Mindfulness* means you consciously notice whatever you experience without any effort to change or resist it. In developing the ability to be mindful, your aim is to notice your different experiences in the present moment and to let them be as they are. That is, to accept them.

We look at mindfulness and how you make contact with the present moment in more detail in Chapter 7, but the best way to understand the concept and how it can be useful is to experience it directly. The following exercise offers a taster.

When the solution becomes the problem

An estimated 1.5 million people in the UK today are addicted to painkillers and experience significant health problems as a result. Research reveals that those who over-use painkillers often have a low threshold for experiencing mental or physical discomfort. This means that when they notice even a small amount of discomfort, they reach for the painkillers to dull the sensation. This strategy works in the short term but over the medium and long term can lead to significant problems. In effect, the 'solution' becomes the problem.

You can practise this exercise anywhere, but outside is particularly effective because it can enable you to experience — and become mindful of — lots of different sensations. Follow these steps:

1. **Take off your shoes and go outside into the garden.**

2. **Stand on the grass with your feet parallel, but slightly apart.**

3. **Take a few moments to focus on your breathing and begin to gently become aware of your thoughts and feelings.**

4. **Allow your awareness to slide down to your feet and notice how they feel.** Observe the gentle swaying and shifting of the weight of your body around the soles of your feet as you maintain your balance. Feel the grass against your skin and the coolness or warmth of the soil beneath.

5. **Breathe slowly in and out through your nostrils.**

6. **Slowly and gently, begin to shift the weight of your body to your right foot and, very gradually and slowly, lift up your left foot.** Slowly take your left foot forward and notice the subtle movements taking place throughout your body as you take a single step.

7. **With your left foot placed slightly in front of your right foot, take a moment to re-establish your sense of balance and stability.** Then repeat the process but with the opposite feet.

8. **Repeat this process a further eight times and then return your feet to a parallel position.**

9. **Take a few last moments to once again observe the gentle sway of your body's weight through the soles of your feet.**

10. **When you feel ready, take a couple of deep breaths and bring the exercise to a close.**

How was this experience of walking different to usual? Are you usually in such a rush to get somewhere that you don't notice the actual sensation of walking? You can practise mindfulness during any and all daily activities, from washing up to chopping vegetables to mowing the lawn. Focusing totally on that one thing creates some space from your thoughts.

Reconnecting with your values

When you fail to achieve a goal, check that the value it's based on still really matters to you at this point in time. Your values are the personal qualities that are most dear to you and provide the motivation for doing the difficult things you experience as you move forward in valued life directions. This means that if the value is no longer important to you, you won't have the motivation to see it through.

A common mistake is choosing values you think you *should* care about. Knowing that a friend is unwell, for instance, you may want to value being a good friend and select goals in relation to that. However, if at that point in time you're actually more interested in pursuing family or community-related values, then seeing through friendship-based goals will be difficult.

You need to prioritise your values. As your life changes, so too does what you care about. Turn to Chapter 4 for more on prioritising your values.

Engaging and taking action

When you've checked that your goals are based on those values most important to you, the next step is to ensure that they're SMART (check out Chapter 5 for more on what makes a goal SMART).

Avoid these common problems associated with setting SMART goals:

- ✔ **Setting unrealistic goals:** Thinking big is admirable, but some things in life just aren't possible. For example, if you want to play a saxophone solo at your best friend's wedding, signing up for lessons a month before the event and hoping to pull it off just isn't realistic. Even if the goal is realistic, you need to give yourself enough time to achieve it. Tasks often take longer to complete than you think.

- ✔ **Setting other people's goals:** Maybe your family and friends want to influence the goals you set yourself. They may think they know what's best for you or want you to do certain things or go down a particular path. While having good relationships with the people around you is important, it's essential that your goals are your own and relate to your underlying values.

- ✔ **Setting negative goals:** Setting negative goals can be problematic because they focus on what you don't want rather than on what you do want. Not only does this make them unappealing, but they also fail to provide any guidance about what to do instead. For example, a negative goal such as 'Stop working late' can be reframed positively as 'Get home in time to eat with the family'.

- ✔ **Setting too many goals:** Each day contains only so many hours and you can't do everything. Instead, work on a small number of goals and do them well rather than doing lots of things badly. Quality over quantity.

Using Failure as Feedback

ACT helps you define and then commit to completing value-based goals. However, no matter how clearly you specify your values and how SMART your goals are, you still won't be successful every time.

While this situation is quite normal, a problem occurs if you over-generalise the failure to complete one goal to this means 'I'm a failure'. Fusing with related negative thoughts, such as 'I can't do it' or 'I give up', will act as a barrier to trying new goals. You may even give up trying altogether; after all, if you're a failure, it makes sense that everything you do will fail.

In reality everyone fails to keep a commitment to achieving a goal at some point. Of course, you may be disappointed, but rather than seeing failures as wholly bad things, you can understand that they're part of how you learn. You can think of your failures as like the wobbling you experience when you're learning to ride a bike. The sensation doesn't feel nice — it's scary even, and sometimes you may fall off completely — but it's this feedback that helps you find your balance. Rather than giving up with each slip and wobble that occurs, you can see them as part of the learning process as you set off in a new life direction. Sure, falling off can hurt, but if you want to master riding a bike you need to get back on and try again.

You may struggle to keep going after failing to achieve a goal (or to stick to a commitment to complete a goal). It can take a lot of effort to pick yourself up and try again. But this is really your only option, to try, try and try again, because no matter how much you try you can never escape failure. French novelist Victor Hugo identified perseverance as 'the secret of all triumphs' and he had a point. All human achievement, be it in science, literature, architecture, medicine or politics, involves overcoming 'failures' and adverse events along the way.

Don't give up!

Kicking the smoking habit is notoriously difficult, and for most people involves up to six prior unsuccessful attempts. Fortunately, the first attempt is the hardest and lasts the shortest time, and each successive attempt is easier. Ultimately, those who persevere are successful.

Succeeding at everything you do simply isn't possible; you'll always meet with failure from time to time. The biggest mistake you can make is not failing to achieve a goal but giving up trying at that point.

Use the elements of DARE (refer to the earlier section, 'Replacing FEAR with DARE') to help you defuse from your thoughts, accept and be open to life, reconnect with your values and set positive goals in their pursuit.

Chapter 7

Being Present through Mindfulness

*H*ave you ever arrived at a destination and not remembered the journey? Or wondered if you've locked the front door behind you because you have no memory of doing so? These are common experiences and they've probably happened to you. Take a moment to consider these situations:

✔ Being introduced to someone and moments later unable to remember his name

✔ Eating a meal and not really tasting or smelling it

✔ Listening to a friend but not really hearing what he's saying

✔ Looking through a magazine but taking none of it in

✔ Turning off the iron but being unable to remember if you've done so

If these seem familiar, you know what it's like to drift off into your thoughts and thereby become a little detached from what's happening in the world. It's almost as though you're on autopilot and you stop noticing what's going on around you. Everyone experiences this from time to time and in fact it's quite normal. However, when you spend too much time in your thoughts, you can become disconnected from the world and this will make it harder for you to live in it. What's more, your thoughts are often negative (Chapter 10 explains why), which means that if you spend too much time in them the world can seem a dark and difficult place.

Mindfulness is the opposite experience. It's about being open and aware and noticing what's going on in the here and now. As this chapter reveals, mindfulness helps you be present in your own life as you purposefully tune in, without judgement or opposition, to your experiences.

Defining Mindfulness

Mindfulness means that you pay active attention to what's happening in the present moment, openly and without resistance. It requires you to slow down so that you can connect with what's happening around you. That probably sounds quite simple, but the power of language makes connecting in this way surprisingly difficult. Language is so pervasive and persistent that you constantly fuse with it and get hooked on its literal content (Chapter 6 delves into fusion in more detail). When this happens you lose contact with the present moment as you drift off into your thoughts, dreams, worries, fears, plans and evaluations. Remaining connected with the here and now is hard to do in practice because the focus of your attention is always shifting and your thoughts will always pull you away. The challenge inherent in mindfulness is not making initial contact with the present moment, but in coming back to it time and again.

Mindfulness isn't a new concept and it's clearly reminiscent of meditation. However, while meditation is often linked to Eastern religions such as Buddhism, mindfulness is secular. Even though mindfulness practices go back thousands of years, the benefits they deliver for psychological well-being and mental health in the modern world are only beginning to be understood by Western science.

Looking at the four core elements of mindfulness

Mindfulness can be broken down into four core elements:

- **Choice:** Mindfulness is a deliberate and conscious act that you purposefully engage in. You choose to pay attention to the present moment and all that it brings.

- **Awareness:** Mindfulness involves being aware of what's happening by focusing your attention on a particular event or process (see the nearby sidebar, 'A good walk lost'). It's *not* a thinking process; it's an awareness process. It may even involve being aware that you're thinking.

- **Openness:** Mindfulness involves being non-judgemental and open to all your experiences at that moment in time, whatever they may be. Maintaining this state of mind can be very difficult if they're unpleasant experiences, but being mindful is about awareness and noticing, not judging or avoiding.

- **Flexibility:** Mindfulness involves being flexible with your attention. Your attention often jumps about from one thing to another and, because of this, mindfulness requires that you can focus your attention on particular events or processes and also be flexible enough to allow it to wander from time to time.

Mindfulness and PTSD

People with post-traumatic stress disorder (PTSD) often report finding it hard to gain any distance from unpleasant thoughts and memories. Seemingly random events can trigger memories of past trauma, which can set off a spiral of difficult thoughts and feelings As a result, those suffering from PTSD may find it hard to stay focused on what matters most in their life, such as relationships with family and friends or other activities that they used to enjoy.

Mindfulness has the opposite effect: it reconnects people with the present moment and reduces the extent to which they fuse with and hence are controlled by unpleasant thoughts and memories.

Being mindful involves slowing down and connecting with the present moment in an open and non-judgemental way. When you do so you can gain a little distance from your thoughts and become more sensitive to all elements of your experiences and what's happening around you. This increased sensitivity is useful because it enables you to relate to yourself and others with more openness and compassion and to begin living your life in line with your values. In this way, mindfulness helps you get on with living your life.

Recognising what mindfulness isn't

As well as defining what mindfulness is, it's also worth spending a little time clarifying what it isn't. The following list counters three common misunderstandings:

- ✔ **Filling your mind:** Mindfulness doesn't mean having a 'full mind' or focusing on something so much that you can't focus on anything else. Filling your mind in this way is a form of distraction, which isn't the purpose of mindfulness. In fact, mindfulness is the opposite of distraction as it involves stepping toward all your experiences, whatever they are.

- ✔ **Emptying your mind:** Having no thoughts, ideas, plans or memories isn't possible. You can't simply stop thinking! You may be able to suppress your cognitive activity or distract yourself to reduce it, but as soon as you stop these efforts your thoughts will soon return.

- ✔ **Relaxation:** Mindfulness isn't a form of relaxation. Feeling relaxed and soothed by the process is quite common, but that's a side effect rather than the aim. In fact, using mindfulness to relax may have the opposite effect because in wanting a particular outcome when you engage in the process, you are by implication also not prepared to experience other things, such as tension or stress. But you can't make yourself relax. You relax when you're open to all of your experiences, not when you're trying to not feel tension or stress.

A good walk lost

Spending too much time in your thoughts can disconnect you from your surroundings. Thinking while walking can be very useful (for instance, if you're planning a party or holiday), but it can also get in the way of noticing the wonderful things in the world outside your skin.

Mark Twain quipped that 'Golf is a good walk spoiled'; so too is not hearing the birdsong or feeling the sun on your face. A good walk may be more than spoilt — you may not notice it in the first place!

Putting Mindfulness into Practice

The only way to really understand mindfulness is to experience it directly. No amount of reading about swimming can teach you how to swim; at some point you have to get in the water and work it out for yourself. Mindfulness is the same.

Staying with the learning to swim metaphor, the best approach is to start in the shallows and gradually move into deeper water as your technique develops. Starting with a one-kilometre swim in cold open water isn't a good idea. With that in mind, we introduce you to two exercises that offer you a gentle introduction to mindfulness.

Odd though it may seem, many people first experience mindfulness with a raisin! Jon Kabat-Zinn, one of the pioneers of mindfulness in Western healthcare systems, likes to use a raisin in a first exercise with people because it demonstrates the everyday, even banal, quality of mindfulness. Because you may not have a raisin to hand for this exercise, instead you can use any piece of fruit and the principle remains the same. This exercise takes about five minutes.

Whenever you find your attention wandering from the task at hand (and it will!), just notice that it's happened and gently return your attention to the piece of fruit and what you're doing with it.

Follow these steps:

1. **Place the piece of fruit in the palm of your hand. Spend a few moments just looking at it.** Study it with a sense of curiosity as though you've never seen such an item before. It may even start to look a little strange as you really notice its details.

2. **Gently pick up the piece of fruit with your thumb and index finger and roll it between them. What does it feel like? What textures are you aware of?** At this stage you may like to close your eyes so that you can really notice what you're feeling.

3. **Smell the piece of fruit and see what aromas you can pick out. Rub the piece of fruit across your lips and notice what that feels like.**

4. **Gently place the piece of fruit on your tongue. Just let it sit there for a few moments.** Don't chew it; simply notice how it feels.

5. **Begin chewing. Bite the piece of fruit very slowly and gently, extending the time it takes to bite through it for as long as possible. What does the piece of fruit feel like between your teeth? What sensations, textures, tastes and smells do you notice?** If you feel the urge to swallow right away, just notice that urge, and slowly chew the piece of fruit for a minute or so, without swallowing. Finally, go ahead and give in to the urge to swallow it.

6. **Notice the absence of the piece of fruit in your mouth and, when you're ready, open your eyes.**

What did you notice? Was it an easy or difficult exercise? Could you focus your attention on the task at hand or did it keep wandering? Did you have any thoughts about how well you were or weren't doing?

This exercise has no right or wrong answers; whatever you experienced was correct. What's interesting is that most people report finding this seemingly simple exercise quite hard to do. They tend to get hooked by a thought or a feeling and find their attention drifting to other things. When you noticed this happening, were you able to redirect your attention back to the exercise? If you did manage to refocus on your piece of fruit, you may have also noticed that a short while later your attention wandered off again.

Flip-flopping between focusing on the moment and your attention wandering onto something else . . . wandering, focusing, wandering, focusing — this is the essence of mindfulness. Steve Hayes, one of the developers of ACT, points out that mindfulness is difficult because it's elusive. It comes and goes as your attention moves from one thing to another.

The essence of mindfulness is contact with the present moment, without resistance or judgement. Just being in the present. This simple and quick exercise helps you do just that.

Follow these steps:

1. **Take a moment to notice where you are.** Look around and really take it in.

2. **Notice five things you can see.** Let your eyes examine and really look at them, as though you're seeing them for the first time.

3. **Notice five things you can hear.** Really listen and hear the things in the world around you (closing your eyes may help).

4. **Notice five things you can feel.** Consider the temperature of the air on your skin, a piece of jewellery you're wearing or the posture of your body.

Mindfulness and the brain

Research undertaken by neuroscientists has shown how the brains of Buddhist monks change significantly as a result of mindfulness meditation. But this finding rather misses the point. First, *every* experience changes your brain in some way. And if you do something an awful lot, you'll undergo an even greater degree of change. Thus, changes in your brain function following the practice of mindfulness aren't a surprise. Second, and more important, mindfulness is a *psychological* experience; making sense of it by reducing it to your neurological functioning just isn't possible. Neuroscience may one day be able to explain how your brain functions during mindfulness, but not why you engage in it, when you do so or what it means. For that, you need a psychological analysis.

As you do this exercise your attention may wander and you may drift off into your thoughts from time to time. When that happens, just acknowledge it and return to the stage in the exercise you'd reached. Keep going until you finish the exercise and that's it! What's great about this exercise is that you can do it anywhere — at work, in a shopping queue or during a mindfulness retreat.

When you become familiar with the mindfulness process through these and other exercises, you can start to bring it into your everyday life. You don't need to practise complicated or lengthy mindfulness exercises to enjoy its benefits. In his wonderful book *The Miracle of Mindfulness*, the Buddhist teacher Thich Nhat Hanh describes how you can be mindful while doing everyday chores or seemingly mundane activities, such as making a cup of tea or brushing your teeth. Mindfulness is there when you want it in any moment you choose. Just make the decision to be present and you're being mindful.

 Try to practise every day initially. Mindfulness is a skill like any other, and the more you practise, the better you get. When you've got the hang of it, you can then use it more flexibly as and when you want or need to.

Measuring Your Mindfulness

Developed by Ruth Baer, the Mindful Attention Awareness Scale (MAAS; you can find it at www.selfcareinsocialwork.com) has been used in many mindfulness research studies and provides a good measure of how mindful you are. Take it and see.

The following list presents a collection of statements about your everyday experiences. Using the scale (from 1 to 6), indicate how frequently or infrequently you currently experience each scenario. Make sure that your ratings genuinely reflect your experience rather than what you think your experience should be. Please treat each item separately from every other item.

> 1 = almost always; 2 = very frequently; 3 = somewhat frequently; 4 = somewhat infrequently; 5 = very infrequently; 6 = almost never

- ✔ I could be experiencing an emotion and not be conscious of it until some time later.
- ✔ I break or spill things as a result of carelessness, not paying attention or thinking about something else.
- ✔ I find it difficult to stay focused on what's happening in the present.
- ✔ I tend to walk quickly to get where I'm going without paying attention to what I experience along the way.
- ✔ I tend not to notice feelings of physical tension or discomfort until they really grab my attention.
- ✔ I forget a person's name almost as soon as I've been told it for the first time.
- ✔ It seems I am 'running on automatic' without much awareness of what I'm doing.
- ✔ I rush through activities without being really attentive to them.
- ✔ I get so focused on the goal I want to achieve that I lose touch with what I'm doing right now to get there.
- ✔ I do jobs or tasks automatically, without being aware of what I'm doing.
- ✔ I find myself listening to someone with one ear, while doing something else at the same time.
- ✔ I drive places on 'automatic pilot' and then wonder why I went there.
- ✔ I find myself preoccupied with the future or the past.
- ✔ I find myself doing things without paying attention.
- ✔ I snack without being aware that I'm eating.

Add up the scores for all 15 answers. Then divide your total by 15 to find your average score. The higher the score, the greater your ability to be mindful. Typically, the average score is around 3.86 (the highest is 6 and the lowest is 1).

If you gained a low score on the MAAS, you may well benefit from some mindfulness practice. Use the exercises in this chapter to help you focus on the present moment.

Being Kind to Yourself

Human beings can be very self-critical, largely as a result of the negative contents of their thoughts and cognitions. The mental repertoires that you commonly refer to as the 'mind' can perform a range of tasks, but they're particularly good at evaluating and analysing things critically (see Chapter 10 for more details on this). They also seem to be predisposed to noticing the negative aspects of the world around you. From an evolutionary perspective, this predisposition makes sense because it can help you avoid potential risks and dangers; it has clear value in terms of survival. For example, your evaluations can help you notice and weigh up the risks when crossing a busy road so that you can cross it safely.

So when your mind's evaluative capacity focuses on yourself, you shouldn't be surprised by its negative and critical tone. After all, that's what it evolved to do. Trying to stop your mind doing what it's set up to do resembles trying to teach a cat to stop chasing mice. You can try all you like, but you're unlikely to be successful!

What can you do to counter your critical thoughts? Well, a little kindness is a start.

Kindness is a much-underrated quality and yet is fundamental to human relationships and ultimately happiness. Your most important relationships are based on kindness. Loving relationships, for example, are defined by sensitive, generous and selfless acts towards another person.

Of course, being kind to those you love is easy (though not always!) because you care about them. But that's the point. Love doesn't mean behaving lovingly only when you feel like it; rather, it also means behaving lovingly when you *don't* feel like it. It's the parent's ability to speak calmly to his child when inside he's fuming, the lover's ability to smile when he's sad and the friend's ability to listen patiently when he has other things to do. Sometimes love means *not* saying an unkind word or performing an unkind act even when you feel like doing so.

'No act of kindness, no matter how small, is ever wasted,' stated Aesop in the fable of *The Lion and the Mouse*. In the next two minutes, do something kind for yourself or someone else and see what follows. You may be pleasantly surprised.

The challenge you face, like everyone else, is how to be kind to yourself when you're having self-critical thoughts or seeing yourself in a negative light. It's in just such situations that defusing from your language and being open to and accepting of all your experiences can help. What results is self-compassion.

Before describing self-compassion in detail (in the following section), it's important to point out that compassion is what emerges from ACT processes, rather than being part of the model directly. When you step back from the literal content of your thoughts and take an open and accepting position towards all your experiences, you're better placed to engage in value-based actions that reflect the things you care about, for example kindness, love, friendship and health. Behaving positively towards yourself even when your mind is telling you that you don't deserve it is an act of self-compassion.

Working on Self-Compassion

According to psychologist Kristin Neff, compassion has three main components:

- ✔ Being kind and gentle to other people and yourself
- ✔ Recognising a shared common humanity and that your struggles are part of human experience
- ✔ Being aware of (mindful) and open to all your experiences

When these three components are in place, you become sensitive to the suffering of other people and motivated to try to alleviate it. According to Neff, compassion and self-compassion are essentially the same; the former is focused on other people and the latter on yourself.

Compassion means being moved in the face of suffering and wanting to try to help. *Self-compassion* means that you notice your own suffering, which motivates you to be kind to yourself. Self-compassion is helpful because it encourages you to become more active in responding to your own suffering and distress. Rather than simply experiencing your suffering, you can reach out to yourself with kindness and concern, which in turn can create the space to move your life forward.

Self-compassion isn't about trying to feel positive about yourself. It doesn't mean replacing negative thoughts with positive ones. Instead, it's about how you choose to respond when those negative thoughts arise. Self-compassion involves behaving kindly to yourself even when you're experiencing negative thoughts or feelings.

Self-compassion in tandem with psychological flexibility

Self-compassion is an important human capacity and it correlates strongly with psychological wellbeing. In fact, evidence suggests that interventions based on self-compassion can be helpful for some people with post-traumatic stress disorder (PTSD).

You may think that those people who are more resistant to self-compassion (that is, they find it hard to be kind to themselves) would fare worse, but actually that's only part of the story. Psychological flexibility and experiential avoidance (see Chapters 6 and 9 for a fuller description of experiential avoidance) also appear to play a role in coping with PTSD.

Research conducted in 2015 found that people who were more resistant to self-compassion and demonstrated higher levels of experiential avoidance presented with more extreme symptoms of PTSD. The researchers thus argued that being unable to show compassion to oneself in combination with attempting to control or avoid difficult experiences actually worsens the symptoms.

Developing psychological flexibility alongside self-compassion appears to be beneficial for these people.

Differentiating between self-compassion and self-pity

Self-compassion is different from self-pity. In general usage, pity (from the Latin root 'pietas' meaning 'duty') refers to a sense of sympathy, sorrow or regret. Compassion (from the Latin root 'compati' meaning 'to suffer together') also refers to a feeling of sympathy or sorrow, but directed toward another person; it's also accompanied by the strong desire to alleviate that person's suffering. Compassion is a more proactive term.

Self-pity typically describes the behaviour of someone who's become immersed in his own problems and simultaneously forgets that other people have difficulties too. Self-pity tends to be more inward-looking, excluding other people's needs or problems, and as such has a more self-indulgent flavour.

Self-compassion, in contrast, is outward-looking and connects your suffering with that of others. It recognises your common humanity and acknowledges that everyone is struggling with his own issues. This sense of connection enables you to develop a more balanced perspective toward your own suffering.

Carry a small pebble or button in your pocket and when your hand touches it, look around until you see someone. Then imagine him as a baby in his mother's arms or as a young child, laughing with friends or crying with sadness. Try to 'see' the real person in front of you, with his own history and life story.

The two wolves

A Native American parable concerning two wolves captures the challenge you face in deciding how you approach life. An old man is teaching his grandson about the choice between good and evil. 'A constant battle is taking place every moment inside each of us', he says. 'It's between two wolves — one good, the other evil. The good wolf wants a world filled with peace, kindness, love, joy, humility, truth and compassion. The evil wolf wants a world filled with anger, pain, regret, pride, greed, guilt and arrogance'. His grandson asks, 'Which wolf will win?' to which the old man replies, 'The one you feed'.

Measuring your self-compassion

Checking in with your self-compassion can be useful. We developed the following ten questions to help you measure your self-compassion and take a look at how you relate to yourself.

Read the following 10 statements and rate each one on a scale of 1–5:

Don't agree → 1 → 2 → 3 → 4 → 5 ·····Agree completely
····Agree
somewhat

- I find it easier to be critical of myself than kind or supportive.
- I don't deserve to be kind to myself.
- To succeed in life by being tough is more important than being kind or caring.
- I don't know how to be kind to myself.
- I worry that if I open up to my own needs and feelings, I will feel overwhelmed.
- Being kind is for other people; I'm about getting things done.
- I've never been really kind to myself.
- Being critical of myself makes me maintain high standards.
- If I'm kinder to myself I may lose my edge.
- I deserve all of the criticism I direct at myself.

Add up your total score. If you score between 10 and 20, you demonstrate high self-compassion and are generally kind to yourself. Scoring between 40 and 50 suggests low self-compassion and that you're very self-critical.

Gaining a high score on this quick self-compassion assessment suggests that you can be quite critical towards yourself. If you fuse with (believe the literal content of) your critical self-statements, you can become your own worst critic, continually undermining yourself. Remaining positive when you're fused with your self-critical thoughts is hard, if not impossible.

While struggling against self-critical thoughts by trying to ignore, change or reject them may initially seem a good idea, doing so is largely ineffective and indeed counterproductive. The alternative proposed by ACT is to increase your openness to all of your experiences, including your negative thoughts, feelings and bodily sensations. Rather than trying to avoid your unwanted psychological content, the challenge becomes to respond to that part of yourself with kindness and self-compassion.

Linking self-compassion and self-esteem

Self-esteem refers to how positively you think or feel about yourself, whereas self-compassion refers to your ability to be open to and accept self-doubt, suffering and negative self-evaluations as part of being human. Researchers have identified an interesting relationship between self-compassion and self-esteem: people with low self-esteem are more likely to experience mental health problems and psychological distress.

An Australian study surveyed the self-esteem and self-compassion of 2,448 adolescents. It found that low self-esteem had little impact on the psychological wellbeing of students demonstrating high self-compassion. The study concluded that self-compassion provided a 'potentially potent buffering effect' in relation to the negative impact of low self-esteem and negative thoughts. In other words, people with higher self-compassion still have negative thoughts and feelings about themselves; however, by treating them as just thoughts and feelings that they occasionally experience, rather than literal truths, the negative impact on their general wellbeing is greatly reduced.

Believing that what goes on in your head represents the world as it really is, is referred to in ACT as being *fused* with your thoughts. At the other end of the scale, when you don't believe the literal content of your thoughts, merely observing them as random words and phrases, you're *defused* from them.

Defusion is important in ACT because it enables you to slip from the grip of your mind and any negativity it brings. When you're not constantly wrestling with your thoughts, you have more time for other — more enjoyable! — things. Chapter 6 looks at the concept of defusion in more detail.

Chapter 8

Understanding Your 'Selves'

In This Chapter

▶ Understanding how you experience yourself

▶ Connecting with yourself as a story and through what you feel and sense

▶ Using your observing self to gain some distance from difficult thoughts and feelings

*H*ow you experience and understand yourself is important in Acceptance and Commitment Therapy (ACT). ACT identifies three distinct ways in which you experience who you are:

✔ **Self as concept:** How you describe yourself in words, for example 'I'm a teacher', 'I'm 4 years old' or 'I'm friendly'.

✔ **Self as awareness:** Your ongoing awareness of what you experience and sense moment by moment, such as the wind in your hair, the sounds you hear or the weight of your body on a chair.

✔ **Self as context:** Your stable sense of being 'me' or 'I'; the perspective from which you look outwards. Wherever you go, your self as context is your sense that you're just behind your eyes, looking out on the world and taking it in.

This chapter looks at these three distinct senses of self and introduces some exercises to help you recognise and differentiate between them.

Using Self as Context to Defuse from Your Thoughts

Distinguishing between the three different aspects of your personal experience — self as concept, self as awareness and self as context — is useful because it enables you to respond more flexibly towards yourself. In particular, it allows you to respond differently to your thoughts, feelings and bodily sensations.

Consider the problem of fusing with your thoughts. *Fusion* is when you look at the world *from* your thoughts and respond to them literally as though they represent the world as it truly is. The difficulty with fusion is that your thoughts are often wrong. And even when they're 'right', they can still be unhelpful. Therefore, spending too much time inside them isn't always productive and can interfere with living a value-based life.

ACT proposes a novel solution to this problem: rather than trying to change or avoid negative thoughts, instead look *at* them and see not just the content of your thinking but also the thinking process itself. In ACT this is called *defusion*. Defusion frees you from some of the more troublesome aspects of the literal content of your language and allows you the space to decide what you actually want to do in that moment. (Chapter 6 explores defusion in more detail.)

Being able to actively discriminate between the three ways in which you experience yourself is critical for defusion. In ACT, it's your experience of yourself as the place where your thoughts and feelings occur (that is, your 'self as context') that allows you to look *at* your thoughts and thereby get some distance from them. It is your self as context that provides the vantage point or perspective from which to see your psychological content and not become entangled in it.

Conversely, when you're unable to differentiate between your three distinct experiences of who you are, disentangling yourself from your problematic thoughts and self-statements becomes much harder.

A Buddhist metaphor illustrates the three facets of your self-experience very nicely. Called the Slit Lamp, it involves walking into a dark room holding an oil lamp, from which emanates light from a narrow opening. We update this idea and use an electric torch.

Imagine walking into a pitch-black room holding a torch. The torch shines a beam of light into the room that enables you to see what's in there. As you look around you see tables, chairs, lamps, pictures and so on. Now, take a look at what's happening. The furniture (and other things you can see) symbolises your *self as concept*. It's the form of the world that you see and describe. The beam of light that moves around the room is your *self as awareness*. It's your ongoing process of seeing and noticing. Finally, the torch itself is your *self as context*. It's the place or perspective from which your awareness emanates and sees the content of your life. Figure 8-1 provides a graphical representation of this metaphor.

The social origin of self-awareness

A small part of the universe in contained within your skin and you learn how to talk about it via the same social process that you use to talk about the world outside your skin. You discover what something is called when someone tells you its name and shows you how to behave towards it. While you're the only person who can directly feel your emotions, you can only talk about them after your social community has given you the language to do so. And when you learn which words relate to which inner experiences, you also learn how to behave towards them.

Consider this situation. A parent walks into the bathroom and sees a spider on the floor.

If she yells, 'It's a spider!', throws her arms in the air and runs out of the room, the child discovers two things. First, that the thing on the floor is called a 'spider', and second, that you respond to it by running away. Your learning process involves finding out what something is called *and* how to behave towards it. For example, if, when a child is crying, her parent labels her experience in a calm and contained way, the message the child receives is, 'I know what you're feeling and it's okay.' Conversely, if the parent becomes angry, shouts or kicks the door, the child receives a different message and example of how to behave in similar situations.

Figure 8-1:
The Slit Lamp metaphor.

Illustration by Joe Munro

Seeing Your Self as Concept

All people have stories to tell about their lives and you tell different parts of it to different people. For instance, on a CV or during an interview you focus mostly on your educational and employment history and say only a little about your personal interests. In contrast, on a date you probably talk more about your personal history and what you like to do at weekends. The stories you tell about yourself are from your self as concept.

Self as concept is how you describe yourself linguistically (for this reason it's often called *self as description*). It's your verbal statements and evaluations about who you are; for example:

- ✔ I am a woman
- ✔ I am British
- ✔ I am married
- ✔ I am unattractive
- ✔ I am funny
- ✔ I am lazy

Some of these statements are *descriptive facts* (the first three) and some are *evaluations* (the last three) and it's quite natural to bundle them all together to tell a story about the sort of person you are. However, it's also important to be able to distinguish between your evaluations and descriptions and not to confuse the two.

Facts about who you are include your age, nationality, marital status, health, employment and so on. Evaluations are subjective statements that attempt to describe features of your character and personal qualities. They include your strengths and weaknesses, nature, traits, hopes and fears. Try the following exercise to help you identify aspects of your conceptualised self.

Complete the following sentences with as many statements about who you are as possible. See if you can include positive and negative statements so that you develop a rounded picture of who you are.

I am _____

I am not _____

I like _____

I dislike _____

What I like best about myself is _____

What I like least about myself is _____

I would describe myself as _____

Other people would describe me as _____

Now look at what you've written and circle the descriptive facts and underline the evaluations. Discriminating descriptive facts ('I am tall') from evaluations ('I am a failure') is useful because you can then see that your self-evaluations may not actually be facts.

When you fuse with your thoughts (or language in general) you respond to them as though they're literally true. While fusing with a descriptive self-statement such as 'I am a teacher' often isn't problematic, doing so with evaluative self-statements is because they tend to be negative. For the reasons set out in Chapter 10, your evaluations about the world in general, and yourself in particular, are more often negative than positive. This means that your self-evaluations are more likely to be self-critical, such as 'I am mean' or 'I am stupid', than supportive, such as 'I'm a good person'. As a result, you're unlikely to find peace with yourself at the level of your evaluative self-statements.

Identifying where self-descriptions come from

Some of the statements and descriptions that make up your self as concept are provided by other people, such as parents, teachers and friends. Parents, for example, tell their children they're 'lovely' or 'beautiful' and teachers say things like 'You're a clever girl' when praising good work. Similarly, friends may describe you as funny, helpful and supportive and adversaries may see you as obstinate, rude or unreasonable. All these descriptions of 'who' you are accumulate and combine as you go through life to shape your self as concept — how you describe yourself.

In addition to how other people describe you, your culture also encourages you to describe your own behaviour ('What are you doing?'), its outcomes ('How did you get on?') and your general traits ('How would you describe yourself?'). These self-statements can be particularly influential in terms of how you think about yourself, as they come directly from you and this makes them easy to fuse with. In ACT, however, the key thing to remember is that they're still just bits of language, regardless of who thought or said them. The more important issue from an ACT perspective is not 'who' said them, but how *useful* they are. And by this we mean, do they help you move forward in the direction of your chosen life values?

Realising that being 'right' isn't always useful

From early childhood you're praised for being 'right', whether that's for providing the correct answers to questions or describing situations accurately. Being 'right' is good and is something you strive for. In addition, Western cultures typically encourage people to behave consistently with what they say; that is, you do what you say and vice versa.

Unfortunately, while being 'right' is often very useful, it's not *always* helpful. For instance, the thought, 'I felt anxious the last time I went on a date; I'll feel better if I stay at home' may be correct, but if someone behaves consistently with this belief (that is, stays at home so as not to feel anxious), she may not be living in line with her desire to meet a possible partner.

Rather than wondering if what you say or think is right or wrong, the more critical question is whether it helps you live in line with your values.

This is the case even when evaluations are broadly accurate. For instance, a major barrier young children face when learning to read is confidence rather than ability. They find reading hard and feel they can't do it. They may say things like 'I can't do it' and 'It's just too difficult'. These statements can be broadly 'true' (that is, a child can't do the task and it is too difficult at that moment), but they're not helpful in terms of encouraging her to engage in the practice required to learn how to read. When the child fuses with these types of evaluative statements they can be a significant barrier to even trying, thereby creating a self-fulfilling cycle.

Recognising Your Self as Awareness

The second way in which you can be aware of yourself is in your moment-by-moment experience. In ACT this is termed your *self as awareness* and refers to what you feel through your five senses — what you can see, hear, touch, smell and taste — together with your emotions and thoughts. Basically, self as awareness refers to all of your bodily and psychological experiences. Because practising mindfulness helps you be more aware of, and open to, your experiences, it also helps you make contact with your self as awareness.

While you can be aware of your bodily experiences and senses at any given moment, you can also be quite insensitive to them. This is particularly the case when you fuse with your thoughts. When this occurs you can miss things happening right in front of you. You can be so wrapped up in your thoughts that you simply don't notice what's going on around you. Everyone experiences this from time to time, but it becomes problematic when it happens a lot.

The following Body Scan exercise allows you to experience directly how challenging focusing on your physical environment can be.

This exercise involves moving your attention gently around different parts of your body and simply noticing what you can feel or sense. From time to time your attention may drift onto your thoughts and, when this happens, you'll stop being aware of your body. Don't worry if your head is full of thoughts, just notice it and gently bring your attention back to the task at hand and continue with the exercise.

Follow these steps:

1. **Find somewhere quiet where you won't be disturbed for 15–20 minutes.** Turn off your mobile phone.

2. **Either lie down on your back or get yourself into a comfortable sitting position.** Take off your shoes and loosen your clothing.

3. **Take a deep breath in through your nose.** Breathe in slowly. Feel your abdomen move outwards as air flows into your lungs. Continue for 4–5 breaths.

4. **Notice the weight of your body under you.** Feel how gravity pulls your body down onto the floor or chair that you're in contact with. Feel the heaviness of your body.

5. **While breathing slowly, imagine your breath going all the way down to your left foot.** Feel your big toe and be curious about what you notice. Does it feel cold or warm? Does it tingle?

6. **With your next breath, let your attention trace along the underside of your foot to your heel.** How does it feel?

7. **Repeat this process with each breath for your calf, knee and thigh.** Continue to breathe slowly.

8. **Move your attention to your right foot and focus on your big toe again.** Repeat the process of gently noticing the different parts of your leg with each breath.

9. **Now shift your attention further up your body to your buttocks, hips and pelvis.** Scan these areas and simply accept all the sensations you experience.

10. **Move your attention onto your torso and back.** With each breath, notice the different feelings you experience in these areas.

11. **As you breathe, focus your attention on your stomach.** Feel it move as you breathe in and out. Be aware of all your sensations as you breathe and relax.

12. **Notice your chest and shoulders as you breathe in and out.** Repeat the process of observing what you feel and sense.

13. **Together, lift both arms into the air and feel how gravity pulls them down.** Drop your arms to your sides and follow the same procedure with your left hand and arm as applied to your legs. Then proceed onto your right hand and arm.

14. **Move your attention onto your neck and jaw.** Feel any sensations such as tension or discomfort. Maybe you simply feel relaxed.

15. **Now be aware of your eyes.** Note the sensations you experience and scan them with each breath.

16. **Finally, as you breathe become aware of how all the different parts of your body are connected.** Feel each breath flow to every part of your body as a whole. Imagine the air of each breath moving to every cell in your body and nourishing it. Continue to breathe deeply as you connect with your whole body.

This exercise brings you into contact with the present moment — and, as an added benefit, it's also very relaxing!

While doing this exercise you'll drift off into your thoughts from time to time, but this is quite normal. In fact, a key part of mindfulness is noticing how easily you can slip into your thoughts and away from contact with the present moment. Slipping back and forth between your thoughts and being mindful is inevitable. (To discover more about mindfulness, check out Chapter 7.)

Mindfulness exercises help you stand back a bit from your thoughts and connect with your other experiences more directly. Mindfulness is a behavioural skill and, like all skills, the more you practise, the easier it becomes. Ultimately, it can become just part of your daily life and you can do it anywhere, from walking to work to washing the dishes.

Knowing Your Self as Context

The third way that you experience yourself is *self as context*, sometimes called the *observing self*. Your *self as context* refers to your sense of observing what's happening in your life. The experience of your observing self is impossible to describe fully in words because it's not a thing or a process; it's a perspective. But you can glimpse it when you stop and ask 'who' is noticing the things in your life. Ask yourself the following questions and listen carefully to your answers:

- ✔ When you have a thought, who has it?

- ✔ When you smell a rose, who smells it?

- ✔ When you have a pain in your body, who feels it?

- ✔ Who is noticing all the thoughts, feelings and sensations that you experience?

Your answers were probably, 'I do'. This may appear banal, but take a moment to consider what 'I' actually refers to. 'I' is that deep sense of yourself, the person who has been there your whole life, looking out from behind your eyes. It is 'you' who is observing and noticing what you are experiencing. It is 'you' who is noticing that you are reading this book right now.

Your observing self — that deep sense of being who you are — is stable over time because it reflects your unchanging viewpoint on life as seen through your eyes. You feel you are the same person throughout your life, from when you're a small child, through adolescence to being a grown adult. Even though your body, behaviours, roles and daily life are completely different, you still feel that you're the same person. In many ways you are completely different now from the person you were at 5 or 10 years old and you'll be completely different again when you're 80 — and yet you still have a sense that you are who you've always been. In spite of all these changes your observing self remains constant, which gives it an enduring, transcendent quality.

The observing self has a transcendent (that is, non-physical) quality because it's not a thing or a process — it's a *perspective*. More specifically, it's your unique perspective on life. It's not a 'description' as in your self as concept ('I am a teacher') or a 'sensation' like your self as awareness ('I feel tired'). Rather, your observing self is the sense of your life's continuity. It's your point of view from where you experience your life happening. For this reason you retain a sense of being the same person in spite of the changes that occur throughout your life. Your life can and does change, but your perspective on it remains the same. This is your self as context.

Emerging as 'I'

As a young child the linguistic community around you shaped your observing self via a series of repeated questions such as, 'What do you want?', 'What did you see?', 'Where are you going?' and so on. Although the content of each of your answers is different, you consistently start each one with 'I'. 'I' is the constant — what's left when you remove all the differences in the content of your replies.

You can simulate the process by superimposing the answers that you may give to a series of questions over a period of time, such as:

- ✔ I want a drink.
- ✔ I saw an albatross.
- ✔ I am going to school.
- ✔ I think it is orange.
- ✔ I wish I had a red car.

Frames of perspective

ACT calls the I–you relationship a *deictic* frame, as it refers to a perspective relationship. Deictic is derived from the ancient Greek *deixis*, meaning *point of reference*. In linguistics it refers to words that require additional contextual information to be understood. For example, left and right are deictic because they refer to a location relative to something else and not a fixed spot. Similarly, pronouns are deictic. If someone says, 'I want him to come here now', the words *I*, *here*, *him* and *now* require that you know who's speaking in order to determine the *who*, *where* and *when* she's referring to.

As the above example shows, 'I' is the only constant that remains when answering these questions and this is how your linguistic community establishes your ability to notice your unique perspective on life — your self as context. And because the pronoun 'I' exists only in relation to 'you', when you learn to answer 'I', you also learn about the perspective of other people, that is, 'you'. This is how your I–you perspective-taking ability emerges, which is the basis of human empathy and interpersonal understanding. Check out the nearby sidebar, 'Frames of perspective', for a fuller explanation of the I–you perspective.

Your ability to connect with your self as context is critical in ACT because it's from this perspective that you can relate to the content of your thoughts in a defused way. Chapter 3 introduces the chessboard metaphor to describe your sense of being the *context* for your psychological content and experience. You're the board and the chess pieces represent your various positive and negative thoughts, feelings and bodily sensations. As the board, you're in contact with and you contain these thoughts, feelings and sensations (the chess pieces), but you're also more than them. You are the context in which they occur.

You are like the blue, blue sky

A well-known Buddhist metaphor likens the observer self to the sky. Thoughts, feelings and sensations are like the clouds and rain that come and go, but the sky is always present. The sky is the place where weather occurs, but it is not the weather. Likewise, you are the place where your psychological content (your thoughts, feelings and sensations) occurs, but you're not the same as it; you're simply the place where these events occur. Even when extreme weather dominates the sky, such as a heavy thunderstorm involving wind, rain and lightning, the sky is still there in the background. Similarly, you're always there, behind your thoughts and feelings, connected to them, aware of them, but not defined by them.

Experiencing this metaphor directly can be fun. Wherever you are right now, can you see the sky? Look out of a window or go outside. Can you see any clouds or the brilliant sun? Notice how the sky is always there; how it's the place where weather takes place. Now say to yourself, 'I am the sky' and imagine clouds floating beneath and around you. Think of the clouds as your thoughts and feelings and notice how, even though you're in contact with them, you're also detached from them. This experience is the essence of the observing self or the self as context in which things occur. Figure 8-2 presents this concept graphically.

Figure 8-2:
The blue, blue sky metaphor.

Illustration by Joe Munro

 Your observing self can only really be understood experientially. Metaphors and explanations are useful, but they cannot fully explain what the observing self *is*. Now try an exercise to experience your observing self directly.

 Find a quiet place where you can sit down and won't be disturbed for 20 minutes. Place both feet on the floor, sit upright and get into a comfortable position. Focus your attention on your breathing and follow four or five breaths in and out. When you feel ready, close your eyes and continue to focus on your breathing, keeping it regular and deep. Notice how your chest rises and falls with each breath. Observe how your stomach moves in and out and your shoulders up and down.

Your mind may wander from time to time; when it does, gently bring it back and focus on your breath. Throughout this exercise your mind may either drift away or make judgements about how you're doing, such as 'this is stupid', 'I don't get it' or 'I'm bored'. When it does so, just notice your mind doing what it does and bring your attention back to the task.

Become aware of the weight of your body pressing down on the chair on which you're sitting. Notice that it's 'you' doing the noticing. Move your attention to the skin at the back of your neck. Feel the air temperature against your skin. Notice that 'you' are noticing this sensation. Now bring your attention to the position of your arms. Notice how they're lying and feel them as part of your body. Notice that 'you' are noticing your arms. It's you. It's always been you. You have been you your whole life.

Now remember a particular event that happened when you were a young child — maybe a birthday or a special moment. Look around you and try to remember as much of the scene as you can. Try to remember your feelings at that time, to recall what you could hear and see. Who else was there? What was the weather like? Notice who is noticing all these experiences. It's you. It's always been you. You were there then and you are here now.

Now think of a more recent event, perhaps one that occurred last month or last week. Picture what was happening and who was there. What were you wearing? What was around you? What were you saying or thinking? What were other people saying or doing? Notice who is noticing all these experiences. It's you. It's always been you. You were there then and you are here now.

Think about your emotions. You've felt happiness, joy, anger, sorrow and disappointment. You've felt boredom, excitement, jealousy, pride, fear and anxiety. Remember the things you once really loved, such as a toy or item of clothing that now you hardly notice. Your life has changed, but you are still here, noticing all these things. You were there then and you are here now.

Think of the roles you have fulfilled in your life as a son, a daughter, a friend, a colleague, a teammate, a neighbour, a lover or an enemy. The list goes on. You've experienced so many roles in relation to so many people, sometimes simultaneously. Your roles have changed over the years and all that time you were there, noticing. You were there then and you are here now.

Your life has been filled with so many different thoughts, feelings, events and relationships — and all that time you've been present, noticing it all. All these things are the content of your life, but you are the place where they all happened. You are the arena where your life is occurring. No matter what you think, feel or see, you are still here. No matter who else is present or how they affect you, you are still here, noticing it all happening. You are the observer of your own life. No one else has seen what you've seen. No one else has your unique perspective on all that has happened. Take a moment to be fully aware of that fact.

Bring your attention back onto your breathing. As you breathe in and out, picture the place you are in, and when you are ready, open your eyes. As you worked through this exercise, did you have a sense of being the same person at different stages in your life? Was that sense of being yourself evident when you were 5, 10, 20 years old, and is it evident now?

This exercise helps you notice how your sense of being 'you' remains constant even though your body, thoughts, feelings, roles and circumstances are ever-changing. In spite of these changes you feel you are still 'you' and this is what's meant by your observing self or self as context.

Transcending your psychological content

Because your observing self/self as context has a transcendent, non-physical quality, it's often associated with a mystical or spiritual dimension. As a perspective, your observing self has no material basis and isn't linked to any physical event or process. But this doesn't mean it's supernatural. The observing self may be incorporeal, but ACT explains it as a perspective experience that emerges as the product of the particular vantage point from which you engage with life.

ACT sees your observing self/self as context as important for your psychological health and wellbeing. It provides a safe place from which to engage with your more troublesome thoughts, feelings and bodily sensations. It enables you to resist the dogma of your thoughts and the pull of your emotions. You're able to *observe* your thoughts and feelings, rather than become entangled in and dominated by them. You're able to contact your psychological content without being defined by it. In ACT, the aim is for your life to be defined by your values and what really matters to you, not by thoughts and feelings that come and go like the weather.

ACT sees human suffering as the product of a futile struggle to control or avoid negative psychological content. It's when you fuse with your thoughts that you stop being guided by your values and your life becomes about avoiding what you don't want rather than seeking what you do want. Your ability to connect with your self as context, your observing self, provides you with an important means to still be in contact with your thoughts and feelings, but not necessarily guided by them. As Oscar Wilde once remarked, 'To become a spectator of one's own life is to escape the suffering of life'.

Part II
ACT Principles and Perspectives

Five Key Tenets of ACT

- ✔ Therapeutic outcomes in ACT tend to be defined and measured in terms of your psychological flexibility rather than symptom reduction.

- ✔ You have little control over your thoughts and feelings. For that reason, ACT encourages you to practise acceptance of them rather than trying to change them.

- ✔ Minds aren't things and neither are they places. Thinking of your mind as a process is more accurate.

- ✔ ACT is based on a behavioural account of human language acquisition called Relational Frame Theory (RFT).

- ✔ ACT, while drawing heavily on Buddhist practices (such as mindful awareness and living a life informed by a core set of values), is firmly based on sound scientific and theoretical principles. RFT research findings are incorporated into practice very quickly.

For a useful introduction to the three pillars of wellbeing described within the ACT model, go to www.dummies.com/extras/acceptanceandcommitment therapy.

In this part . . .

- ✔ Discover what experiential avoidance costs you.
- ✔ Explore how avoiding unwanted thoughts and feelings stops you from living a full and meaningful life.
- ✔ See the human mind and consciousness from an ACT perspective.
- ✔ Understand the origins of language and cognition.
- ✔ Consider the theoretical principles underpinning ACT.

Chapter 9

Counting the Cost of Avoiding Yourself

In This Chapter

▶ Accepting that you can't always avoid painful or difficult experiences

▶ Understanding the process of experiential avoidance

▶ Seeing that resisting pain isn't the answer to reducing suffering

▶ Questioning if you'd trade avoiding pain for experiencing nothing

'*D*o what matters' is the central tenet of Acceptance and Commitment Therapy (ACT). ACT terms the things that matter to you, the things you really care about, your *values*. Chapters 4 and 5 cover how you can identify your values and then start taking steps to make your life about those things. When the actions you take are consistent with your values, you can truly say that you're living the life you want to be living.

That's it — nice and simple. Only it isn't. For many people, doing the things that they really want to do can be very difficult indeed. Why is this? According to ACT, people face a major barrier in the shape of their quite natural desire to avoid or remove unpleasant experiences. Avoiding negative experiences sounds like a good idea and, under most circumstances, it is. For instance, running away from a hungry lion or putting on a coat to keep warm are clearly good things to do as they aid your survival and comfort.

But a problem emerges when you try to avoid parts of your own experience, such as your thoughts, feelings and bodily sensations. The less willing you are to remain in contact with these private (that is, internal) events, the more likely you are to engage in counterproductive, or even harmful, behaviours that serve to avoid or change them. This is called experiential avoidance and it is the basis for human suffering and mental health difficulties.

This chapter shows you how to allow rather than avoid negative experiences so that you can experience all that life has to offer — warts and all!

Avoiding the Bad Stuff Is the Bad Stuff

Taking actions to avoid unpleasant situations or events is quite natural and probably a regular occurrence. Consider pausing before opening a letter that you think contains bad news, delaying making a difficult phone call or avoiding looking in the mirror because you believe you have a big spot on your face. These are common examples and in many ways make a lot of sense. If something's unpleasant, why connect with it? However, although avoiding negative situations (or situations that you think will be negative) is quite natural, in some circumstances this behaviour can lead to significant problems. For example:

- ✔ People with diabetes often avoid monitoring their blood glucose even though they're aware of the implications for their health.

- ✔ Financial surveys regularly find that people who worry about their financial situation tend to avoid checking their bank balance.

- ✔ People who think they'll receive negative feedback avoid asking their boss or coach how they're getting on.

Being able to avoid experiences, people and sharp objects that can cause harm has clear advantages in terms of survival, and for this reason human beings are acutely sensitive to what's going on around them. Unfortunately, avoidance isn't always in your best interests.

Evaluating yourself

While avoiding negative events in the external world is often sensible, avoiding negative events inside you — unpleasant thoughts, feelings and bodily sensations — isn't such a good idea. It just isn't possible to escape from your own body, and attempts to do so are simply a waste of your time and energy. Human beings evaluate the world through language; language enables you to compare and label different events as either positive or negative. This ability isn't problematic until you turn it inwards and evaluate yourself. When this happens, it can be a short step to treating your internal experiences (thoughts and feelings) in the same way as you address external events; that is, you apply the same avoidance strategies to the world inside and outside your skin.

You can evaluate both internal events (thoughts and feelings) and external events (your actions) as either positive or negative but that doesn't mean that internal and external events can be healthily treated in the same way. In particular, evaluating your actions can often be helpful because doing so can inform more skilled action going forward. But you don't have enough control over the movement of thoughts and feelings inside your skin to be able to apply the same strategy at this level of human experience. This key point is all too often overlooked, however, as culturally you're encouraged to change or control your inner world.

Considering the misapplied control agenda

Doing what works and stopping doing what doesn't work sounds simple, right? Unfortunately, it isn't. Human beings often get trapped into using a *misapplied change agenda*; that is, they try to change things that can't be changed. You may think that you'd notice when this happens, but cultural influences are so strong that they override what your own experiences tell you and you just keep on doing the same thing, even if it isn't working.

The assumption that you can control what you think and feel is often so deeply engrained that you don't even notice it. As a child, your parents and other caregivers say things such as, 'Don't be sad', 'Put those silly thoughts out of your head', 'Stop being so grumpy' and 'Cheer up'. These may seem like reasonable things to say, but take a moment to look at the underlying message — 'You can control what you think and feel if you just put a bit of effort into it'. This message implies that if you continue to have negative thoughts and feelings, this is somehow your own fault because you didn't try hard enough.

This observation isn't a criticism of your parents and other caregivers, because they received the same message from the adults in their own lives. This message is buried deep in people's cultural subconscious and extends across generations. Indeed, many traditional psychotherapies are based on the same premise. For example, anger or anxiety management courses encourage you to address your feelings or restructure your cognitions to deal with negative thoughts. And if things are really bad, a medical doctor may prescribe antidepressants, tranquillisers or even anti-psychotic medication.

All these different strategies have the same thing in common — they attempt to control or change your thoughts and feelings. The implicit assumption is that when you don't feel or think negatively, your life will be fine. Unfortunately, a problem exists here: a positive life doesn't depend on the absence of unhappiness or negative feelings. It involves much more than that.

Trying to avoid or remove negative or unwanted thoughts and feelings can make perfect sense when you first start to think about it. But what if doing so isn't actually possible? You can end up wasting enormous amounts of effort on something that can't be achieved.

Don't think about the white bear (or why trying to control your thoughts doesn't work)

In 1863, Russian writer Fyodor Dostoevsky wrote, 'Try to pose for yourself this task: not to think of a polar bear, and you will see that the cursed thing will come to mind every minute.' He was drawing attention to an almost universal experience — if you try not to think about something, you then think about it even more.

Modern research into thought suppression supports this supposition. In the 1980s the psychologist Daniel Wegner undertook a series of experiments in which he asked people not to think about, among other things, a white bear. What he found verified Dostoevsky's original complaint. The explanation for this finding is quite simple: when you tell yourself not to think about something, you are actually referring to that thing. For example, if you instruct yourself to not think about a red car, you're referring to the thing you want to avoid (the 'red car'), thereby bringing it to your attention.

This knowledge has profound implications for psychotherapy, because it means you can't simply get rid of negative or unwanted thoughts or memories just by trying not to have them. Trying to suppress unwanted thoughts doesn't work and creates a nasty paradox — the more you push a thought away, the more it pops into your head.

Acknowledging that you feel your history

Despite the cultural belief that people can control their thoughts and consequently their emotions, ACT research has demonstrated that this isn't the case. Try the following short exercise, which demonstrates the limits of your control.

Put this book down, close your eyes and take a moment to notice what you're feeling. You may be hungry, tired, inquisitive or confused. Just notice that feeling. Now make a decision to push that feeling aside and replace it with its opposite. For instance, if you're hungry, make yourself feel satiated; if you're tired, make yourself feel alert. Try really hard to make yourself feel the second feeling for 15 seconds, then stop and notice what's happened.

Did you manage to change how you were feeling simply by deciding to do so? Could you actually control your emotions in any meaningful way? If you couldn't, consider what that inability means for how you relate to your inner world (Chapter 6 covers why you can't change your feelings at will and what effect that has on you).

The reason you can't change how you feel is because what you feel is related to the condition of your body — and that depends on what's happened to you. What you feel right now is the result of your past. Put differently, your emotions are your past showing up in the present. You thus can't change how you feel at any point in time because you can't change your past. The only way to feel differently in the future is to give yourself new histories. ACT encourages you to do so by engaging in value-based actions.

While you can't change the past, you can act in ways today that will make you more fulfilled tomorrow. Some things you can change and some you can't, and spending your time on the latter simply isn't productive. In fact, the situation is even worse than that, because every moment you spend trying to change the unchangeable takes precious time and energy away from doing the things you want to do instead. Such is your commitment to the belief that you can change, remove or decrease unwanted thoughts and feelings that you can spend minutes, days, weeks, decades and even entire lifetimes in pursuit of the unattainable. And that's a tragedy.

Identifying what you can and cannot change about your life is a major focus of ACT and many of its exercises are directed at helping you discriminate between the two. And the main tool that ACT practitioners use is *workability*. You simply ask, 'Is this working?' If it isn't, stop doing it and try something else, because if what you're doing hasn't worked so far, it probably never will. Albert Einstein defined insanity as 'doing the same thing over and over again and expecting different results'. It's this kind of unworkability that ACT seeks to address.

Seeing Experiential Avoidance as Short-Term Gain for Long-Term Pain

Steve Hayes (one of the founders of ACT) and colleagues define experiential avoidance as:

> [the] phenomenon that occurs when a person is unwilling to remain in contact with particular private experiences (for example, bodily sensations, emotions, thoughts, memories behavioral dispositions) and takes steps to alter the form or frequency of these events and the contexts that occasion them.

Experiential avoidance is what occurs when you try to minimise, change or escape from your own negatively evaluated private experiences. Some means of avoiding things, such as abusing alcohol or drugs, engaging in self-harm or withdrawing from society, can 'work' in the short term, but in the longer term lead to significant secondary problems.

While experiential avoidance can lead to short-term relief, it also creates problems in the longer term. For instance, if you have anxious thoughts and feelings about job interviews (and most people do), you can avoid this unpleasant experience by not applying for any jobs. That solves the immediate problem and avoids any unpleasant thoughts and feelings you may have, but it also means that you don't progress in your career. Most people engage in experiential avoidance from time to time, from pushing away a traumatic memory to procrastination in the face of a deadline. But experiential avoidance always has a cost. The following exercise aims to help you understand the direct effects of experiential avoidance.

Complete the statements below to identify the type of experiential avoidance you engage in and what such behaviour costs you.

The memories I most avoid include:

_____

_____

(For example, memories of my father.)

Avoiding these memories costs me in the following ways:

_____

_____

(For example, I don't think about my childhood.)

The bodily sensations I most avoid include:

_____

_____

(For example, boredom.)

Avoiding these bodily sensations costs me in the following ways:

_____

_____

(For example, I'm overweight because I eat when I'm bored instead of when I'm hungry.)

The emotions I most avoid include:

_____

_____

(For example, sadness.)

Avoiding these emotions costs me in the following ways:

_____

_____

(For example, I avoid having conversations about our relationship difficulties with my partner because such discussions may lead to feeling sad
about how little we talk nowadays.)

The thoughts I most avoid include:

_____

_____

(For example, I could never get a job like that.)

Avoiding these thoughts costs me in the following ways:

_____

_____

(For example, I don't apply for a promotion even though I think I'd love
being a team leader.)

Avoidance undermines relationships

Have you ever been so anxious while on a date that you found it hard to speak? You may have had uncomfortable thoughts such as, 'I can't think of anything to say' or 'He must think I'm boring'. Bear in mind that how you respond to these common thoughts and feelings determines the success, or otherwise, of your interpersonal relationships.

In a 2014 study conducted with 159 college students, James Gerhart and colleagues looked at the link between experiential avoidance and relationship success. They found that higher experiential avoidance predicted higher levels of interpersonal difficulties. The more the students attempted to control or avoid their own cognitions and emotions, the less successful were their relationships. When students directed their attention and energy toward monitoring and suppressing their subjective experience, the less they engaged with the person in front of them and the more they missed important signals in the relationship, thus undermining it. The anxious thoughts and feelings weren't problematic (indeed, they're quite natural); rather, the students' attempts to avoid or control them made it difficult for them to form relationships.

From an ACT perspective, unpleasant thoughts and feelings aren't the problem. Indeed, they're a natural part of life and can't be avoided. How you respond to these thoughts and feelings is what creates difficulties. If you're unwilling to experience any uncomfortable thoughts or feelings, you'll behave in ways that try to avoid or minimise the events that cause them, which can get in the way of living in line with your values.

Resisting Pain Leads to Suffering

Pain is inevitable in life. Things go wrong and bad things happen and when they do, painful experiences inevitably follow. You have no choice about feeling pain because it's an inescapable part of living (check out the nearby sidebar 'Recognising the importance of pain'). But how you respond to pain determines whether you suffer or not. If you're unwilling to experience any pain, this resistance comes at an additional cost. It uses up your time and effort and distracts you from moving your life in a direction that focuses on your values. Your efforts to avoid the negative things in life get in the way of you doing the things that you want to do. And that's the root of your suffering; your life will pass you by as you waste your time and energy engaging in an unwinnable battle with pain avoidance.

So what can you do? Stop resisting! The following formula represents the idea that it's your resistance to pain that causes your suffering:

pain + resistance = suffering

However, if you draw a line through '+ resistance', what you're left with is 'suffering' equal to your 'pain' — nothing more and nothing less. When you give up struggling to resist your pain, all you're left with is the original pain. That pain is unavoidable, but at least you won't be adding to it with negative feelings such as anger, resentment or regret.

According to the new formula — 'pain = suffering' — although you can't get rid of your pain completely, you can reduce it to the level dictated by your history. If you stop resisting your psychological pain, you still feel it but it no longer controls your life.

Removing Your Pain . . . for a Price

One of the developers of ACT, Kelly Wilson, likes to pose a question about pain. He asks people how much they'd be prepared to pay to avoid suffering. He poses that question to people whose lives have been dominated by feelings of anxiety, depression, paranoia, or disturbing memories of trauma or abuse — people who have more reason than most to want their pain to go away.

Kelly offers them a hypothetical scenario; a thought experiment about a choice they might make. What if I can take your pain away, he says, but for a price? And that price is that you no longer feel *anything*. Nothing. To people who experience great pain, that can be a very appealing offer. He then asks, would you pay that price?

Take a moment to think about painful experiences in your own life, such as an actual event like a bereavement, or negative emotions such as low self-esteem or depression. Everyone experiences moments and events in his life that he wishes hadn't happened.

Consider this pain and ask yourself how much you'd pay to never again experience it. Would you be prepared to give up feeling altogether in order to escape your suffering? Your pain would be gone but so too would your passions. A beautiful sunrise or a moment with your family or a wonderful meal would mean nothing to you. You wouldn't hurt anymore, but neither would you love. Your heart would never be broken, but neither would it ever race with passion and desire. If your child fell over and cried out in pain, you'd be disinterested. You'd feel no pain and care about nothing. Is that a price worth paying?

Recognising the importance of pain

Wouldn't it be great to be impervious to pain, rather like a comic book superhero? Superficially, this ability may appear attractive, particularly when you've just slammed your hand in a door! But not feeling pain is actually very dangerous. Some people suffer from a rare genetic condition which means they don't feel physical pain and are thus very vulnerable to injury. They don't notice if a cup of tea is too hot, if a shoe is causing a blister or a knife is cutting their skin. Pain is your body's way of signalling danger and is essential for survival. Pain may not feel very nice (that's the point!), but it does provide important feedback from the world. Pain is part of life and the challenge is not to find ways to avoid it but, rather, to live with it.

Chapter 10

Linking the Human Mind and Consciousness

*H*ave you ever thought about what you notice when you walk down a street? Is your attention drawn to the positive or negative things you see? When a stranger walks towards you, is your mind filled with warm and friendly thoughts or does it jump to more negative evaluations? Your answers to these questions provide an interesting insight into your mental functioning and what your 'mind' does.

This chapter covers the ACT perspective on the human mind and consciousness. We explore in detail how the term *mind* is used in ACT and make important distinctions between the mind and the brain. We also look at how the mind appears to have evolved to perform certain tasks.

Understanding the Human Mind

Acceptance and Commitment Therapy (ACT) talks about the 'mind' a lot. At first glance, doing so may seem inconsistent with a scientific approach such as ACT. Many psychologists, for instance, avoid referring to the mind because it's associated with a number of problems, chief among them the fact that it's never been precisely defined. After all, if you can't reliably agree on what something is, you can't study it scientifically.

The ghost in the machine

French philosopher, mathematician and scientist René Descartes suggested that the mind was the seat of the human soul and the source of human agency. However, lots of problems were associated with this idea, such as how the non-material mind interacted with the material body and broader physical world. British philosopher Gilbert Ryle called this problem — the relationship between the mind and the body — 'the dogma of the ghost in the machine'.

In his 1949 book, *The Concept of the Mind*, Ryle described how the idea that the mind is a causal entity is logically flawed. He pointed out that because you infer the presence of the mind from behaviour, you can't then use the concept of the mind to explain behaviour. According to Ryle, the mind is not a separate entity to the body; it's simply what the body does. ACT also takes this position.

Another issue is that the mind is often seen as a thing or entity that causes your behaviour. This is the problem that the philosopher Gilbert Ryle referred to as the 'ghost in the machine' (see the nearby sidebar). Transforming the functioning of the mind into a physical thing probably results from the grammatical tendency to change verbs (processes) into nouns (structures, or *things*) that then become seen as discrete objects in their own right.

This problem isn't new. Nineteenth-century political philosopher John Stuart Mill noted how nouns often become endowed with mysterious, causal properties:

> *The tendency has always been strong to believe that whatever received a name must be an entity or thing, having an independent existence of its own; and if no real entity answering to the name could be found, men did not for that reason suppose that none existed, but imagined that it was something peculiarly abstruse and mysterious, too high to be an object of sense.*

Rather than being considered a causal entity, in ACT the *mind* is simply a summary label for your mental or cognitive functioning. It's a way of referring to thinking, describing, evaluating, analysing, considering, planning, wondering, dreaming, aspiring and so on. The word 'mind' is used as a convenient shorthand to refer to these processes — nothing more than this.

Recognising that Your Mind Is more than Your Brain

Consider the relationship between the mind and the brain. People commonly use these two words synonymously in everyday conversation as though they're the same thing. But in ACT the mind is not simply what the brain does. The brain is a physical thing and is clearly important in human mental functioning; however, it's the *whole* human being who thinks, analyses, plans and wonders (as Figure 10-1 demonstrates). Mental functioning is something the whole person does, not simply what your brain does.

Figure 10-1:
The brain can't function without a body.

Illustration by Joe Munro

Science fiction and horror stories are fond of presenting the mind as solely the product of brain function. It's a popular image in films, novels and television drama, from *The Man with Two Brains* to *Frankenstein* and *Doctor Who*. Remove the brain, put it in a bowl of special fluid, wire it up to an interface and, hey presto, you have a disembodied mind that thinks, senses and functions. While it's a great idea full of comic and horrific potential, it's not really relevant from a scientific perspective.

One day separating a living brain from its body may well be possible, but it remains to be seen whether that 1.5 kilograms of grey matter will be able to think or perform other mental functions. Until then, a more pragmatic course of action is to deal with the phenomenon at the level it occurs. That is, at the level of the whole organism and the context within which it lives.

Considering What Your Mind Is For

Defining the mind as the general label for your mental or cognitive processes deals with some of the conceptual issues surrounding it. But you're still left with the question of what the mind is for? Why do you have a mental repertoire at all? What's the point of being able to think, evaluate, criticise, assess or plan?

No one knows the answer to these questions for sure, but from an evolutionary perspective it seems unlikely that your mind (that is, your mental repertoire) emerged to make you feel good about yourself. Simply feeling positive has no immediate value in terms of survival. What seems more likely is that human mental functioning developed because it helped to tackle some of the risks and dangers in the evolutionary past. The ability to think, assess, evaluate, plan and so on evolved because these processes aided survival through noticing and avoiding environmental risks.

Your mind is still noticing and avoiding risks today. You're constantly using your mental functions to evaluate people and situations in the world around you in case they present opportunities or threats.

If this is correct then it can help you to understand why your general thinking and evaluation processes are often negative. Your mental processes are biased towards noticing the negatives in the world around you because this helps you identify any possible risks in the environment. In effect, your mind is like an internalised 'health and safety' officer, continually scanning the environment for potential dangers to avoid.

Holding a Negative Mental Bias

While your mind is very useful and enables you to do lots of amazing things, its negative bias can present problems. If you've never noticed that your mind sees the world through a generally negative lens, try the following exercise.

Use the following chart to keep a simple diary over the period of a single day and notice the different types of thoughts that you have. For example, maybe you're worrying about something, thinking about lunch or noting what the weather's doing. As you notice a thought, write it down.

Briefly Describe Where You Are	*Write Down the Thought You Noticed*	*How Positive Was the Thought (on a scale where −10 = very negative, 0 = neutral and +10 = very positive)?*

You probably found, like most people, that a lot of your thoughts and evaluations about the world are indeed negative. Obviously you also have some positive and neutral thoughts too, but overall it's common to see life's negatives ahead of the positives.

Unfortunately, this negative bias means that if you spend too much time in your thoughts rather than engaging with life around you, the world can seem a hostile or scary place, full of bad things and risks. And when you turn your attention onto yourself, you tend to pick out the negatives about who you are, what you did wrong, what you can't do and so on, rather than focus on what's gone well. You can become so caught up in your thoughts that they stop feeling like transient mental events and start to define you.

Take a moment to recall three thoughts you might regularly have about yourself. Write them down.

Now evaluate what you've written. Are you more often kind and supportive or sharp and critical?

Your mind enables you to do truly amazing and wonderful things — things that no other species appears capable of — and you should celebrate that. But your mind also has a darker side. It tunes you into life's negatives and enables you to ruminate about the past or worry about the future.

If you were designing your mind from scratch, you'd obviously keep all the upsides and engineer out the downsides. But you don't get to choose your mental capacities; they come as a package that evolved over millennia. However, even though your head may be filled with worries, doubts, anxieties and generally negative stuff, these thoughts don't have to dominate your life.

While you don't have a lot of control over your thoughts, memories and so on, you can change how you relate to them and thereby change their meaning.

Think of your mind as a tool that you can use. Like all tools, your mind is better suited to some tasks than others. A screwdriver, for example, is great for putting up shelves but useless at washing the car. Likewise, your mind is great at problem solving, planning and evaluating risks but not much good at helping you feel more positively about or at ease in the world. That's just not what it evolved to do. Your challenge is to learn to engage your mental processes for the jobs they're good at while you go about living your life according to your values.

Examining human language and cognition

Language is one of the key abilities that distinguishes humans from other animals. While other members of the animal kingdom, from insects to chimpanzees, are capable of sophisticated communication, only humans have developed a complex symbolic language composed of sounds, images, words, facial expressions and gestures.

Human language occurs in two domains — the public and the private:

- ✔ **Public language:** Speaking, writing, singing dancing, miming and so on. Basically, any display of symbolic communication that can be seen by another person.

- ✔ **Private language:** Thinking, planning, remembering, dreaming, evaluating, worrying and so on. Basically, any symbolic process that you experience as taking place inside you. Human language processes that take place inside you are typically called *cognitions*.

ACT is based on a theory of language called *Relational Frame Theory* (RFT), which describes how different words or stimuli become arbitrarily linked together (see Chapter 11 for more about RFT and the origins of ACT). For instance, imagine you're very afraid of mice and you then learn that 'benza' is another word for 'mouse'. If you then hear someone say a 'benza' is under the table, your heart may start racing. Even though there's nothing mouse-like about the word 'benza', you can respond to it in the same way as you do upon hearing the word 'mouse' because you now link the two words together.

Linking sounds, symbols and signs together in arbitrary relationships enables you to connect anything together. This is the basis of the huge generativity and creativity of human language. However, the relational capacity of language doesn't discriminate between positive and negative events; rather, it links things together irrespective of how you evaluate them. For example, seeing a flower that you associate with a departed loved one can release a flood of memories that can make you feel happy *and* sad.

Exploring the trouble with thoughts

Thinking, planning, evaluating, remembering and so on are doubtless very useful, indeed essential, for solving many of the problems you face in the world day to day. However, a good number of your thoughts are negatively biased, and they can also be pretty random, bizarre, unsettling or just plain wrong. Like everyone, you've probably experienced disturbing, unwanted or odd thoughts from time to time. They come out of the blue and sometimes are set off by something in the environment. Either way, some thoughts are just not very nice and you'd prefer not to have them.

Thoughts are fine as long as they stay just that — thoughts (that is, bits of private language that occur in your head). But trouble occurs when you believe your thoughts to be accurate descriptions of the world and, in so doing, elevate them to a level of 'truth'. And when you believe something to be 'true', you're more likely to take it seriously and act accordingly. ACT calls believing your thoughts in this way *fusion* (Chapter 6 covers fusion in detail).

For instance, if you fuse with the thought 'I'm not smart enough to do it', that notion is highly likely to impact on how you behave. You may not sign up for a training course or apply for that new job. The thoughts themselves aren't the problem here; it's your fusion with them that's problematic and the resulting impact this has on your life.

Understanding Consciousness

Some people believe that all animate and inanimate things possess consciousness — a belief called *panpsychism*. Others, conversely, adopt a narrower definition, seeing consciousness as roughly synonymous with awareness or attention. From this perspective you can be said to be unconscious when you're sleeping, as you lack awareness of events taking place around you.

Philosophers have been speculating about consciousness for centuries as they've attempted to define and understand the concept. However, to date no agreed-upon definition exists and, instead, *consciousness* has become an umbrella term for a number of more complex mental processes, including self-awareness.

Unravelling the brain and consciousness

A currently popular explanation of consciousness put forward by neuroscientists is that it's an emergent property of the brain. That is, it's the product of large networks of neurons working together in the brain. While neurological processes do co-occur alongside conscious experience, good reasons exist for thinking that it can't be fully understood in this way.

While neuroscience is shedding light on *how* your neurology relates to your behaviour, it cannot explain what your behaviour means or *why* it occurs in the first place. One day it may well reveal what happens in your brain when you think and do different things, but not *why* you do or think those things. For instance, neuroscientists can already identify which parts of your brain are active when you think about a rugby match or Shakespeare, but this knowledge doesn't explain why you're thinking about these subjects or what they mean. To understand that, you need to understand the context within which these thoughts occur.

Understanding how brain function underpins consciousness may one day be possible, but it won't explain the experience of consciousness or what it does.

ACT sees consciousness as a psychological phenomenon and, as such, aims to understand it at the level at which it occurs rather than by reference to events occurring on another level (for example, neurons firing in the brain). This isn't to deny that neurological correlates of consciousness are taking place somewhere inside you; they are, just as chemical, atomic and subatomic correlates exist too. What's at issue is whether understanding one set of phenomena by referring to phenomena taking place at another level is practical (or even possible). Check out the following sidebar, 'Psychology and neuroscience: Good bedfellows'.

Psychology and neuroscience: Good bedfellows

With each experiment, neuroscience deepens the understanding of human functioning by filling in the temporal gaps in what is known and explaining how past events affect future behaviour. At the same time, psychological science is setting the research agenda for neuroscientists by pointing them to particular areas of interest. For example, Shallice and Cooper, in *The Organisation of Mind* (2011), wrote: 'Without putative task analysis, interpreting functional imaging results is little better than reading the tea leaves'. Neuroscience is dependent on a coherent contextual analysis provided by psychology to organise its activity and help make sense of its data.

Discovering the social origin of self-knowledge

ACT sees your ability to be consciously aware of yourself as emerging from your social interactions with other people.

Just as your ability to talk about and relate to the world outside your skin is shaped by other people, your ability to relate to your internal world is also shaped by those around you. For instance, you can only label an orange an 'orange' because you were taught to do so by other people. If you lived in Sweden, you'd be taught to call an orange 'apelsin' and in Spain a 'naranja'. Similarly, you only learn to talk about events taking place inside your body when other people give you the language to do so. For instance, if a child hasn't eaten for a while she'll feel hunger, but will only know that feeling is called hunger when someone labels it so for her.

In 1974, philosopher and psychologist B.F. Skinner wrote:

> Self-knowledge is of social origin. It is only when a person's private world becomes important to others that it is made important to him . . . self-knowledge has a special value to the individual himself. A person who has been 'made aware of himself' is in a better position to predict and control his own behavior.

In other words, the social community teaches you to talk about your internal or personal experiences because it's useful for the community to know what's happening inside you. When a parent teaches her child to label what's happening inside her, she increases her ability to support that child's needs. For instance, a parent can respond differently to a child when she says that she has a toothache or feels lonely or is hungry. It's useful for other people to know what's going on inside you and hence your social community teaches you to describe it accurately.

Viewing consciousness as a social product

ACT sees consciousness as a social process. You become aware of yourself when the community in which you live teaches you to notice and label what you're doing. And during this process, you also become aware of yourself in relation to other people. You learn to discriminate *I* as distinct from *you* when you appreciate that people have different perspectives on life. Consciousness is your awareness of yourself in relation to other people — the *I–you* relationship. (Chapter 8 explores the ACT perspective on selfhood, including the I–you relationship, in more detail.)

The self–other (or I–you) relationship is an important aspect of human experience. You're aware of it when you really connect with someone else. When a parent looks into her baby's eyes, she experiences a wonderful moment when she sees that the infant is seeing her in return. In that moment a deep connection exists between parent and child. Similarly, you also become aware of yourself in relation to other people. In this way, consciousness is not *I*, it's *we* — as shown in Figure 10-2. Consciousness isn't just a social product — it's also a social experience.

Figure 10-2:
The social nature of conscious experience.

Illustration by Joe Munro

Chapter 11

Tracing the Origins of ACT and Relational Frame Theory

*T*his chapter looks at the history and theoretical models that led to the development of Acceptance and Commitment Therapy (ACT). It describes how scientific breakthroughs in the understanding of language in the 1980s led to the development of Relational Frame Theory (RFT) and, later, the ACT model.

ACT has its roots in the philosophical and theoretical position outlined by the psychologist B.F. Skinner. Skinner laid down the foundations for a radically functionalist view of psychological science that sought to understand all human activity in relation to the context in which it occurred. The ideas Skinner first articulated are today broadly referred to as the field of *behaviour analysis*. RFT and ACT are part of this tradition and represent contemporary efforts to realise Skinner's understanding of human lives in context so that this knowledge can be used to build a better world for everyone.

Today, ACT is part of what's often called the 'third wave' of behavioural therapy. The first wave emerged as practitioners applied the early laboratory findings of psychological science to everyday clinical problems. While successful, these therapies generally ignored what people were thinking and so, in the 1960s and 1970s, practitioners extended their models to include cognitions and the second wave of behavioural therapy — cognitive behavioural therapy (CBT) — was born. But problems with the empirical, theoretical and philosophical basis of traditional CBT were soon identified, which led on to the development of third wave behaviour therapies that emphasise mindfulness and acceptance rather than efforts to change your psychological experiences. We outline the three waves of behavioural therapy in the sidebars in this chapter.

Warning! This chapter is quite technical and at times a bit of an intellectual workout, so it won't be for everyone. But if you stick with it, you'll gain some understanding of the underlying psychological processes that ACT targets, which will help you understand *how* ACT works.

You don't need to understand these processes in order to gain the benefits of ACT, in the same way that knowledge of how a car engine works isn't a prerequisite of driving. The ACT 'engine' works whether or not you know about the psychological science that informs it. However, if you're interested in what's under ACT's bonnet, read on.

Explaining the Initial Breakthrough

The story of ACT begins in what may seem an unusual place — learning to read. In the 1970s a team of American behaviour analytic psychologists led by Murray Sidman was investigating how people with learning disabilities learn to read. The team arranged simple 'matching to sample' procedures to see how people learned to link symbolic labels such as the sound 'dog' and the letters DOG to a picture of a dog.

A *matching to sample* procedure is basically a form of conditional discrimination whereby you learn to select one stimulus in the presence of another. Typically, a subject is presented with a sample stimulus (for example, the sound 'dog') and asked to choose from an array of comparison stimuli (in this case, perhaps pictures of a dog, cat and pig). If he chooses the correct stimulus he's provided with positive feedback (technically, his behaviour is reinforced) and the process continues.

In the early 1980s, Sidman extended this procedure to teach children to select the correct picture and word in the presence of a sample stimulus. He found that after a child learned to point to a picture of a dog when he heard 'dog' and later to point to the word DOG when he heard 'dog', the child could match the picture with the corresponding word without any direct training — as shown in Figure 11-1. Sidman also found that children could reverse the original learned relationships and match the picture to the sound and the word to the sound without any further training.

First wave behavioural therapy

Different phases or waves of behavioural therapy have occurred and ACT is in the current, third wave. The first wave of *behavioural therapy* appeared in the early twentieth century as clinicians began to apply new research findings emerging from university laboratories demonstrating how human behaviour and emotions could be 'conditioned' or changed by particular environmental events. These interventions were usually brief and short term, such as graded exposure for phobias. For instance, a behavioural therapy intervention for someone with a phobia of beetles typically involves graded exposure to the wee beasties so that they can learn directly that they're not harmful — a process called 'habituation'.

Prior to the development of the first wave therapies, psychotherapy had been mostly psychoanalytic (that is, based on the work of Freud). Early behavioural therapy interventions may appear quite basic today, but at the time they were quite revolutionary as they represented the first attempt to develop psychotherapeutic interventions based on the findings of empirical research.

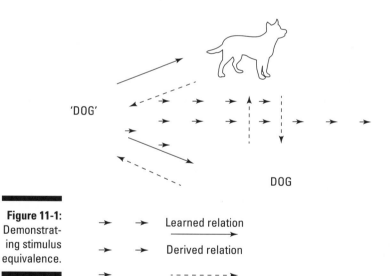

Figure 11-1: Demonstrating stimulus equivalence.

→ → Learned relation

→ → Derived relation

→ - - - - - →

The solid lines in Figure 11-1 show the taught relations and the dotted lines show the relationships that emerged without any further training. After learning two basic relationships, four other relationships automatically emerge, linking together previously unrelated stimuli.

This ability may appear trivial and indeed you take it for granted as a basic human ability, but it caused a great deal of excitement when it was first discovered because what Sidman had found couldn't be explained easily by existing theoretical models. The children had no learning history linking the arbitrary stimuli and their performance couldn't be explained by stimulus generalisation because no physical similarities existed between the picture and the word — that is, there's nothing dog-like about the word 'dog'; the relationship is arbitrary. Clearly something else was going on — but what?

Demonstrating Sidman's stimulus equivalence

Sidman and his team demonstrated that, in effect, the children had learned to behave towards the three stimuli (the sound, picture and word) as though they were equivalent (refer to the preceding section and Figure 11-1 for more). In general terms, you can represent the reversal of learned relationships as:

$$\text{If } A = B, \text{ then } B = A$$

You can then represent the derivation of new relationships across existing stimulus relations as:

$$\text{If } A = B \text{ and } B = C, \text{ then } A = C \text{ and } C = A$$

Sidman called the phenomenon *stimulus equivalence* — and a whole new area of research was born.

Subsequent investigations confirmed the importance of Sidman's initial studies. Extensive research has shown that only human beings can reverse and combine stimulus relationships following only minimal training; other animals can't. While there is some evidence that under particular experimental conditions some animals, such as pigeons, can reverse learned relationships, they require extensive training and this ability isn't robust. No other animal, not even so-called 'language-able' chimpanzees, has yet been seen to reverse or combine learned relationships via the matching to sample procedures first used by Sidman.

Not only is reversing and combining learned relationships a peculiarly human ability, to date only language-able humans have demonstrated it. This ability appears to emerge at around the same time as complex language (approximately 16–18 months of age) and is absent in people who've lost the ability to speak (for example, following a stroke). It would appear that this seemingly minor ability is at the heart of human language.

Second wave behavioural therapy

Second wave behavioural therapy developed in the late 1960s and early 1970s, as researchers extended their models to include thoughts. Early behavioural therapy (refer to the earlier sidebar, 'First wave behavioural therapy'), while effective, often ignored what people were thinking. A typical behavioural therapy intervention for phobias, for instance, involved gradual exposure to the object/event causing the fear without necessarily considering what the person may have been thinking at the time.

The problem was that what people thought about the fearful object/event affected how readily they engaged in the exposure process. As a consequence, a new wave of behavioural therapy interventions began to target people's thoughts and cognitions (the processes of gaining knowledge and understanding via thought, experience and the senses) and sought to change them to more positive or accurate ones. For example, if someone with a fear of spiders thinks 'Spiders can hurt me', an intervention might seek to challenge these thoughts and help him to produce verbal statements that are more accurate, such as 'Spiders in the UK aren't dangerous and can't hurt me'. This approach was applied alongside the exposure techniques developed in first wave behavioural therapy and the new intervention models that emerged came to be referred to as 'cognitive behavioural therapy', or CBT.

Including what people were thinking in psychological interventions also made common sense in terms of people's everyday experiences, and the CBT model quickly became popular.

Recognising the benefits of deriving novel relationships

The ability to reverse and combine stimulus relationships is important because it enables humans to connect events and objects in ways that other animals can't. Consider the example of someone taking a dog for a walk in the park. Before he sets off he may call out to the dog 'walkies'. Because that word precedes going for a walk to the park, when the dog hears 'walkies' it wags its tail and becomes excited. But if the owner had only ever said 'walkies' *after* he returned from the park and not before, and if one day he then said 'walkies' before setting off, the dog wouldn't react. The dog cannot reverse the park — 'walkies' relationship — it is one way only.

Now consider an equivalent situation involving a language-able human. A parent gives a child a sweet and only afterwards says 'sweet'. On another occasion, the parent asks the child if he'd like a sweet and he still knows what this term means and immediately says, 'Yes, please!' This situation is possible because a language-able child can reverse the sweet–'sweet' relationship.

Third wave behavioural therapy

Third wave behavioural therapy emerged in the 1980s from a number of different sources. Some drew heavily on Eastern philosophies, such as Buddhism, and others, such as ACT, emerged in response to new scientific findings about how human language functions, and specifically the development of Relational Frame Theory. Whatever their origin, these approaches had something new to say about the role thoughts and feelings play in people's lives. Whereas second wave behavioural therapy viewed negative thoughts as needing to be changed so that a person could feel more positive, third wave practitioners wondered if trying to control thoughts and emotions was actually part of the problem. A niggling problem lay at the core of the second wave models: a growing body of research and reports from clinical practice indicating that the more people tried to control their thoughts, the more those thoughts occurred. The third wave of behavioural therapy sought to address this issue.

The ability to reverse and combine learned and derived relationships means human beings can connect all sorts of arbitrary stimuli and events together, and this ability is at the heart of their symbolic communication.

Introducing Relational Frame Theory

Relational Frame Theory (*RFT*) was developed by a group of behavioural psychologists working mostly in the United States and Ireland in the 1990s. It sought to provide a theoretical explanation of Sidman's initial findings on stimulus equivalence, and to account for the whole range of other arbitrarily derived relationships, such as bigger/faster/hotter/opposite and so on. This section describes RFT and how generalised relational responding (see the following section) is the basis of people's ability to respond to stimulus relationships in novel and generative ways.

Explaining relational responding

Critical to understanding RFT is the concept of *relational responding*. All complex organisms can respond to the physical features of a stimulus, such as its colour, shape, texture, smell, sound or location. Basically anything you can sense about a stimulus, you can respond to. Relational responding is a more complex way of interacting with the environment. It involves responding to the relationship *between* stimuli rather than merely their formal physical properties, that is, what they look like.

Look at the shapes in Figure 11-2. You can choose one based simply on its physical appearance.

Figure 11-2:
Responding
to an item
based
purely on
what it looks
like.

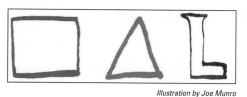

Illustration by Joe Munro

Relational responding goes a step further, however, and you respond to the relationship between two or more stimuli. For instance, consider the three different-sized balls in Figure 11-3. If presented with the small and medium-size balls and asked, 'Which is the biggest?', the correct answer is the medium-size one. If presented with the medium-size and large ball and asked the same question, the correct answer is the large ball. The correct answer depends on the contextual relationship *between* the stimuli and not their formal characteristics.

Figure 11-3:
Responding
to items
according to
the relation-
ships
between
them.

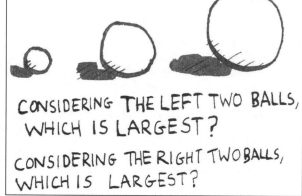

Illustration by Joe Munro

RFT understands *relational responding* to be a generalised *operant*: a functional unit of analysis that's influenced by its context — that is, antecedents, consequences and motivational factors. In other words, relational responding is a concept that helps you understand how you respond to contextually cued relationships *between* stimuli. Reconsider the example of the balls in Figure 11-3: language-able humans can apply the relational term 'bigger' to a range of stimuli, not just different-sized balls, and as such it's a generalised ability.

What's an operant?

The term operant was coined by American psychologist and philosopher B.F. Skinner to describe a functional class of behaviour. That is, a group of behaviours that have the same effect even though they may appear quite different. Consider all the different ways in which you can say 'hello'. You can say hi, hey or wotcha; you can nod, wink or wave your hand; you can write, text or sing. These behaviours look different, but they all belong to the same operant because they have the same function. Operants are important because they provide the basis for a functional understanding of behaviour, which is critical for ACT and RFT.

RFT argues that human beings can learn different types of relational responding, which enable them to relate stimuli in a variety of ways based on their contextual cues. Stimuli can be related in a variety of ways, for example:

- **Equivalence:** The chairs are the same.
- **Difference:** A bike and a car are different.
- **Co-ordination:** Apples and oranges are similar.
- **Opposition:** Good is the opposite of bad.
- **Comparison:** Louis is faster than Aadi.
- **Time:** Tomorrow is after today.
- **Perspective:** I–you, here–there, now–then.

The ability to derive relationships between stimuli enables human beings to do things that wouldn't be possible if you were restricted to responding to only learned relationships. If, for example, you're told that A is bigger than B (A > B) and B is bigger than C (B > C), without any further training you know that A is bigger than C (A > C) and, vice versa, C is smaller than A (C < A).

An everyday example is learning the value of coins. Because young children typically learn that big is better (think pieces of cake and bags of sweets!), they tend to see larger coins as being worth more than smaller coins. However, as Figure 11-4 demonstrates, 10p and 50p coins are worth less than £1 coins even though they're physically larger, which is often a source of confusion for young children. But if they're taught that £1 buys more sweets than 50p (A > B) and 50p buys more sweets than 10p (B > C), children will opt for the £1 coin (A > C) when asked which coin is worth more (£1 or 10p). In effect, the children *derive* their response (A > C) by combining two learned relationships (A > B and B > C). Other animals are unable to do so.

Figure 11-4:
Combining and reversing stimulus relationships — considering the value of coins.

Deriving a novel relationship between two or more stimuli is an everyday occurrence. ACT calls this process *derived relational responding*. Consider this scenario: you go to an Indian restaurant for the first time and want to know how spicy the curries are. The waiter goes through the menu and explains that a korma (A) is the mildest, a bhuna (B) is hotter than a korma (B > A), a madras (C) is hotter than a bhuna (C > B) and a vindaloo (D) is hotter than a madras (D > C). From this information you instantly know that a vindaloo is hotter than a korma and a bhuna, even though these curries were never mentioned together. In short, you're able to respond to relationships between different things without any explicit training or exposure.

Work through the following exercises to experience directly how you naturally engage in relational responding.

To see how you can relate the same two stimuli, CAT and DOG, together in different ways, answer the following questions:

- ✔ How are a cat and a dog different?
- ✔ How are a cat and a dog similar?
- ✔ How are a cat and a dog opposite?
- ✔ How is a cat better than a dog?
- ✔ How is a dog nicer than a cat?

Did you notice how the contextual relational cues drew your attention to different aspects of the two stimuli (in this case cat and dog, but the same process works for any two or more stimuli)? Here, the contextual cues *different*, *similar*, *opposite*, *better* and *nicer* engage particular types of relational responding that enable you to identify different relations between cats and dogs. This process is automatic and pervasive. For instance, you may also have experienced mental images of different features of cats and dogs in response to the questions.

This exercise involves relating different words together. Write down two different things (for example, an animal, a fruit, a skateboard):

 ✔ First noun: _____

 ✔ Second noun: _____

Now ask yourself:

 ✔ How are these things different?

 ✔ How are these things alike?

 ✔ What is better about the second thing?

 ✔ How is the first thing smaller than the second?

How did you get on? These two exercises demonstrate how you can relate anything to anything else depending on the contextual cues you're provided with. This ability is a central feature of human language and it enables you to have a hugely flexible and creative relationship with the world around you.

Looking at the transformation of stimulus function

A *relational frame* is a particular type of relational responding that involves the ability to reverse and combine stimulus relationships. It also includes the *transformation of stimulus function*, which describes how the function (that is, the effect) of one stimulus can be changed or altered by participating in a particular relationship with another stimulus.

For example, if you hear that 'betrang' is another word for lemon, when you're asked to imagine biting into a betrang you can experience a sour taste in your mouth and perhaps even some mild discomfort. Via the contextual cue 'is another word for', the functions of *lemon* have transferred to the word *betrang*, which now elicits the same reaction from you as a lemon, even though moments earlier it was a neutral stimulus (take a look at Figure 11-5).

Figure 11-5:
The trans-
formation of
stimulus
function
transfers
the defining
properties
of a lemon
to a betrang;
for instance,
you can
now picture
it as sour,
yellow,
bumpy and
waxy.

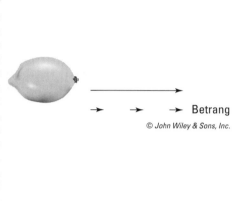

Betrang

© *John Wiley & Sons, Inc.*

The transformation of stimulus function explains how people are able to respond to events or stimuli with which they have no prior direct experience. The issue is particularly relevant in relation to mental health difficulties, such as anxiety or phobia, in which people often report being fearful and avoidant of events with which they have had no direct history of aversive contact. For example, if a child who's scared of crane flies is told that they live in plugholes, he can become reluctant to get in the bath. He has no prior history of baths being unpleasant, but the prospect of sitting in one can still lead to anxiety or fear.

Post-traumatic stress disorder (PTSD) provides another example of the transformation of stimulus function. If a person is involved in a serious car accident and remembers a strong smell of petrol as part of the experience, he may later try to avoid petrol stations because of the thoughts and feelings they provoke. The smell of petrol is a reminder of his past trauma. Further, if one day someone remarks that BBQ lighter fluid smells like petrol, the lighter fluid, or indeed even the BBQ, can also make him remember the accident. In this way, arbitrary stimuli that were not present at the original event can nonetheless evoke the same memories and physiological responses.

Moving from RFT to ACT

Often a lengthy time lag exists between breakthroughs in the laboratory and practical application. Scientists engaged in pure research don't necessarily consider the potential applications of their work and instead focus on the pursuit of new knowledge for its own sake.

Fortunately that wasn't the case with RFT and ACT. As both a researcher *and* practising clinician, Steve Hayes, together with Kirk Strosahl, Kelly Wilson and others, immediately began to use the concept of RFT to formulate a therapeutic model that's come to be known as Acceptance and Commitment Therapy.

RFT has profound implications for language-based therapies and interventions, as reflected in ACT. Because relational frames specify *relationships* between stimuli, when one stimulus rears its head, other stimuli to which it's contextually related also come along for the ride. The following exercise demonstrates this idea.

Read the following words and write down next to them the first words that come into your head:

- ✔ Up _____
- ✔ Hot _____
- ✔ Bat _____
- ✔ Stupid _____
- ✔ Anxious _____
- ✔ Happy _____

Did other words automatically come to mind? Your words (arbitrary stimuli) are automatically related to other words, memories, mental images, feelings and events. Obviously the associations you make will depend on your history and may well be different to those chosen by other people. Which stimuli appear in the presence of other stimuli depends on the contextual cues. For instance, if you hear the word 'bat' while sitting in a field on a sunny day, you may think of cricket; in a campsite at night, however, you may look up to see if small winged creatures are flying above you. Lots of different contextual cues exist. If you're looking at pictures of animals, you may be more likely to think of that type of bat — and talking about sport may result in associations with men in white trousers.

Clarifying why you can't fix language with language

One of the most important implications of RFT for therapeutic practice is that language can't be used to combat language. If you have a negative thought, such as 'I'm stupid', trying to counter it with a positive thought such as 'I'm smart' is unlikely to work.

You can represent the substitution of a negative statement with a positive statement in the following way:

If 'I'm stupid' (stimulus A), then 'I'm smart' (stimulus B).

Or, more simply, 'If A, then B'.

When you've related two stimuli, A and B, the relationship can also be reversed: 'If B, then A'. This means that when you think 'I'm smart', 'I'm stupid' will show up too. You can't stop that occurring because, in language-able humans, verbal relationships are reversible (sometimes called bi-directional).

You can't escape your psychological content at the level at which it occurs. You can't get rid of disturbing memories by simply trying not to have them or replacing negative with positive thoughts. If doing so was that easy, you'd never have a negative psychological experience again. The reality is different. Every day people struggle with low self-esteem, overwhelming and distressing feelings, and sad or upsetting memories from their past. These experiences don't continue just because people haven't tried hard enough to forget them or replace them with positive alternatives. Quite the contrary, in fact: part of their difficulty may result from spending too much time and energy engaged in the futile attempt to get rid of or control their psychological content.

What does your own experience tell you about how effective you are at controlling or minimising negative thoughts and feelings? If it's a struggle, you're not alone. Research persistently demonstrates that the more you try to control, avoid or minimise your thoughts and feelings, the more your life is dominated by them (check out the nearby sidebar 'Thought suppression increases thoughts' for more details).

Try the following quick exercise to see how good you are at controlling your thoughts.

Do *not* think about a red bus for 30 seconds. Don't think about what it looks like or any of its features.

Thought suppression increases thoughts

Psychologists Richard McNally and Joseph Ricciardi demonstrated that suppressing negative thoughts works only in the short term. As soon as you stop actively trying to suppress them, they're three times more likely to return.

The situation is the same for emotions and even physical pain. Cioffi and Holloway, for example, found that attempts to suppress pain resulted in actually increasing the sensation of pain.

Did you manage to do so? In our experience, 80 per cent of people say they do think about a red bus at some point. The remaining 20 per cent calmly state that they thought about something else instead. If you fall into that 20 per cent, fine, but the next question is, how do you know that what you were thinking about was correct? Take a moment to consider that question because the answer is interesting. How do you know you completed the exercise successfully? The answer, of course, is that you know you were doing it right because whatever it was you were thinking about was *not* a red bus. And there, implicit in your efforts to do the opposite, is the red bus. This little exercise explains why thought suppression techniques don't work. The act of trying *not* to have a thought actually invokes it and makes that thought more present in your life.

Considering rule-governed behaviour

Words linking arbitrarily with other words is one thing, but words can also become organised together to form rules. Psychologists have long understood that an important difference exists between behaviour that's directly shaped by feedback from the environment and behaviour that's influenced by rules — that is, *rule-governed behaviour.*

Verbal rules specifying salient features of the world can be very useful because they shortcut the need for learning by direct experience. A child can learn to be safe on the road, for instance, by following the instruction, 'Stop, look and listen before crossing the road'. Similarly, you can cook new and exotic meals by reading a recipe or find your way to a destination by following directions from a stranger (for example, 'Turn left at the traffic lights').

The downside is that rule-governed behaviour tends to be less sensitive to what's happening around you than behaviour shaped directly by the environment. This may result from a long history of following rules to lead to favourable outcomes. Indeed, societies work hard to establish positive consequences for following instructions, obeying laws and heeding warnings — and negative consequences for not doing so.

Whatever the reason, the relative environmental insensitivity of rule-governed behaviour is well established. In a typical experiment, for example, participants may learn that pressing a button *occasionally* turns on a light and that when that light is on, additional button presses produce points that can later be exchanged for money. The participants who are given verbal instructions about what to do are generally much less sensitive when the task changes than participants who learn the task directly. For instance, if participants are told, 'Press the button for money', they're less likely to stop when the light is off. They continue to follow the verbal rule about what to do rather than respond to the direct environmental feedback; that is, that the light comes on only occasionally.

Acceptance versus change: A shift of focus

Third wave behavioural therapy shifted the therapeutic focus from trying to change the literal content of your thoughts on to the process of thinking itself. Therapy now involves helping you learn new ways to relate to your own thoughts and feelings rather than actively seeking to change them. Working through acceptance and mindfulness processes helps you learn how to do this, and hence they're at the heart of third wave behavioural therapy.

Because of the heavy emphasis placed on acceptance and mindfulness in the third wave, you can be forgiven for thinking that they're end goals in themselves. But useful as these processes are in terms of reducing the impact of negative thoughts and feelings, the ultimate aim of third wave behavioural therapy is not just to be more mindful and accepting. That would be quite a passive position to take and life has so much more to offer than that. No, the aim of third wave behavioural therapy is to help people live their lives with vitality and purpose. In other words, the goal is to identify what matters to you and make your life about those things.

A whole range of third wave behavioural therapies exist today, such as ACT, Dialectical Behaviour Therapy (DBT), Behavioural Activation (BA), Functional Analytic Psychotherapy (FAP) and Mindfulness Based Cognitive Therapy (MBCT).

Perhaps because of their general usefulness, it can be very easy for your life to become dominated by rules. When this happens you can end up doing what the rule stipulates rather than what really matters to you (that is, living in accordance with your values). For example, if you're asked to give a presentation, you may think, 'I'm terrible at public speaking so I'd better not do it'. If you follow that self-generated rule, you may decline the invitation even though, deep down, you want to give the presentation.

Showing how ACT leads on from RFT

Language, and rule following in particular, can exert a great deal of control over what you do. Some language is helpful but some of it is problematic. When it's not helpful, ideally you need to weaken its control over your behaviour. RFT, however, implies that you can't weaken or undermine the influence of language by tackling it head-on with more language. For instance, you can't just say the opposite and expect the two statements to cancel each other out. So instead, ACT helps you learn to change the meaning of language by changing your relationship with it. This is achieved by learning from experiential exercises to see your thoughts as bits of language you're experiencing rather than 'truths' that must be obeyed. ACT calls this process defusion (see Chapter 6 for the lowdown on this concept).

Via a range of defusion and acceptance exercises (see Chapters 5 and 6) you can discover how to observe your own thinking and to see it as part of your experience — over which you often have little control.

A thought is just a thought. And a verbal rule is just a verbal rule. You can choose whether or not to follow them.

When you engage in defusion exercises, the meaning of the language you experience changes, even though its form doesn't. This is because defusion exercises change the context in which language occurs and thereby how you relate to it and its meaning. When the control your language processes exert over your behaviour is loosened, you're more able to connect with the values that matter to you and to make your life about those things. For example, if you really want to be a loving partner, you can engage in loving and caring actions even when you think 'I'm tired'. Or if you genuinely want to make a positive contribution at work, you can do things that reflect that value rather than being pushed around by angry or resentful thoughts. In short, you can get on with living a life in line with your values, rather than being controlled by worrisome thoughts and unhelpful psychological content.

Part III
ACT for Everyday Life

Five Ways to Incorporate ACT into Your Everyday Life

- ✔ Do five minutes of mindful breathing each day, either when you wake up or before you go to sleep.

- ✔ When you feel angry with someone, reflect on your underlying emotions: what are you worried about, afraid of or concerned may happen? Take a leap of faith and communicate these emotions to the other person.

- ✔ Work through a values exercise every once in a while to help you connect with what's important to you right now.

- ✔ Set yourself one SMART goal each day, no matter how small, that's consistent with your personal values.

- ✔ As an opportunity to practise acceptance, occasionally set yourself a goal that places you in an emotionally uncomfortable position.

Check out some great examples of how to explore your values and set value-based goals at www.dummies.com/extras/acceptanceandcommitment therapy.

In this part . . .

- ✔ Discover how to use ACT to enhance your work life.

- ✔ Explore some of the many ways in which ACT can improve your relationships with others.

- ✔ Understand anger from an ACT and evolutionary perspective – and find out how to better manage it.

- ✔ Find out how ACT can help you cope with chronic pain.

Chapter 12

Overcoming Work-Related Stress

. . . .

. . . .

*A*ccording to the UK Health and Safety Executive (HSE), just under 0.5 million cases of work-related stress were reported in 2013/14. Believe it or not, this figure accounts for 39 per cent of the total number of recorded cases of work-related health conditions over that same period. Work-related stress is clearly a major issue and while stress management training programmes do exist, few access them.

This situation is obviously very costly, not only for those involved but also to society at large. More than 11 million working days were lost as a result of work-related stress, anxiety and depression during 2013/14 — an average of 23 days of work lost per case. Among those most severely affected are health and social care professionals, teachers and those working in public administration and defence. And as well as high levels of absenteeism, work-related stress has also been linked to poor job performance and high rates of job turnover.

This chapter covers how the Acceptance and Commitment Therapy (ACT) model can be used in the workplace to promote psychological health and wellbeing and to help you work effectively and positively with work-related stress. We hope you find the information useful but do bear in mind that work-related stress is a complex and serious experience and this chapter alone is unlikely to be sufficient to address it. If you're experiencing work-related stress, talk to your employer and, if necessary, contact a specialist (either via your GP or your organisation's occupational health department).

Stress doesn't turn you into a grey old badger

A widespread belief exists that stress can turn your hair grey. Marie Antoinette's hair apparently whitened before her execution and Barack Obama rapidly greyed during his first term as US president. Actually, however, no scientific evidence backs up this assertion. Rather, stress can cause hair loss, although it often isn't noticed at the time because it usually begins weeks or months after the stressful event occurred.

Defining Work-Related Stress

No single definition of stress exists. In general, work-related stress results from the gap between what people are required to do and what they can do. The HSE, for example, defines it as, 'The adverse reaction people have to excessive pressures or other types of demand placed on them at work'.

People can experience work-related stress in a range of ways (as the nearby sidebar 'Stress doesn't turn you into a grey old badger' shows!) and across three major domains: mental, emotional and behavioural. For example, they can experience one or many of the following symptoms in relation to the workplace:

- ✔ **Mental:** Having many negative and critical thoughts; indecisive; being unable to concentrate; and noticing problems with memory.

- ✔ **Emotional:** Feeling depressed or highly anxious; lacking self-confidence; reacting more emotionally, such as being tearful, over-sensitive or aggressive; feeling isolated or lonely; lacking motivation and commitment; and experiencing mood swings.

- ✔ **Behavioural:** Losing appetite; smoking and drinking more or abusing drugs 'to cope'; experiencing changes in sleeping patterns or getting too little sleep; sweating excessively; and having to take time off work.

These symptoms need to be recognised and acknowledged so that you can help yourself or seek help from others.

Training Your Way through Stress at Work

When applied to workplace settings, interventions based on the ACT model are often referred to as Acceptance and Commitment *Training*, rather than Acceptance and Commitment *Therapy*. This slight reframing reflects the fact that these interventions are designed for general staff groups experiencing stress, rather than people needing therapy for mental health difficulties. That said, some 40–50 per cent of people attending stress management programmes meet the threshold for experiencing clinically significant mental health difficulties.

Most stress management programmes draw heavily on techniques used in the field of traditional Cognitive Behavioural Therapy (CBT). For example, interventions may focus on building personal resilience by directly changing negative thought processes, using relaxation techniques and/or altering professional behaviour (such as time management, efficient record-keeping, delegation and so on).

ACT takes a different approach, in both work-based training and therapy sessions. Rather than trying to change or reduce stressful thoughts and feelings directly, ACT looks to change your *relationship* with these events and thereby change their meaning. ACT works to help you:

- ✔ See your thoughts for what they are — transient events taking place inside your skin, rather than statements about the world that are literally true.

- ✔ Embrace your emotions as a reflection of your history — what you feel depends on what's happened to you.

- ✔ Clarify your values and then set goals that represent them so you can begin living a life that matters to you.

ACT calls being able to change how you relate in this way, psychological flexibility.

Responding to stress with laughter

Laughter is a great antidote to stress. Not only does it feel good, but laughing lowers stress hormones (such as cortisol and adrenaline), strengthens your immune system and boosts your physical health. In addition, a good laugh:

- ✔ Builds and strengthens your social relationships

- ✔ Relieves physical tension and increases your ability to relax

- ✔ Triggers endorphins so that you feel better

- ✔ Protects your heart by increasing blood flow and dilating blood vessels

The trick, of course, is finding something to laugh about!

Responding to Work-Related Stress in a Psychologically Flexible Way

ACT aims to increase your psychological flexibility so that you can be more effective in relation to your chosen value-based goals. Chapter 3 covers psychological flexibility in detail so here we simply state that it involves the following six interrelated processes: acceptance, defusion, contact with the present moment, self as context, values and committed action. We describe each process as it relates to work-related stress in the following sections.

Practising acceptance in the workplace

You may wonder why you can't simply set practical and realistic goals and then get on with it. Work is where you're professional and proper, so why do you need all this emotional awareness and acceptance stuff too?

The answer is because you're still a human being at work and what you think and feel are still important. If the path to reach your goals was always happy and painless, you wouldn't need to be more accepting of stressful or unwanted psychological experiences because you wouldn't have them. But goals worth achieving are seldom easily reached and you'll probably experience difficult thoughts and emotions along the way, such as self-doubt, worry, anxiety, confusion and uncertainty. Having a way to respond positively to these thoughts and emotions so that they don't knock you off course can be helpful.

While a value-based goal can help organise what you want to do, trying to avoid or control negative thoughts and feelings, such as doubts, anxiety or lack of confidence, can reinforce a set of actions that move you in a very different direction. For this reason, being more accepting of your difficult psychological experiences helps you stay on course in the direction defined by your chosen values. In this sense, acceptance is like a beam of light you can shine in the direction of your valued work-related goals, as shown in Figure 12-1. When a self-doubting thought such as 'I can't do it' appears in the beam of light, you can see it for what it is — a transient thought that will pass as quickly as it arrived. It need not deter you from your path toward important goals.

Working out your own level of acceptance can help you understand more about your reactions to negative events inside and around you. Complete the following questionnaire to assess how able you think you are to accept and deal with difficult internal experiences.

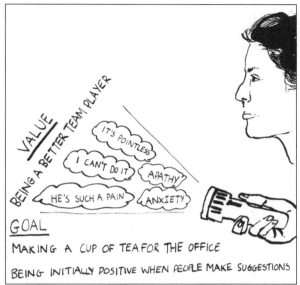

Figure 12-1: Acceptance is like a beam of light.

Rate the following statements on a scale from 1–10, where 1 = 'This is never true for me' and 10 = 'This is always true for me'.

1. For me, feeling anxious or depressed at work sometimes isn't okay.

2. I find anxiety at work to be a really bad thing.

3. I try to control or run away from my feelings at work.

4. I feel I need to be in control of my feelings, even if they're painful or uncomfortable.

5. It would be great if I never again experienced painful or difficult thoughts or feelings in relation to my work.

6. When I experience thoughts and feelings about work that I don't like, I try not to think about them.

Add up your total score (which will be up to a total of 60). The higher you score, the less able you are to accept and cope with difficult experiences. This inability to accept thoughts and feelings that make you uncomfortable or unhappy acts as a barrier to engaging in valued work-related goals.

Creating mental space with defusion

Defusion and acceptance are closely related in ACT because defusing from your thoughts means that you accept them for what they are — just thoughts. Defusion is the opposite of fusion, which is when you believe the content of your thoughts (and language in general) to be literally true. Fusion is problematic because you're more likely to do as your thoughts suggest when you think they're true, even when these actions run counter to your values. For example, having thoughts such as, 'They don't think I'm any good', 'He doesn't like me' or 'This is a waste of time' may make pursuing value-based goals with your work colleagues difficult. (You can read more about defusion and fusion in Chapter 6.)

Whether or not your thoughts are true/accurate is less important from an ACT perspective. What is important, however, is the effect that they have on your actions. If you're convinced, for example, that you're too busy at work to buy your partner some flowers, you're very unlikely to ever present her with those roses! But if you defuse from your thoughts and accept them for what they are, just transient mental events, you can then get on with doing what's important (expressing your love for your partner, in this case).

Your relationship with colleagues has a huge impact on how you experience and cope with the work environment. Developing your awareness of how negative thoughts can lead to ineffective interactions with them is essential in order to function at your best at work.

Consider this scenario. Following a disagreement with a colleague, you find yourself wrapped up in your thoughts about what happened and what was said. You ruminate on what you wish you'd said and rehearse what you'll say next. You wonder what your colleague thinks of you and even begin to consider whether you're in the right job. At just this point, two new members of staff enter the room and introduce themselves to the team. They begin chatting and discussing the roles they'll be carrying out. Later you realise you can't remember their names or much about what they said. You may think that you have a poor memory, but in fact you didn't really hear what they said in the first place because you were listening to your internal voice rather than paying attention to them — you lost contact with the present moment.

Making contact with the present moment

When you spend too much time in your thoughts you lose contact with the present moment and can become insensitive to what's going on around you. Rather than concentrating on your work environment, your colleagues and indeed what you need to be achieving, you're tuned into your internal thought processes instead. ACT uses mindfulness exercises, alongside defusion and acceptance, to increase your contact with the present moment.

Contact with the present moment connects you more fully with your sur-roundings and enables you to use your time more effectively doing the things that really matter to you (that is, working on your value-based goals). For example, if developing effective relationships with your colleagues is impor-tant to you, you can set yourself the goals of really listening to them, offering support if needed and valuing their contributions to team projects.

Seeing your self as context

Your *self as context* is that sense of who you are that's stable while your thoughts feelings and bodily sensations come and go. You are the context, the setting, where these events take place.

This is a really important point in ACT because your experience of yourself as the context for your thoughts and emotions provides you with a safe and stable place from which to relate to them. It enables you to gain some dis-tance from your thoughts and to see them for what they are — just thoughts. It enables you to feel the emotions in your body and relate to them as part of your history showing up in the present.

The following exercise aims to help you see *who* is noticing your thoughts.

Stop what you're doing and notice the first thought that comes into your head.

Really notice that thought, even if it's simply 'My mind is blank' or 'I can't notice anything'. Repeat it to yourself several times to really get a feel for it. Now say it out loud several times so that you can hear what it sounds like. Finally, write it down so that you can look at it.

Now as you notice, repeat, say, write and rate your thought, notice who is doing all those things. Who is thinking, speaking, writing and rating?

What exercises such as these reveal is that thoughts, on the one hand, and the thinker, on the other hand, are distinct from one another. Your thoughts are transient mental events but your sense of being who you are persists over time — at work and anywhere else.

Recognising your work-related values

From an ACT perspective, your values reflect and describe the things that you really care about. They give your life meaning and describe the direction you want your life to be heading in. Being clear about your values, at work as else-where, helps you identify what's important to you and then set relevant goals.

ACT-based interventions aim to support the *whole person* and not merely the employee. ACT sees the wellbeing of the individual as the central concern. The division between your work and home life is less significant when you can see that you're the same underlying person in both places. If you're psychologically inflexible in one setting, you're likely to behave in the same way in other settings too. For that reason, ACT aims to help you become more psychologically flexible (that is, more aware, accepting and values-driven) generally because this will have an impact across every aspect of your life.

The implication for employers is quite clear. If they want to improve the effectiveness of their staff, they need to support their general wellbeing (check out the nearby sidebar, 'Addressing presenteeism results in greater productivity'). Although supporting employees' wellbeing across the board may not be an obvious priority, evidence increasingly demonstrates that improved general wellbeing leads to improved productivity and workforce effectiveness.

Does this mean a happy workforce is an effective workforce? Yes, in short (though the full relationship is a little more complicated).

A sense of fulfilment is what you feel when you're living in line with your values in an open and accepting way. Thus simply trying to make their workforce 'happy' isn't enough; employers need to help their employees to identify their values and to set related meaningful goals at work and at home.

Also in our experience staff can sometimes be a little cynical about stress management programmes that are only tied to their workplace. They see them as attempts to get them to work harder and to be more productive without addressing any wider systemic issues. The ACT model provides a positive alternative message here: it genuinely supports the global wellbeing of staff. While doing so can lead to a happier and more effective workforce, that outcome is a by-product of living a fuller and more value-consistent life.

Addressing presenteeism results in greater productivity

Presenteeism is the phenomenon whereby people don't function at full or usual capacity at work. It's increasingly recognised as an important issue affecting the workforce and is estimated by the Sainsbury Centre for Mental Health to cost the UK up to three times more than sickness absence. While some level of work-related stress is inevitable, growing evidence exists that psychological interventions can reduce its negative impact by improving psychological wellbeing and, correspondingly, workforce productivity. For instance, data supplied by Australian employers suggested that interventions supporting staff wellbeing delivered a five-fold return on their investment. A happy workforce is clearly good for business!

Take some time to reflect on the following questions, which are adapted from the ACT Conversation Cards developed by ACT therapist and researcher Dr Louise Hayes.

- ✔ What is your main purpose in your work life?
- ✔ What is the most important thing happening to you at work right now?
- ✔ Imagine that you could achieve anything at work — what would it be?
- ✔ What does it mean to feel seen or heard at work?
- ✔ What is it like to learn?
- ✔ What makes a good working life?
- ✔ What do you hope people you work with will remember about you?
- ✔ What do you hope for in your job/career?

Your answers to these questions can help you to clarify your work-related values.

Working through these questions with a colleague can be a useful process because you may see things from a different perspective. Having to justify your answers to another person also means that you need to be specific about your values, which can make setting work-related goals based on them easier. (Check out Chapter 4 for more on identifying your values.)

You can identify values specifically for your working life, which then inform your actions in the workplace. Maybe you value being a supportive colleague or being creative. If so, these statements represent the global ongoing actions that you want to engage in at work. The next step is to set specific goals in relation to these values. For example, you could ask colleagues how they are every day, or research and discuss a new idea every week. You can express your values in numerous ways; the only limit is your creativity.

Setting goals and taking committed action

When you've identified clear values, the next step is to set SMART (specific, measurable, achievable, relevant and time-framed; see Chapter 5 for the details) goals to aim for. Remember, your value-based goals don't necessarily need to be specifically related to work performance or achievements. For example, your responses to the reflection questions in the preceding section may have made it clear that what's important to you right now is setting aside more time for friends or family rather than letting the pressures of work act as a barrier to doing so.

Use the chart in Table 12-1 as a guide to set your value-based goals. We provide one example goal in each of the four value domains, but you can have more than one goal in any single domain and, if it feels right to you at the time, none in one or more of the others.

Table 12-1	Setting Value-Based Work-Related Goals		
Value Domain	*Goal*	*Why This Is Important to Me*	*When I Will Achieve this Goal*
Work/ education	To apply for the upcoming promotion.	Because I want a chance to make positive changes to existing systems at work and because more money would mean we could move to a bigger house and the children could have their own bedrooms.	I will submit my application next week.
Health	To go running for at least 15 minutes twice a week.	Because I feel more fulfilled, calm and healthy when I regularly exercise, which helps me put things into perspective at work and deal with stress better.	I will stick to this exercise regime for the next three months at least.
Leisure time	To read half a chapter of a novel each day.	Because work priorities always get in the way of reading fiction, which I used to love and know helps me unwind before sleep. I will not read work reports in bed!	I will end my days like this for the next three months at least.
Relationships	To have at least one day of family time every weekend.	Because I often feel I devote too much time to work and not enough time to my family.	I will enjoy activities with my family every weekend for the next year.

When you've set your value-based goals, the next step is to begin achieving them. Although you may encounter barriers along the way (Chapter 6 covers overcoming obstacles), at least you know what you want to do with your life — at work and at home.

Establishing a Better Work–Life Balance

On average you spend more than one-fifth of your waking life in the workplace. Here you expend a great deal of your creative energy and form some of your most important relationships. Who you think you are — your conceptualised self (see Chapter 8 for more on your different 'selves') — is closely tied to your job and the work you do. And, of course, working is how you earn a living and pay the bills.

Work can also be a huge source of stress and difficulty in your life, however. Figuring out how to manage and respond to this stress can make your life a whole lot easier. While some stress in the workplace is inevitable, ACT can help you limit its impact and reduce the suffering that results from it.

What happens at work often spills over into other parts of your life. A less stressful existence in the workplace will have positive knock-on effects on everything else you do.

Chapter 13

Looking at Love and Relationships through an ACT Lens

*H*uman beings are social animals. That aspect of human nature is so pervasive and universal that you can easily overlook it. Just as fish don't notice the water in which they swim, so human beings can be unaware of the social world in which they live. But it takes only a moment of reflection to understand how interconnected human lives are. Almost everything human beings do takes place in a social context. The social world teaches you to communicate and live and ultimately it's where you form partnerships, fall in love and reproduce.

Love is often seen as the ultimate human emotion and survey after survey rates it as people's number one concern. Finding love, being in love and dealing with the absence of love consume lots of time and energy. But even though loving relationships are essential for life and happiness, they're not simple or straightforward. Interpersonal behaviours demonstrating nurture and care are necessary but may be absent when you're dominated by your thoughts, feelings and emotions. This situation has grave implications for your ability to engage in a loving relationship.

In this chapter, we explore how the Acceptance and Commitment Therapy (ACT) model can be applied to loving and intimate relationships. We show you how you can connect — or reconnect — with your partner so that you make your relationships as positive and value-based as possible. We help you address some of the typical, daily challenges inherent in human relationships and look at ways in which you can use ACT to overcome them.

This chapter doesn't address complex relationship difficulties or criminal behaviour such as domestic violence or sexual abuse. We recommend you seek professional advice and support if these issues affect you.

Ruminating on What Love Is

Love is commonly seen as a powerful emotion that you feel. It's endlessly described in poems, novels, songs, plays and indeed every form of popular culture. We're surrounded by romantic (and sometimes tragic) stories about people falling in love and being overwhelmed by the experience. Indeed, most people have first-hand knowledge of the feeling of being in love.

But what happens when this feeling is no longer present? Does it mean you no longer love your partner? And if, instead of love, you feel angry, irritated or bored, does it signify that you're no longer *in* love? If you see love as just a feeling, it's easy to come to these conclusions, which can have a serious impact on how you see the relationship you're in.

ACT understands love to be both a feeling and a value. Values are statements that describe what's important to you; they inform your freely chosen, ongoing actions (refer to Chapter 4 for more on identifying your values). According to that definition, you're in a loving relationship when you behave in loving ways, not simply when you feel romantically connected to someone. If you value being in a loving relationship, you can choose to behave in ways that reflect that even when you feel annoyed or upset with your partner.

Rather than being pushed around by negative thoughts and emotions, when you consciously choose to live in line with the value of being a loving partner, you can continue to be kind and respectful towards that person. For example, instead of shouting at your partner when you're angry, you can choose to speak in a calm and clear voice. Or when you have negative thoughts about your partner's behaviour, rather than withdrawing you can continue to talk to him and even make him a cup of tea. Of course, engaging in these actions isn't easy, but doing so reaps obvious benefits in terms of the stability and warmth of your relationship. When you behave in this way you can go to bed at night knowing that you've lived according to the values that matter to you and you're not filled with a sense of guilt or regret about what you've said and done that day.

The art of loving

ACT isn't alone in seeing love as both an emotion and a way of behaving. In his 1956 book *The Art of Loving*, psychoanalyst and social philosopher Erich Fromm argued that love is a skill that can be taught and is not merely a feeling. He rejected the popular idea of 'falling in love' as a sentimentality — you do not fall in love; rather, you behave lovingly. According to Fromm, true love involves four basic elements: care, responsibility, respect and knowledge. These elements define your behaviour. From an ACT perspective, these elements are values that you choose to reflect in your behaviour.

Fromm also talked about 'self-love', which he differentiated from narcissism or arrogance. Self-love involves behaving in a caring, respectful, honest and supportive way towards yourself. Again, this is similar to the emphasis ACT places on self-compassion and kindness towards yourself and others as the basis for forming positive relationships and enjoying a happy life.

Breaking down Barriers

Australian author and ACT trainer Russ Harris outlines five key issues that commonly run through relationship problems, summed up using the acronym DRAIN (and presented graphically in Figure 13-1):

- ✔ **D**isconnection
- ✔ **R**eactivity
- ✔ **A**voidance
- ✔ **I**nside your mind
- ✔ **N**eglecting values

Here is some more detail on the five key issues in DRAIN:

- ✔ **Disconnection:** You feel that you can't connect with your partner. This often manifests in a lack of mutual interest in one another and the absence of open and honest communication. You may feel that you're not being listened to and that your partner doesn't pay you enough attention — or enough of the right kind of attention.

- ✔ **Reactivity:** This is the tendency to react, in both words and actions, quickly and without consideration for the needs and feelings of your partner. Reactivity can often lead to big arguments because something that you said or did has made your partner feel upset or undervalued in some way.

Illustration by Joe Munro

Figure 13-1:
Watching your relationship go down the drain.

✔ **Avoidance:** Everyone has a tendency to want to avoid negative thoughts and feelings or situations that may lead to them. However, your unwillingness to remain in contact with painful psychological content can lead to counterproductive efforts to control or avoid it. This *experiential avoidance* is at the root of many of the problems people face (check out Chapter 9 for more).

While avoiding painful or uncomfortable experiences may be appealing in the short term, doing so in a relationship can interfere with behaving in a loving or supportive way. For example, wanting to avoid negative feelings may stop you talking openly about an issue that needs to be addressed, such as a lack of intimacy or the division of household chores.

✔ **Inside your mind:** You tend to spend a lot of time caught up in, or fused with, negative thoughts about your relationship, ruminating on what should be that isn't and what shouldn't be that is.

> ✔ **Neglecting values:** You lose contact with your values. For example, while you may want to be a kind, caring and loving partner, your actions are unkind and unloving; your behaviour is thus inconsistent with your values.

Fortunately, ACT can help you before your relationship disappears down the plughole.

Plugging the Drain

Consider this excerpt from an argument between Tom and Sarah:

> **Sarah:** Do you remember when we used to curl up together in front of the fire, hold each other and talk about all the wonderful things we were going to do together? We used to get on so well. Now we hardly ever speak about anything important. We just exist; that's all.

> **Tom:** You never want to do that kind of thing anymore anyway! And besides, I work all day and when I come home I'm exhausted. I just want to relax and all you do is moan about what we don't do anymore. I can't get a break!

> **Sarah:** I work too, you know! What am I supposed to do, just accept that our relationship is non-existent? We may as well live on different planets for all the communicating we do. I'm sick of it.

> **Tom:** At least I'd have some peace and quiet if we did. I don't know what you want from me. If I did, I might be able to do something about it. But even if I did the things you complain I don't do, you'd still find something to have a go at me for, I'm sure!

> **Sarah:** Why are you so angry all the time? It's impossible to have a conversation with you. All you do is lash out and then we have a huge argument. What's the point?

Tom and Sarah are clearly feeling completely disconnected from each another. This situation is made all the more painful by the fact that they used to feel so close. Part of the problem is that neither is acting in a way that creates the conditions for the other to feel safe enough to let go of their reactive, anger-fuelled behaviour and tune into the more tender emotions that lie underneath that anger — feelings of inadequacy, self-doubt, worry (about being hated by someone you love, perhaps), disappointment or anxiety (the list could go on).

Maybe you recognise this scenario. Possibly you're wondering whether your anger with your partner is masking more tender emotions beneath. Anger can stop you making contact with these emotions and prevent you from sharing them with someone else.

The problem is that anger is even more contagious than the common cold — its incubation period is microseconds! Almost always, when one person in a relationship is exposed to anger, the other catches it.

The most effective response to (or medicine for) anger in your relationship is not reciprocal anger. Rather, you need to reach the more tender issues underlying it. For this, you need to open up, show your vulnerabilities and communicate in a way that doesn't make the other person feel threatened or attacked.

Take a moment to reflect on a recent argument with your partner (or a close friend, if you prefer). Now, being as honest as possible, write down your answers to the following questions:

- What was the fight about?
- How did you feel before, during and after the argument (describe any physical sensations in your body as well as particular emotions)?
- What kind of thoughts were you having about your partner?
- On reflection, what more sensitive and tender emotions were you aware of beneath the anger that you were unwilling to show at the time?

From an ACT perspective, anger can be a natural response to feeling under threat — physical or emotional. When you feel angry (just after a heated discussion or full-on argument, for example), it can be hard to see past the anger response. Reflecting on the previous questions can help put you in touch with the more tender emotions that your anger may have been masking and thus protecting you from experiencing during the argument.

Symbolising love the Chinese way

© John Wiley & Sons, Inc.

Ai is the traditional Chinese character for love, consisting of a heart inside the symbols for *accept* and *feel* (or *perceive*). Feeling or perceiving is similar to being aware, which ACT likewise sees as a prerequisite for love. In addition, Ai is interpreted visually as one hand offering a heart to another hand. This act of openness and giving also reflects the ACT position that love is built on loving actions.

Listening Actively, Responding Openly

When you feel threatened by the words of another person, you typically become defensive and enter either *fight* or *flight* mode. That is, you prepare to run from the source of the threat or fight against it. In everyday terms, this means you either walk away or stand and argue. Arguing can involve heated exchanges as you seek to justify your actions, deny anything's wrong or blame the other person for what's happening. Clearly, these behaviours aren't conducive to good communication. A valid point that needs to be discussed is usually at the bottom of every argument, but it's lost when you slip into defensive behaviour.

So what's the alternative? ACT proposes that, rather than reacting defensively against the difficult thoughts and feelings that emerge during an argument, you accept them and try to behave in ways that are more consistent with your values. In the heat of an argument you can't control what you think or feel (because these responses are the product of your history, which you can't change), but you can control how you behave — what you say and how you engage in conversations with your partner.

Doing so may not be easy, but if you want to get beyond the anger to address the underlying issues, controlling your behaviour can help:

✔ Your partner to know that he's being heard.

✔ You to minimise the sense of threat you experience and your resulting angry behaviour.

✔ You to communicate effectively your own thoughts and feelings.

Try the following ten active listening tips to help you get started:

1. **Face your partner and make lots of eye contact.**

2. **Really listen to and be aware of what your partner is saying.** Thoughts and feelings will inevitably emerge and distract you. When this happens, gently bring your attention back to the conversation.

3. **If you sense that your partner is feeling angry (which may then lead to a similar response within you), remind yourself that tender emotions and needs lie beneath that anger.**

4. **Wait for your partner to finish speaking before responding.**

5. **Actively engage in listening as well as speaking.**

6. **Confirm what you think you've heard in an enquiring, curious and non-judgemental manner.** For example, ask, 'What I think you're saying is . . . Is that right?'

7. **Take at least one breath before responding.** Allowing even a couple of seconds to elapse can provide the space for you to reply considerately rather than react critically.

8. **Don't be too quick to offer solutions.** You may need to solve the issue, but do so after you've both had a chance to communicate how you feel and to validate each other's feelings.

9. **Ask questions to clarify your understanding.** Even if you think you've understood what's been said, asking a clarifying question or two can help reassure your partner that you've listened to him and understood what he's said.

10. **If you feel yourself becoming angry and find it hard to respond with compassion, ask your partner if, in the service of making this a helpful conversation, the two of you can return to it later.** It's important that your partner understands that you're not trying to avoid the conversation, but rather that you're trying to make it a helpful one in which the two of you can show compassion towards one another.

Defusing Unhelpful Thoughts

Thoughts can act as a barrier to engaging in a loving relationship. When you encounter difficulties in your relationship, you probably ruminate and dwell on what your partner did or didn't say or do. Similarly, you can spend a lot of time wondering or speculating about what he may or may not be doing. Having these thoughts is quite natural, of course, but when you fuse with them (that is, believe them as the literal truth; check out Chapter 6 for more on fusion) they can become problematic.

Fusing with your thoughts means that you spend too much time in your head, which gets in the way of living the life you want to live. You stop paying attention to the things that are important to you in all areas of your life — in your relationships, work or leisure time.

Consider the following scenario. Your relationship with your partner is going through a rough patch and you keep thinking that he's no longer attracted to you. You get caught up in these thoughts frequently, believing them to be literally and completely true. And even though you deeply love your partner and desperately want the relationship to work, when you fuse with these thoughts you become less inclined to be physically intimate with him. You also avoid having a conversation about the situation because you worry it can only confirm your fears.

These thoughts may or may not be accurate, but that's not the point. What's significant is that you're expending so much time and energy fusing with them, which is causing you pain and, even more importantly, moving you no closer to the kind of relationship you really want to have.

From an ACT perspective, defusion is the solution to your dilemma. You need to gain some distance from your thoughts — not by trying to change or avoid them directly, but by noticing *thinking as a process* and not getting hooked onto particular negative thought patterns. One way in which to do so is to add to each negative thought as it emerges, *I'm noticing a thought about . . .*

For example:

- ✔ *I'm noticing a thought about* feeling fat and overweight.
- ✔ *I'm noticing a thought about* how he hasn't touched me in days.
- ✔ *I'm noticing a thought about* being rejected if I try to kiss him.
- ✔ *I'm noticing a thought about* how he never seems interested in what I have to say.
- ✔ *I'm noticing a thought about* being boring and uninteresting.

Altering your thoughts in this way makes you more aware of what you're actually saying so that you can choose to dismiss it.

Being Mindful in Your Relationships

Emotions are neither good nor bad; they just are what they are depending on what's happened to you. They also provide you with valuable information about the contexts in which you find yourself. This isn't to say that emotions aren't pleasurable or painful; of course, to varying degrees they're generally one or the other. However, the key point is that you have no control over them in the present moment. The emotions you feel reflect your past history, and as you can't change that, you can't change how you feel at any single point in time.

When you can't change something, your best option is to accept it.

ACT shows you how to become more accepting and aware of the whole range of human emotions — pleasurable and painful. This therapeutic agenda contrasts with those that see positive outcomes in terms of an increase in pleasurable emotions alone. Although that may initially seem somewhat counterintuitive, ACT partially defines positive outcomes as the ability to accept and become more aware of painful emotional experiences — *in the service of something bigger and more important*: being able to live and experience a rich, meaningful and fulfilling life. And that includes in your intimate relationships.

Mindfulness exercises can help you to open up to the full range of your feelings, and in so doing develop your shared intimacy with your partner. ACT uses many such exercises; the following exercise is designed for a couple to work through together. Try it if you feel willing and able to engage in a direct, intimate experience with your partner.

Put two cushions on the floor and sit on them facing each other. (If you prefer, use two chairs instead.) Take a moment to centre yourselves, sitting with your backs straight and with a sense of being firmly rooted to the floor.

Place your hands on your knees, with one of your palms facing up and your partner's palm facing down on top of it. Place your other palm facing down on top of your partner's upward-facing palm.

Begin to find a natural and steady rhythm to your breathing. You'll probably notice that the rhythm of your breathing has aligned with that of your partner. Don't worry if it hasn't, however; it's not essential to feeling connected to one another.

Spend approximately ten minutes in this position, noticing your breathing and the sensation of your palms touching. This exercise has no other agenda — just simply *be* together. You may notice your eyes wandering toward those of your partner and that's fine. But don't force yourself and don't be deterred if your partner's eyes are closed or looking elsewhere. Just be with one another and be with your experience for these ten minutes or so.

How did you find this experience? Did you and your partner talk to each other afterwards? And, if so, how would you describe the quality of the conversation?

Finding the time to *just be* with your partner can be difficult in your busy life. This exercise, and others like it, can help you to reconnect with your partner by putting all other priorities aside, taking time to enjoy each other's company and remembering what you love about doing so.

Creating the Relationship You Want

Projecting into the future can be a good way to understand the values you hold within your intimate relationships. Picturing yourself in the future can make you reflect on the kind of person you are now and possibly how you would rather be. Try out the following exercise.

Imagine you're attending your ruby anniversary party. You and your partner have invited your family and friends. This event is a joyous occasion because your relationship has seen many happy times and also managed to weather the more challenging periods.

At the end of the celebration dinner, your partner stands up to make a speech. At the clink of a wine glass, the room falls silent and he begins to talk. Take a few minutes to think about what you would like him to say about you. What qualities would he describe? What values would he say you have embodied in your relationship? What would he say about how you conducted yourself during the tough times? What particular experiences may he refer to and what would he say about them?

Now consider what your answers to these questions tell you about the values you hold in terms of your relationship.

Your values are those things most important to you and which you can embody by acting in particular ways.

When you've considered your values, pick two or three that you feel are currently most important. (You're not abandoning the other values you identified; you're simply picking some to work on in this exercise.)

Now, for each value, write a statement defining what it means to you. Next, set two personal goals that you can work towards in the service of each value: one that you can do today and one to achieve over the next two weeks. Table 13-1 provides an example.

Table 13-1	Defining Your Values and Setting Related Goals		
Relationship Value	Definition	Goal for Today	Goal for the Next Two Weeks
Honesty	Being open with my loved ones about my thoughts and feelings, even when doing so is hard and means talking about difficult things.	Talk to my partner about something at work that is currently really exciting me.	Practise ten minutes of mindfulness at least four times (with my partner if he's willing) and share those experiences at the next convenient time.
Kindness	Acting in a caring and compassionate way. Taking into account my partner's feelings before doing things that directly affect him.	Buy a nice bottle of wine for my partner on the way home from work today.	Cook a selection of my partner's favourite meals.
Intimacy	Sharing my thoughts, feelings and body with my partner.	Offer to give my partner a back massage before bedtime this evening.	Initiate physical intimacy at least twice.

When things are tough, bring to mind this 'best self' you visualised in the future — this person your heart most desires to be. Reconnect with the values that he or she represents, and then set goals to help you live up to them in your relationship.

Disagreeing Rather Than Fighting

All relationships involve disagreements and differences. The challenge is to address them without descending into angry arguments. What characterises a healthy or an unhealthy relationship is not the presence or absence of disagreements, but *how* they're dealt with.

Keeping in mind the kind of partner you want to be is hardest when you're immersed in an argument. You probably fuse with negative thoughts about yourself and then become defensive, using anger or avoidance to shield your vulnerabilities from the perceived attack. Using the techniques described in this chapter, such as active listening, being aware of the pain your partner is hiding beneath his anger, saying 'I'm noticing that . . .' and 'I'm wondering if . . . ' before replying, and so on, can help you avoid inflicting or incurring serious emotional damage during arguments with your partner.

Often, however, acting in a value-consistent manner in your relationships means going back after a row and carrying out some repair work. Strong and resilient relationships aren't problem- or challenge-free. They result from two people having a history of working effectively through difference and challenge. Why? Because partners in such relationships have learned to work through disagreements by having had them in the first place! If they'd never argued, they wouldn't have developed the skills to deal with them effectively.

Try asking your partner these questions when you feel a bit of reparation is needed:

- What do you feel happened then?
- What's happening for you now?
- How are you feeling?
- What do you need (and what do you need from me) in order to be able to move on from this?
- What can I/we do to work through these kinds of difficulties more effectively in the future?

Questions like these aren't threatening because the answers they prompt don't incite blame or deny responsibility. And while you can't control your partner's feelings any more than you can change the past, engaging in reparation in this way increases the chance that your partner won't feel threatened by your responses. It also signals how much you value your relationship with your partner.

Facing a Positive Future Together

People need relationships with others in order to survive, learn and ultimately reproduce. In spite of their necessity, however, social and intimate relationships aren't always easy. And neither do they just happen all by themselves — they're the product of your actions and take time, energy and effort. This chapter demonstrates how ACT can help you connect with your partner and behave in line with your core values, rather than your thoughts or feelings.

Building the foundations of your relationship on the things that really matter to you both means that you and your partner can create the life you want together.

Chapter 14

Dealing with Problem Anger

· ·

In This Chapter

▶ Considering when anger becomes a problem

▶ Working out the personal cost of anger

▶ Using defusion, acceptance and compassion to deal with anger

▶ Establishing some realistic goals to help you respond to anger positively

· ·

*A*nger is a powerful emotion that everyone experiences from time to time when things don't go her way. Fortunately, most people express their anger in healthy and socially appropriate ways most of the time. For some, however, anger is a huge problem, expressed in outbursts of violence towards others or as an inner rage that eats away at them.

The consequences of problem anger can be so harmful that it's easy to overlook the fact that the angry person is also hurting. She'll be feeling negative emotions, such as pain, fear, hurt or confusion, and dark and difficult thoughts. These experiences, while unpleasant and challenging, are also quite natural. While minimising or removing your anger may seem an obvious solution, this isn't actually possible in practice because you don't have direct control over your feelings. Rather than changing the experience of problem anger directly, the challenge is to change how you respond to it. Crucially, you don't fight fire with fire. That is, you don't deal with your negativity with more negativity; instead, you respond with kindness, compassion and acceptance.

This chapter covers the emotional experience of anger from an Acceptance and Commitment Therapy (ACT) perspective. It shows you how to reduce the suffering your anger causes by helping you to become compassionate towards, and accepting of, your own experiences, and, by extension, the angry behaviour of other people too.

This chapter isn't a substitute for specialist support if anger behaviour is a serious issue for you or someone you know. Your GP can make a referral to a suitable therapist if that's the case.

Defining Anger

Feeling angry is part of being human, but it can become problematic when you express it in violent or aggressive ways.

We define *problem anger* as a way of expressing angry thoughts and feelings that leads to persistent and significant difficulties in a person's life. Problem anger and associated violence are a big problem in the UK. An Office for National Statistics report showed that 2.1 million violent incidents occurred in England and Wales in 2013. Domestic violence figures were also high, with an estimated 7 per cent of women and 5 per cent of men experiencing domestic abuse each year.

Of those surveyed by the Mental Health Foundation in 2008:

- ✔ 32 per cent reported that a close friend or family member had trouble controlling his or her anger.
- ✔ 12 per cent reported that they had trouble controlling their own anger.
- ✔ 28 per cent reported feeling worried about how angry they feel.
- ✔ 20 per cent reported that they had ended a relationship or friendship with someone because of how that person behaved when they were angry.

Anger typically occurs when you feel threatened, attacked, insulted or wronged in some way. In these circumstances, a *fight or flight* response (that is, fleeing from or attacking the source of anger when your arousal levels feel overwhelming) is quite natural. Your survival response means you can experience a wide range of difficult thoughts, emotions and bodily sensations, such as:

- ✔ Feeling tense, angry and anxious
- ✔ Making negative evaluations of people around you
- ✔ Being less inhibited in your behaviour (for example, saying or doing things you ordinarily wouldn't and then wondering why)
- ✔ Experiencing a faster pulse rate, muscular tension and increased perspiration
- ✔ Ruminating to an excessive degree (especially after the event)

The fight or flight survival response can be helpful when you feel threatened because it propels you into action (standing your ground or running away), but this is partly what makes it so difficult to manage. Intense, action-orientated emotions such as anger can feel as though they automatically lead to particular acts and this can make them hard to respond to differently. Fortunately, ACT can give you the tools to do so.

Considering the Cost of Anger

Sometimes you don't fully appreciate (or don't want to appreciate) what your anger really costs you and the people around you. Use Table 14-1 to help you reflect on how you typically respond to angry feelings.

Consider your responses to anger over the last six months and how they've made you feel or behave. Indicate, by ticking in the relevant boxes, how often these events or feelings occurred and see if a pattern emerges. Maybe you become depressed more often than you pick a fight, for example.

Table 14-1	What Has My Anger Cost Me?		
Over the Last Six Months, When I Became Angry I Have:	**Never**	**Once**	**More than Once**
Become depressed			
Had a fight			
Broken something			
Argued with a loved one			
Physically hurt myself			
Said horrible things to others			
Jeopardised potential opportunities at work			
Got into trouble with the police			
Felt ashamed or guilty			
Driven unsafely			

Were you surprised by your answers? What do they tell you about your current relationship with feelings of anger and how you manage them? If you answered 'Once' or 'More than once' to several questions, to some degree you're likely to feel that you need to find new strategies to address how you deal with the situations, people, feelings and thoughts that make you angry. Knowing the particular ways in which you're prone to respond means you can work out new ways of managing your anger in the future.

Dividing Anger into Five Elements

In their book *ACT on Life Not on Anger* (New Harbinger Publications, 2006), Eifert, McKay and Forsyth suggest that anger can usefully be thought of as involving five elements, or phases:

1. **Pre-anger feelings:** You experience these feelings and sensations in your body, typically before you actually feel angry. Pre-anger feelings are *aversive stimuli*, which means that they should induce changes in your behaviour because they're unpleasant. However, they're not thought to be associated with hostile emotions, such as shame, guilt, worry, anxiety and fear. When anger finally emerges, one of its functions can be to mask, or avoid further experience of, these painful emotions.

2. **Trigger thoughts:** These can be in the form of painful or uncomfortable memories, often triggered by an event taking place in the here and now. Such thoughts are usually highly evaluative, judgemental and negative. You can easily fuse with trigger thoughts (believe them to be literally true), becoming lost in them and desensitised to what's taking place around you.

3. **Anger feeling:** Together with feeling angry, you may also experience bodily sensations such as muscular tension, a quickening pulse rate, waves of heat and shakiness.

4. **Impulse to act:** Whether or not your feeling of anger results in anger behaviour (described in the next point), the impulse to act on anger almost always occurs, and usually very quickly after the anger itself. Often, the impulse is to do something that's unlikely to result in a positive outcome for you — as the person experiencing the anger — or the people around you.

5. **Anger behaviour:** The preceding four elements take place inside your skin (they're internal events). When you're unable to work with anger positively and effectively, anger behaviour occurs either in the form of being acted out or suppressed. *Acting out* usually involves physical or verbal aggression, often towards other people. *Suppression* means you try to push your anger back down, rather than giving it a healthy outlet. In extreme cases, this approach can lead to self-harming behaviours, which can function to numb the pain of aversive internal events.

Sometimes you're not fully aware of your anger and what's going on when you experience it. Work through the following exercise to explore your own experience of the five elements of anger.

Get a pen and paper and jot down notes for each point:

1. **Pre-anger feelings:** Reflect on a recent experience of feeling angry. Describe the emotions and bodily sensations you felt before your anger emerged.

2. **Trigger thoughts:** Make a note of any prominent or particularly relevant thoughts, memories or images you experienced during or immediately following your pre-anger feelings. With what (or about whom) were they concerned?

3. **Anger feeling:** Rate (on a scale from 1–10 if it helps) how angry you felt. Did your anger grow slowly or erupt very suddenly? How long did it last? What bodily sensations co-occurred with your anger? Rather than answer this quickly (which is often the urge), allow yourself to reflect and, if you can, relive the experience a little. Doing so will really help bring the activity to life and make it more meaningful to you (remember, ACT is primarily an experiential learning process, not simply an intellectual one).

4. **Impulse to act:** What did you want to do and to whom (or what) did you want to do it? Do you feel that you made (or were able to make) a conscious decision about what to do when you felt the impulse; that is, whether or not to act on it? Remember, the impulse to act on anger is always present (whether you chose to act on it eventually or not).

5. **Anger behaviour:** What happened? Did your behaviour result in a positive or negative outcome — for you and anyone else who was involved? What feelings did you experience when you expressed your anger? Did those feelings change immediately afterwards? What about an hour later and the next day? Did you feel a sense of control over your eventual action or was it a knee-jerk reaction?

If you find reflecting on a previous incident difficult, keep this exercise in mind ready for the next time you feel angry. Work through the exercise as soon as possible after the event so that you can easily remember the thoughts and feelings you experienced.

Hopefully this exercise gave you a deeper understanding of how the experience of anger is part of a much more complex psychological process involving a range of other difficult emotions, such as shame, fear, embarrassment or loneliness. Maybe thinking about an actual experience of anger rather than viewing it hypothetically allowed you to see that you can make a choice between the *impulse to act* and the *act itself*. These two elements of the anger process are separated by one critical thing — a choice. You didn't choose to experience the impulse but you did choose how to act in response to it.

In ACT, working positively with anger involves becoming more aware of this *choice-space*. Recognising that you can pause to consider how to respond to a situation that makes you angry means you can choose to effect outcomes that nurture, protect and invest in what's most important to you — your partner, your job, your friends and so on — rather than destroying or endangering it.

Defusing Angry Thoughts

Moments of anger are usually accompanied by dark, aggressive or resentful thoughts. You may think:

- ✔ I'm going to get her for this.
- ✔ What he did just isn't right.
- ✔ She's totally wrong.
- ✔ He's crazy and nasty.

You may even drift off into vengeful fantasies about what you'd like to do.

These thoughts and imaginings, while natural, can be problematic. For a start, the very nature of their content means you won't feel very positive or upbeat when you have them. Also, if you fuse with your thoughts (that is, believe their literal content) they can exert quite a lot of influence over your behaviour.

When you fuse with your thoughts you believe them to be true/accurate and this means you're more likely to act on them.

Consider this scenario. In conversation with a colleague, you have the thought, 'She's being rude and disrespectful'. If you fuse with this thought you're then more inclined to form a negative opinion of her, which will increase the tension between you. Alternatively, you can respond to your thought as just a thought and, as a result, its literal content will be less influential. You can use the prefix, '*I'm having the thought that* she's being rude and disrespectful on purpose' (Chapter 13 has more on defusing from specific unhelpful thoughts). Adding that prefix reminds you that a thought is just a bit of private language going through your head and not necessarily the best basis for action.

Defusing from the language you use (check out Chapter 6 on how to do so) enables you to step back from the literal content of what you say or think and to create a space in which to decide how you want to behave. This means your behaviour can then be directed by your values rather than your angry thoughts.

Fighting the Anger Monster

If you have a problem with anger, you've probably already tried to do something about it. Maybe you've attempted keeping calm or distracting yourself. Possibly you've worked on trying to change or control your thoughts or feelings. You may even have attended an anger management course. What these approaches typically have in common is that they all try to directly control or reduce your angry thoughts and feelings. Unfortunately, you simply don't have enough control over what you think and feel to make doing so a viable strategy (as Chapter 9 explains in detail). If you've tried and failed to do this in the past, it's not for want of effort that you didn't succeed; rather, it was because your thoughts and feelings aren't very controllable. If dealing with anger simply involved deciding to feel differently, you wouldn't have a problem!

Picture your struggle with problem anger as a tug-of-war with a huge and very strong monster (see Figure 14-1). Between you and the monster is a dark and rather scary-looking hole; it's so deep that you can't see the bottom. As you pull on the rope you can feel the monster's strength and, initially, you match it with your own. As you become increasingly fatigued, however, the monster laughs in your face, its strength undiminished. Finally you acknowledge that you can't win this fight. But losing isn't an option either because you don't want to fall into the hole. You have too much at stake, so you struggle on.

Figure 14-1:
Doing battle
with the
anger
monster.

Illustration by Joe Munro

Take a moment to consider your options here. You can continue expending your energy fighting a monster you can't defeat — but where will that lead you? Won't you be pulled into the gaping hole before you? Actually, you can adopt a different strategy: put down the rope and stop struggling with the monster! ACT encourages you to do just that — to give up trying to control or win the battle against the monster of your anger.

Giving up the struggle to control your anger can be extremely difficult because it means accepting that you can't win. You can't rid yourself of the anger monster by pulling it into a bottomless pit. And, obviously, if you can't get rid of your anger, and the thoughts and feelings that accompany it, you simply have to accept that they'll always be there.

Accepting anger (and any other thoughts and feelings associated with it) can feel counterintuitive because humans evolved to avoid or minimise painful experiences. For this reason, the idea of acceptance may not be particularly appealing when first encountered, but in fact it's your best option. Why? Because trying to control your angry thoughts and feelings (your internal 'monsters') is a futile task that takes up valuable time and energy.

Abandon your efforts to control the uncontrollable and focus on doing the things that really matter to you instead. Begin living a life defined by your values and not your fears.

Tackling Your Anger with Acceptance, Compassion and Mindfulness

You can deal with your problem anger by following these four steps:

1. **Acknowledge your anger as and when you feel it.** This is the first step towards understanding why you're experiencing the anger and what lies beneath it.

2. **Accept the situation as it is.** You can't turn back the clock — and expending your energy on fusing with thoughts about what you would do if you could is as pointless as trying to control your emotions.

3. **Explore and understand what lies beneath your anger.** What painful and tender emotions underlie the harsh, prickly exterior of your anger? What do they achieve or help you avoid? If you don't discover the source of your anger, you can't respond to it differently.

4. **Respond to your feelings with kindness and compassion.** Rather than allowing anger to mask sensitive or painful issues, acknowledge that you find dealing with them difficult and allow yourself to respond in a way that makes you feel better.

Restorative justice and acceptance

The restorative justice (RJ) process brings stakeholders in a crime or harmful incident together in order for the harm to be repaired. Following preparatory sessions with both parties, an RJ practitioner mediates during a face-to-face encounter between the victim and perpetrator. For the person who may have been bullied, assaulted, stolen from or lied to, for example, the RJ process involves reliving, working through and accepting some very difficult experiences. However, the same can be true for the perpetrator because she's likely to experience all kinds of difficult emotions too, such as shame, guilt, regret, remorse, and even anger and resentment. Like the victim, she needs to accept these experiences if she's to be able to participate in the RJ process. Research consistently indicates that both parties reap considerable benefits from the RJ process, and perpetrators typically find it an emotionally difficult experience — not a get-out-of-jail-free card — and something they don't want to go through again.

Acceptance involves being open to your experiences without trying to avoid or change them. It's not easy because it involves being willing to be in contact with unwanted or painful experiences in your life — which doesn't come naturally. And to make acceptance even harder, it's an ongoing process that you have to keep engaging in, not a single event. You can't switch it on or off like a lightbulb. Acceptance is a choice that you have to keep making. Fortunately, being accepting is perfectly possible (though admittedly difficult at first) and with practice you can get better at it.

When you experience dark and angry thoughts or feel a sense of rage coursing through your body, it can be very difficult to be accepting of those thoughts and sensations. This is where a bit of compassion and kindness is essential. Compassion allows you to recognise suffering at the heart of anger and directs you to be proactive in your response. Compassion means:

- ✔ Treating yourself and other people with kindness and gentleness
- ✔ Recognising that all people share a common humanity and everyone struggles
- ✔ Being aware of and open to all your experiences

When you're compassionate, you become sensitive to the suffering of other people and yourself, and motivated to try to alleviate it. When you feel angry or have angry thoughts, underneath you're suffering. Being compassionate towards yourself is an important step in responding differently in these circumstances. It can also motivate you to alleviate the suffering of others by not inflicting your anger on them. You can choose to no longer respond to internal anger with external aggression.

You can practise acceptance and self-compassion through mindfulness. Mindfulness involves purposefully paying attention to the present moment, openly and without defence (check out Chapter 7 for more details). It's an awareness process rather than a thinking process, which aims to help you recognise and accept your experiences, be they good or bad.

Practising mindful awareness allows you to *own* your feelings, rather than your feelings owning you. When you're mindful, you allow your thoughts, feelings and bodily sensations to emerge and pass by without response. You simply watch them come and watch them go. Although your mind may be busy with lots of thoughts and evaluations when you're practising mindfulness, they too are just part of what you notice.

Mindfulness also has the benefit of increasing your sensitivity to events unfolding within and around you. Angry thoughts and emotions can be very persistent and can dominate your life as you struggle with them. Focusing on that struggle reduces your ability to respond to the world effectively and to make choices that are consistent with your chosen values.

Practising mindfulness is the best way to experience its benefits. Have a go at the following simple mindfulness exercise, which helps you focus on noticing your feelings.

Find a comfortable sitting position and ensure that your spine is straight and upright; on a chair or cross-legged on the floor is fine. Take a deep breath and then either close your eyes or settle your gaze on a single point near the floor, maybe a knot in a wooden door or a pattern in the carpet.

Notice how you feel right now. Give that emotion a name; for example, you may be sad, uncertain, happy, relaxed, excited or worried. Possibly you feel a combination of emotions. Rate the strength of the emotion on a scale of 1–10, where 1 is low and 10 high. You may also notice thoughts and bodily sensations, such as aches and pains. Allow yourself to be aware of these thoughts and sensations and rate them too.

If the emotion, thought or sensation is a little uncomfortable, you may notice that you're resisting it. Just notice this sense of resistance and, rather than responding to it, simply stay with the emotion or sensation that you're experiencing — just let it be.

Notice that you may be feeling the emotion more prominently in certain parts of your body. Possibly you even ascribe it a certain quality, such as a colour or texture. Whatever you're experiencing — be it positive and enjoyable or negative and uncomfortable — like all emotions it will pass in time. So allow it to be knowing that, by its very nature, it's transient and will eventually subside.

From time to time you'll drift off into your thoughts, which will take you away from the present moment. When this happens, acknowledge those thoughts and then gently bring your awareness back to the task of focusing on your emotions and bodily sensations.

After five minutes, or whenever you feel ready, gradually begin to roll your shoulders and neck a little, and take a deep and slow breath before opening your eyes or beginning to shift your gaze from its focus near the floor.

This mindfulness exercise is about being present with your emotions and bodily sensations without seeking to change or avoid them. It enabled you to make contact with an emotion and *accept* what you encountered. You can apply this same process to your anger by observing it, giving it the space to bubble up in your experience and seeing it for what it is: your natural response to feeling under threat.

Letting Go of Your Anger

When you let go of anger, it lets go of you. You free yourself from its grip and can then live according to your values and what matters to you. You can begin to make a choice when angry thoughts and feelings emerge. You can respond to them aggressively — and accept the negative consequences! Or you can accept them as a valid part of your experience, and *then* choose how you want to respond to them. Knowing your values is useful here because they help you decide what to do.

Values define the life you want to be living (and Chapter 4 helps you determine them). They're deeply personal statements about the ongoing actions that you want your life to stand for, such as:

- ✔ I want to be a loving, responsible parent.
- ✔ I want to make a positive contribution to my community.
- ✔ I want to be a loving and caring partner.
- ✔ I want to be physically and mentally healthy.
- ✔ I want to be good at my job.
- ✔ I want to be a charitable human being.
- ✔ I want to be a good and reliable friend.

Notice that none of these statements mentions *not* being angry. Values describes what you want, not what you don't want. However, your value statements can nonetheless provide guidance regarding how you behave when you're angry. Use the following exercise to gain a sense of your values as they relate to anger.

If anger has been a dominant force in your life, the epitaph on your head-stone may read something like this:

> *Here lies David. He was short-tempered and regularly shouted at people. He wasn't a nice person to be around because no one knew when his anger would erupt. He didn't mean to hurt people and often felt guilty after an outburst. But people were hurt, emotionally and sometimes even physically. May he rest in peace?*

Now take a moment to reflect on what you'd really want it to say. What do you want your life to be about, and what do you want to be remembered for? Rather than concrete actions (such as the fact that you gained a degree in chemistry or took the kids to Greece every year), focus on the values you want your life to represent, such as, 'Here lies a kind and generous person'. Now write your own epitaph on the headstone in Figure 14-2, reflecting the person you want to become.

Figure 14-2:
Writing your
own
epitaph.

Illustration by Joe Munro

Working through this exercise helps you to see how anger can be a pow-erful internal barrier to your quest to live a life that's value-consistent. Acknowledging how you *don't* want to behave can help provide you with a clear sense of how to live in line with your values.

Setting Yourself Some Helpful Goals

You don't overcome problematic anger by trying to manage, control or get rid of it. The solution lies in developing a new relationship with your angry thoughts and feelings so that you can respond to them differently. You do this by accepting your experiences and showing compassion and kindness toward yourself and others in the process.

To help you respond to your anger in a new and less damaging way, set yourself some goals that will help bring about positive outcomes when you feel angry. Goals are the actions you take to live according to your values. You may find it helpful to express your goals as statements, for example:

> 'I value being kind and considerate. Therefore, when I become angry I will count to three, take three deep breaths and speak politely and calmly'.

> 'When I experience thoughts such as "You should listen to me" or "Don't speak to me like that", I will mindfully notice these thoughts before reminding myself of the values that I want to define my life by'.

Reflect on how you'd like to be remembered in situations that typically incite anger and frustration (the writing your own epitaph exercise in the preceding section may help here). Then establish three related value-based goals by completing this sentence: 'When I feel angry I will . . .' (for example, '. . . calmly explain why').

You can deal with your anger in the same way that you manage any other difficult emotion or behaviour — by choosing how to respond to it.

Accept your thoughts and feelings, Choose a valued life direction and Take action.

Chapter 15

Helping You Live with Chronic Pain

In This Chapter

▶ Understanding what chronic pain means

▶ Accepting that you can't avoid your pain

▶ Using ACT to help you cope

*A*cceptance and Commitment Therapy (ACT) is one of the leading intervention frameworks for people experiencing chronic pain. Over the past 20 years researchers and clinicians have developed a range of evidence-based intervention protocols based on the ACT model that have improved the quality of people's lives and reduced their pain-related difficulties. A reduction in levels of pain may also result, but that's not the primary goal. Rather, ACT aims to help you live as rich and meaningful a life as possible alongside your pain. That might not seem an appealing prospect, but when it isn't possible to control or minimise your pain then the only other option is to find a way to live with it.

The effects of chronic pain can be debilitating and have a huge impact on your quality of life, work and relationships. In addition, chronic pain exacts a heavy emotional toll and can make you feel fearful, anxious, depressed, angry and fatigued. The exercises in this chapter help you to view your pain from a different perspective and hopefully increase the extent to which your life is defined by your values rather than your pain.

If you're experiencing chronic pain, we hope you find this chapter of some use. However, it's no substitute for a full consultation with a pain specialist. Ask your GP for a referral if you need one.

Defining Chronic Pain

The term *chronic pain* generally refers to pain that's lasted for more than three months. It may be intermittent or constant and is usually associated with some form of soreness, aching, tightness or stiffness.

Accompanying the physical pain, people often report experiencing problems with:

- ✔ Anxiety, anger and depression
- ✔ Relationships
- ✔ Work activities and opportunities
- ✔ Fatigue and energy levels
- ✔ Sleep
- ✔ Libido

Chronic pain is a big issue worldwide. In a large-scale European study conducted in 2006, 19 per cent of people reported experiencing significant levels of pain for more than six months; in 2014, US researchers estimated that 20 per cent of the population (39.4 million people) suffered persistent pain.

Chronic pain has an enormous impact on people's lives. A 2008 UK Department of Health report estimated that chronic pain reduces quality of life more than any other health condition. And a pain survey conducted across Europe found that 21 per cent of people with chronic pain had been diagnosed with depression, 61 per cent were unable or less able to work outside the home and 19 per cent had lost their job.

The economic costs are also huge. Pain is the second most common reason given for claiming incapacity benefit in the UK (after mental health), and in 2014 the Office for National Statistics reported that more days were lost to back, neck and muscle pain than any other cause (26 million days). Europe-wide, the healthcare costs could be as high as £220 billion.

Whichever way you look at it, chronic pain is a major issue. Take a moment to consider the individual suffering behind those mindboggling statistics. Each percentage point represents *thousands* of human beings; thousands of people whose lives are dominated by constant, gnawing, inescapable pain.

Recognising that Avoiding Pain Isn't the Answer

Pain, by definition, hurts, and that's not nice. If something can be done to reduce your level of pain, then it makes sense to do it. A range of biomedical and other interventions exist that can address your pain — allowing it to persist when you can remove or reduce it makes no sense. But what can be done when your pain cannot be removed completely?

Nettle urtication

Urtication refers to the 2000-year-old practice of brushing stinging nettles against the skin to reduce the effects of joint or muscle pain. The term derives from the nettle's botanical name, *Urtica dioica*. The hairs on the nettle's leaves inject several chemicals that cause a stinging sensation. These can trigger an anti-inflammatory and/or pain-killing effect. Another explanation for its remedial effect is that the nettle stings distract you from the original pain, which provides some relief because it's a different kind of pain and it's more under your control (you can rub the affected area with a dock leaf, for example). Whatever the explanation, some people do find urtication an effective form of pain relief.

Warning! **Seek medical advice before engaging in urtication.**

When you experience physical pain, it's quite natural to want to do things that reduce or minimise it (check out the nearby sidebar, 'Nettle urtication', for an example!). You may avoid particular activities or move in certain ways to guard against aggravating it. You may take pain-killing drugs or use other remedies such as massage, ice or heat. In more extreme cases you may even engage in emotional denial by trying to stop noticing or talking about how you feel. Often these activities provide some form of short-term relief, which is why you persist in them.

In your efforts to not feel pain, you might also engage in avoidance behaviours that are themselves harmful and counterproductive. Addiction to pain-killers, for example, can lead to serious health problems, even death. Similarly, not going for a walk may be an effective means of reducing the pain in your knees, but it may also result in you missing out on a spectacular view and the lack of exercise can have unintended cardiovascular consequences.

Avoidance behaviours often come at a cost and are increasingly recognised to be the main reason for pain-related suffering and disability rather than the pain itself. That is, your efforts to avoid physical pain have a bigger impact on your lifestyle than the experience of pain itself. For example, a 2014 study led by Kevin Vowles, at the University of New Mexico, found that disability levels correlated with the extent to which people attempted to control their pain and the degree to which they engaged in actions based on their values. People who made fewer efforts to control their pain and did things that held meaning for them experienced lower levels of disability and vice versa.

Considering the ACT Alternative

The strong link between pain and disability makes it easy to think of pain reduction as your main priority. The logic goes that to reduce any pain-related problem, you first need to reduce the pain. Sometimes, however, reducing the pain just isn't possible. If you can, then go ahead and do it, but if you can't this logic implies there's nothing you can do. You're left thinking that if you can't get rid of your pain, then you can't lessen its impact on your life either. In these circumstances you may end up feeling hopeless and trapped in your predicament.

If you accept the reasoning that you need to reduce your pain before you can move forward in life, it's true that your choices are limited. But it turns out that this isn't the only option on the table. While you may not be able to change the pain you experience, you can change how you *respond* to it and in the process reduce its impact on your life. This is what ACT helps you to do.

Instead of trying to change the pain experience itself, ACT aims to help you engage in value-based activities and goals while staying in contact with the original pain — an approach based on developing *psychological flexibility* (that is, being open to and accepting of all your thoughts and feelings while simultaneously getting on with what you want to do in life; check out Chapter 3 for more details).

In particular, ACT works on two related areas:

- *Reducing* your unsuccessful efforts to control or remove pain. Trying to control the experiences associated with pain that can't actually change is a futile activity and expends a great deal of your time and energy.

- *Increasing* the degree to which you live according to your values because ultimately they will give your life meaning and purpose.

Research shows that reducing your efforts to avoid unavoidable pain and engaging in value-based activities diminishes your pain-related disability, even if the pain level remains broadly the same. For instance, in 2011 Lance MacCracken, Professor of Behavioural Medicine at Kings College London, and colleagues published results of a study demonstrating that participants in an ACT intervention reported significantly lower levels of anxiety, depression and physical and psychosocial disability, which were maintained at three-month follow-up. Interestingly, the data showed that participants did not report a discernible change in the degree of pain they experienced. This finding challenges the view that you need to reduce pain in order to reduce your level of disability. The relationship between pain, disability and quality of life is more complex than that. Fortunately, rather than concentrating only on pain reduction, other approaches are also available to you that can make a difference to your life.

Fearing pain can lead to real pain

The *fear avoidance* model describes how the fear of pain can encourage avoidant behaviour that in turn leads to the development of real musculoskeletal pain and disability. If an individual can minimise his experience of pain by engaging in avoidant behaviour, that outcome will reinforce this behaviour and increase its likelihood of reoccurrence. For example, he may avoid putting weight on a sore knee until it's healed. In that circumstance his avoidant behaviour is adaptive — he changes the way he walks to protect his knee. However, if he continues walking in an unnatural manner after the original injury has healed because of the fear of any pain, his limited mobility will restrict the normal functioning of his body and his physiology will change accordingly. This can lead to other sources of pain; for example, twisting his body to avoid walking on a painful knee may create secondary back pain.

Giving up what doesn't work

The *control agenda* is the main obstacle facing people experiencing chronic pain: their strong and entirely understandable desire not to experience pain fuels their efforts to get rid of it. Trying to control and change unavoidable pain can only lead to failure, frustration and a host of other undesirable outcomes, however.

Human beings are strongly disposed to want to avoid certain internal experiences, such as negative thoughts, feelings and bodily sensations. Cultural norms reinforce that natural disposition. The desire to avoid unpleasant experiences may be even stronger in chronic pain sufferers because of the (false!) assumption that pain and disability are intractably linked. The end result is that you can spend so much time and effort trying to minimise or get rid of your pain that your avoidant behaviour dominates your life. The challenge you face is to give up that pattern of behaviour and try something new.

To help you recognise how effective your past efforts to control your pain have been, complete Table 15-1. Rate the success of each strategy on a scale of –5 to 5, where –5 = your pain is much worse, 0 = no change in your pain and +5 = your pain is considerably better. We've provided an example to get you started.

When you've completed Table 15-1, reflect on the results. Consider abandoning those strategies scoring –5 to 0 because they're clearly not working. You need to try something else!

Table 15-1	How Successful Are My Pain Control Strategies?
Strategies I Have Used To Cope with or Treat My Pain	*Success of This Strategy*
Avoided going out	0

Building openness and awareness through mindfulness

Trying to control or avoid unavoidable chronic pain is a bit like trying to dig your way out of a hole. Try as you might, you simply won't be able to do so and all your efforts will come to nothing. When you find yourself in a hole, therefore, the first thing to do is to stop digging and put down the spade. Doing so stops you getting any deeper and gives you the opportunity to do something different.

An alternative to trying to get rid of or reduce your chronic pain is to work out what really matters to you (your values) and begin making your life about those things. This requires increasing your psychological flexibility (see Chapter 3) so that you become more open to, and aware of, all your experiences and active in pursuit of your value-based goals.

Mindfulness exercises offer a tried and tested way to gain contact with the present moment and become more open and aware (Chapter 7 covers mindfulness in depth). Mindfulness helps you to slow down and develops your awareness of, and openness to, your immediate experiences. This in turn enables you to experience yourself as the context or setting in which your thoughts and feelings occur. Mindfulness helps you understand that, while you continue to experience your thoughts and feelings, you're also more than them. You contain them, like the sky contains the clouds. From this vantage point you can observe your thoughts and feelings from a safe and stable place without becoming entangled in them (Chapter 8 describes your *self as context* in more detail). When you gain some distance from your thoughts, feelings and bodily sensations, you're then in a better position to engage with your values and decide what you want your life to be about and stand for.

To experience this directly, try the following mindfulness exercise.

Find a quiet spot and sit down with the soles of your feet resting comfortably on the floor. Now follow these steps:

1. **Breathe in deeply and look around you.** When you feel ready, close your eyes and take two more deep breaths.

2. **Focus your attention on your feet.** If you're wearing socks or shoes, notice the sensation of the fabric or leather against your skin. Notice them and let them be as they are.

3. **Consider your heels on the floor or in your shoes.** Notice what you feel. Slowly move your attention along the curves of the arches of your feet towards your toes. Notice what you feel. Now focus on your toes, starting with your little toes and moving slowly from toe to toe until your attention reaches your big toes. Notice what you feel.

4. **Focus on your feet in their entirety.** Feel all the interconnected parts of the bones and muscles. Your feet are always with you, helping to transport you wherever you go. Take a moment to marvel at their quiet functionality.

5. **When you drift off into your thoughts and forget about your feet — and you will! — simply notice that it's happened and gently and without judgement return your attention to your feet.**

6. **Continue to breathe slowly and deeply for one minute, maintaining your attention on your feet and observing the sensations you experience.**

7. **Move your attention away from your feet and become aware of what you can hear around you.** When you're ready, open your eyes.

Take a moment to reflect on what you thought and felt. The aim of the exercise is to practise your present moment awareness and the focus this time just happens to be your feet. Other exercises in this book focus on your breathing or what you can hear. As you did this exercise you probably noticed how easily you could slip into your thoughts and away from your immediate experiences. This is the essence of mindfulness, the constant need to keep bring your attention back to the present moment.

When you're being mindful you're taking the conscious step to accept all that life brings, the good and the bad. Doing so isn't easy if you've made resisting and defeating your pain your life's mission. Possibly, working through a mindfulness exercise is the first time you've ever taken a different approach toward your pain. Mindfulness can actually be the beginning of a different relationship with your pain.

Becoming more accepting

Acceptance is important because it's your only option when you can't change something.

Battling to change things that can't be changed takes you on a road to nowhere and is a waste of time and energy. Despite your best efforts, you can't achieve the impossible and they are doomed to failure.

However, even though acceptance may be your best option, that doesn't make it an easy choice. Acceptance of your pain, particularly when you've resisted it for so long, is profoundly difficult.

Treat yourself with compassion if you initially find accepting your pain difficult to manage. Adopting a different approach takes time and practice, and experiencing 'off days' doesn't mean you've failed.

Acceptance can be tricky for another reason. For some people it can feel like giving up hope. If you accept your pain it means giving up on the possibility of one day not experiencing it. However, losing hope is not the aim of acceptance. If one day an intervention is developed that can reduce or remove your pain, go for it. But until then your time is better spent accepting your pain as part of your life in the here and now rather than resisting it. Acceptance doesn't mean you want to experience pain (far from it), but it does mean you no longer need to engage in an unwinnable battle against it.

In ACT the term *willingness* is often used as a more positive, active alternative to *acceptance*. The question then becomes, 'Are you willing to have your pain in your life?' Not because you want it, but because when you accept your pain you give up digging a hole (as described in the earlier 'Building openness and awareness through mindfulness' section) and give yourself the chance to live a different life — one based on your values and what really matters to you rather than on trying to get rid of your pain.

Resistance is futile (for pain, at least)

While wanting to pull back from pain and resist it makes complete sense, research demonstrates that this approach actually worsens the situation. Efforts to resist your pain come to dominate your life and also make you even more sensitive to it. A 2006 study by Matthew Feldner and colleagues at the University of Arkansas, for example, demonstrated that subjects who were more experientially avoidant were less able to tolerate pain and recovered more slowly from adverse events. Research also shows that subjects who were instructed to notice their pain but not react to it were more able to engage in physical activities than those who attempted to control their pain.

Defusing from your thoughts

Defusion — looking *at* your thoughts rather than *from* your thoughts — is helpful because believing the thoughts you experience (that is, fusing with them) can stop you getting on with life. Maybe you've believed for years that if you could just get rid of your pain everything would be better. Possibly you have angry and resentful thoughts such as, 'It's not fair; other people don't struggle like I do' or 'If only I hadn't damaged my back in the first place, I'd be okay now'.

These thoughts may be true, but that's not the most important issue from the ACT perspective. What matters is whether they help you move forward in valued life directions. Remember, thoughts are just thoughts — bits of language in your head. Yes, they're immediate, pervasive and insistent, but they're just thoughts nonetheless. If you fuse with your thoughts, your behaviour is much more likely to be directed by them and not your values.

ACT uses a number of exercises to help you develop the ability to relate to your thoughts without being dominated by them. Try out the following exercise for an example.

In Table 15-2, record the thoughts you regularly experience regarding your pain: for example 'I'll never get better'. Then rate how useful these thoughts are in terms of helping you live according to your values. (Use a scale of 1–10, where 1 = not at all useful, and 10 = very useful.)

Table 15-2	How Useful Are My Pain-Related Thoughts?
Thoughts I Often Experience about My Pain	*How Useful Is This Thought? (1–10)*

Review your results. If your thoughts are useful in moving your life forward, embracing them makes sense. If they're not, however, next time they pop into your head you can make a choice about how you respond to them.

Committing to your values

Value-based living is the end goal for ACT, whether you're experiencing chronic pain or any other difficulty. Values are freely chosen ongoing actions that represent what you want your life to stand for and be defined by (see Chapter 4). Your values describe how you want to behave in life and you set goals to reflect them. You can think of your values as your direction of travel and your goals as what you achieve along the way.

To identify your values, use the Valued Living Questionnaire in Chapter 4 or the Values Bull's-Eye in Chapter 17. You can clarify what matters to you in lots of different ways — the key thing is to stop and think about it.

Try the following exercise to help you identify the attitudes, behaviours and actions you value.

Write the eulogy that you'd like your best friend to read at your funeral. Don't write what you think he'd say; write what you'd *want* him to say. Really let yourself go; no one else needs to read it and the more personal you make this ideal version of yourself, the more meaningful it will be.

Use how you want to be remembered as a guide to how to behave today. You can repeat this exercise and imagine the words of your partner, children, parents, friends, colleagues or anyone else you care about.

Living with chronic pain is very hard. If we could take it away from you, we would! However, when the elimination of your pain isn't achievable, you have only one option — to accept it and move your life forward in ways that are important to you nonetheless by engaging in value-based goals. Your experience of pain may remain the same but at least you won't be adding to your difficulties by allowing it to stop you doing the things that matter to you.

Part IV
Mental Health Issues from an ACT Perspective

Five Useful Points to Bear in Mind

- How you feel matters, but feelings don't cause your behaviour. Though not always easy, it's quite possible to feel one way and behave in another.

- Make how you live a conscious choice informed by your values, not dictated by your thoughts and feelings. Remember that you own your thoughts and feelings – they don't own you.

- You have more control over how you act than over your thoughts and feelings.

- While reducing or minimising unpleasant thoughts, feelings and memories can seem appealing, spending your life trying to avoid the 'bad' stuff can greatly restrict what you do.

- The achievement of even the smallest value-consistent goal means that your life is moving forward in ways that matter.

web extras

Read an excellent example of how an ACT-based intervention helped a teenage boy experiencing paranoid delusions to relate differently, and more helpfully, to his thoughts at www.dummies.com/extras/acceptanceandcommitmenttherapy.

In this part . . .

- ✔ Explore new ways to live a meaningful life, even in the presence of anxiety.

- ✔ Discover how to practise mindfulness and accept depressive thoughts and feelings.

- ✔ Find out how to use acceptance and defusion processes to work positively with stigma and shame within the context of addiction and substance misuse.

- ✔ See psychosis from an ACT perspective and find out about effective ACT-based experiential activities and interventions for this condition.

Chapter 16

Addressing Anxiety with ACT

. . . .

In This Chapter

▶ Recognising the symptoms of anxiety

▶ Understanding that avoidance doesn't help

▶ Responding to your anxiety in three stages

▶ Taking action to manage your anxiety

. . . .

The Mental Health Foundation identifies anxiety as the most prevalent of all mental health problems in the UK, with just under 10 per cent of the population reporting anxiety-related problems each year. Considering the common under-reporting of mental health difficulties, this percentage is likely to be an underestimation. In short, anxiety is a major mental health issue that affects millions of people each year.

This chapter provides an introduction to some of the ACT-based (Acceptance and Commitment Therapy) approaches that can be useful for people experiencing anxiety-related difficulties. It provides a variety of exercises for you to work through to help you develop a new relationship with your anxiety.

Defining Anxiety

Anxiety is defined as thoughts and feelings of unease, apprehension, uncertainty, worry or fear. Most people experience these things at some point in their life, of course, such as before an exam or when going on a date. For people with anxiety difficulties, however, these experiences dominate their life and interfere with their daily functioning.

Over 100 signs and symptoms exist for a range of anxiety-related conditions, such as panic attacks, phobias and more generalised problems. The NHS website (www.nhs.uk/Conditions/Anxiety/) lists the following experiences as linked to anxiety:

- ✔ Dizziness
- ✔ Dry mouth
- ✔ Excessive sweating
- ✔ Headache
- ✔ Insomnia
- ✔ Muscle aches and tension
- ✔ Nausea
- ✔ Noticeably strong, fast or irregular heartbeat (palpitations)
- ✔ Pins and needles
- ✔ Shortness of breath
- ✔ Stomach ache
- ✔ Tiredness
- ✔ Trembling or shaking

These symptoms are unpleasant and can also be very distressing. They can be set off by specific phobias (of spiders or flying, for example), but in generalised conditions what's causing the anxiety is less clear and almost anything can provoke an episode.

ACT explains the fact that you can experience anxiety in relation to almost anything by attributing it to your linguistic ability to link stimuli together in arbitrary ways. This ability (which we describe in more detail in Chapter 11) enables you to connect things in novel and seemingly unrelated ways. Even if you've never seen or heard of a kakapo, for example, you can feel anxious, and experience some of the symptoms described in the earlier list, if you're told it's a large green parrot and you have a parrot phobia. And because anything can become linked to anything else via your language, anything can become liked to anxiety.

Linking Anxiety and Avoidance

The symptoms of anxiety are so unpleasant that it's quite natural to want to avoid them. While this may initially seem a sensible approach, it often leads to more problems further down the line. This is because avoiding situations that lead to anxiety means that your life gradually begins to narrow and shrink. You may begin by avoiding one anxiety-provoking situation, and then another and another, and before you know it you're avoiding large parts of your life. Although you may experience lower levels of anxiety, your life is more focused on avoiding what you don't want than on doing the things that really matter to you, and this isn't particularly fulfilling. In a nutshell, in your efforts to solve one problem, you step straight into another.

While avoiding external situations that lead to anxiety can be problematic, things get even worse when you try to avoid or control anxiety-related experiences inside your body. You simply don't have enough control over your internal experiences (thoughts, feelings and bodily sensations) to be able to avoid them, and therefore efforts to do so are counterproductive.

Avoiding events outside your body is possible and can, in the short term at least, be effective at reducing anxiety. If you're scared of parrots, you can avoid pirate-themed parties. But you create difficulties for yourself when you try to do the same with your private internal experiences, because they can't be so easily avoided. You can't just 'leave them behind' like Captain Flint at the buffet (Long John Silver's parrot, for those of you who haven't read *Treasure Island*!). Wherever you go, your body comes too. A great deal of evidence indicates that the more you try to control or avoid negative thoughts and feelings, the more they come to dominate your life. In the absence of an alternative strategy, this often leads to yet more efforts to avoid and control your private experiences and the negative cycle continues. *Experiential avoidance* (trying to avoid or control your thoughts and feelings — check out Chapter 9 for more on this concept) is a major factor in a great many psychological problems.

Imagine that you're a bug — a cricket, perhaps. You're wandering around looking for food, minding your own business. Suddenly, you feel a snag behind you. You turn around and realise that one of your rear legs is caught on a single thread in a spider's web. Almost instinctively, you react by shaking your leg to try to free it from the web, but in doing so you only succeed in getting stuck to another strand.

You shake more vigorously but soon several legs and a wing are firmly entangled in the spider's charming abode. The more you shake, the more caught up in the web you become and, ironically, the less you're able to move. Ultimately, you're completely trapped, barely able to wriggle the tips of your wings.

The spider's web metaphor illustrates the futility of trying to beat anxiety by struggling against it. The web represents the anxious thoughts, feelings and sensations that you want to escape from or gain control over. But just as the cricket's efforts actually made things worse, so your efforts to wriggle free of your thoughts and feelings is similarly destined to fail. Indeed, the more the cricket struggled against the web, the more it became dominated by it, thus restricting its chances of living the life it wants to live — eating more flies, meeting Mrs Cricket, producing lots of little crickets, whatever a cricket values!

But what might the cricket have done differently? One option would be to simply hang from the web rather than struggle to be free. Maybe then it would avoid getting further caught up in the web and maybe, just maybe, the grip of that initial strand would be loosened by the weight of its body and who knows what might happen next.

By not struggling to avoid unwanted anxious thoughts and feelings, you may not lessen or avoid them, but you can reduce how entangled you become in them.

When the cricket stops struggling, other options become available. Rather than focusing on the web and its increasingly strong hold on it, it could start paying greater attention to the things going on around it — that is, it could practise mindfulness (Chapter 7 shows you how). As a result, maybe the cricket might notice something within reach that it could grab hold of and then use to gently pull itself free.

An alternative to struggling with your anxiety exists — you can stop trying to control, reduce or avoid it and instead mindfully be aware that it is part of your life. This gives you a chance to do something different.

Seeing acceptance as an alternative to avoidance

In their book, *The Mindfulness and Acceptance Workbook for Social Anxiety and Shyness* (New Harbinger Publications, 2013), Jan Fleming and Nancy Kocovski define acceptance and willingness as 'opening up to and allowing your experience to be exactly as it is, without trying to avoid it, escape it or change it'. Accepting unpleasant experiences isn't initially an appealing prospect, but being accepting and willing is very different to wanting. You can be willing to experience something even though you don't want to if doing so enables you to do the things that matter to you. For example, if you have agoraphobia (a fear of open or public spaces) you may become highly anxious when you walk your children to school. This is an unpleasant experience and one option is to simply stay at home. However, by doing so you miss out on kissing your kids at the school gate and greeting them at the end of the day.

The question ACT asks you is this: are you willing to experience anxious thoughts and feelings, not because you want them, but because doing so allows you to engage with the things that matter to you?

Acceptance and public speaking

Speaking in public always makes the top five when people are asked to identify what makes them most anxious. In fact, most people find standing up in front of a crowd hard to do. But here's a secret — even experienced professional public speakers feel some degree of anxiety beforehand. *Not* having anxious thoughts and feelings isn't the key to being able to speak in public; rather, it's that accepting them is worth it. Imagine how good you'd feel after delivering a heartfelt speech at your daughter's wedding or addressing members of your local sports club at the annual prize ceremony. Research has shown that people who participate in acceptance interventions (allowing difficult thoughts and feelings to come and go without trying to alter or control them) do better at public speaking than those who engage solely in exposure interventions (doing lots of what they find difficult). This indicates that practice on its own isn't enough; adding some acceptance also helps.

Approaching anxiety mindfully

Mindfulness is a very helpful approach to understanding your anxiety and allowing it to simply be present in your life. It involves purposefully paying attention in the present moment to your ever-unfolding experiences openly and non-judgementally. That doesn't mean you won't ever experience judgemental, evaluative thoughts when you're practising mindfulness, of course. Insisting on that would run counter to ACT's premise that you have relatively little control over internal events such as your thoughts and emotions. Rather, mindfulness allows you to notice those thoughts in a *non-judgemental* way.

As you practise mindfulness you may, for example, notice thoughts such as, 'I'm not good at maintaining my concentration' or 'I wonder whether my new colleagues like me?' Evaluative thoughts like these, which can sometimes be laden with anxiety, are normal — inevitable even — when practising mindfulness. Practising may or may not lead to you experiencing fewer anxious thoughts or feelings over time, but that's not the purpose of mindfulness. Rather, the aim is for you to simply notice them and, in so doing, gradually change your relationship to these thoughts and feelings. With practice (even just a few minutes a few times a week), you can begin to be less fused with the contents of your thoughts and how you think about yourself (Chapter 8 introduces you to the notion of your *self as content/description*).

Gaining some distance from anxious thoughts

Anxious thoughts can show up in many different ways. You can classify such thoughts as follows:

- ✔ **Fortune telling:** When you're anxious about the future. For example, you may worry that something bad will happen if you engage in a particular activity: 'If I go to the party, I'm bound to make a fool of myself'.

- ✔ **Mind reading:** When you worry about what other people think of you. For example: 'They all think I'm an idiot' or 'She doesn't like me, so what's the point of asking her on a date?'

- ✔ **Post mortem:** When you ruminate on what you did wrong in a social situation. For example: 'I can't believe I did that. Why did I ask about her husband when I knew he'd left her?'

When anxious thoughts like these pop into your head, gaining some distance from them can be useful. ACT calls this process *defusion* — you step back from the literal content of your thoughts and see them as just thoughts, bits of language in your head.

You can use a range of different defusion exercises, depending on what works best for you.

You can simply name the thought you're having as it occurs, perhaps labelling it under one of the three classifications described earlier in this section or giving it your own new label. You can also 'thank your mind' for your thoughts as they show up.

Another option is to add a pre-fix to a particular thought to remind you that it is just a thought. For example, when you notice yourself thinking, 'Everyone at work thinks I'm rubbish at my job', you can take a deep breath and add the precursor, 'I'm noticing a thought that . . .'. That thought then becomes, 'I'm noticing a thought that everyone at work thinks I'm rubbish at my job'. Having noticed it, you can then choose whether to believe it!

These short defusion exercises don't make anxious thoughts go away. But they can loosen the grip they have on you, which in turn creates a space in which you can respond to them differently.

Tackling Anxiety with a Three-Stage Approach

A very useful 'three-stage' approach to building up your mindfulness and acceptance skills in the face of anxiety is provided by Fleming and Kocovski in their mindfulness workbook. Each approach is a type of mindfulness activity and the first stage is a body scan exercise. Try it for yourself.

You can work through this entire process in about five minutes but you can also take as long as you like. Follow these steps:

1. **Find a comfortable position.** You can adopt a sitting position (in a chair or on the floor cross-legged) with a straight and upright spine or lie flat on your back.

2. **Take a deep breath and then either close your eyes or settle your gaze on a single point.** If you don't want to close your eyes, focus on a detail in the wallpaper or on a door knob, for example.

3. **Shift your awareness to the little toe of your left foot, notice for a moment or two how it feels and, if it feels tense, gently allow it to relax.** Do the same for each toe on your left foot.

4. **Allow your awareness to gently shift to the rest of your left foot, noticing how each part feels, from the sole to the sides and top.**

5. **Shift your attention to your left ankle for a few moments and then slowly upwards from your calf to your knee to your thigh.**

6. **Focus on the muscles in the front of your left thigh, followed by those in your inside leg and the back of your leg.**

7. **Notice for a moment any differences in sensation between your left and right legs.**

8. **Repeat Steps 1–7 for your right leg.**

9. **When you've scanned both legs, gradually shift your attention to your hips.** Begin with your left hip and notice how it feels.

10. **Move your attention to your abdomen. Notice, as you breathe in and out, the slow, rhythmic motion of your abdomen as it rises and falls.** Observe this motion for a few breaths.

11. **Now focus on your chest area.** Unlike your abdomen, it remains relatively still as your breath comes and goes.

12. **Next, focus on your spine.** Gradually work your way up your back, noticing what you feel.

13. **Now bring your attention to your shoulder, upper arm, elbow, lower arm, wrist, palm, back of your hand, and the fingers and thumbs on your left side.** Then repeat the process on your right side.

14. **Settle your awareness on your neck and throat area, noticing any sensations you feel there.** Shift up to your jaw, mouth and nose. Notice the cool sensation inside your nose as you breathe out and the warmer sensation as you breathe in. Focus on your eyes, eyelids, brows, forehead, temples, crown and back of your head, again noticing how they feel.

15. **Finally, take a few moments to broaden the scope of your awareness to notice how your whole body feels, from the tips of your toes to the crown of your head.** Spend as much time as you like focusing on your whole body.

16. **When you feel ready, gently begin to move your body, take a deep and long breath and open your eyes.**

How did you get on? This first stage is intended to help you begin to open up to the sensations in your body under a condition of no, or relatively little, anxiety. Your ultimate aim is to be able to develop awareness and acceptance of your bodily sensations under more anxious conditions. However, initially it's helpful to begin developing this skill when you don't feel the pull of experiential avoidance as soon as anxiety rears its head.

The second stage is practising mindfulness during physical movement. You can do this in a number of ways. You can adopt a few gentle yoga positions (called asanas) while being mindful of the physical changes and sensations you experience in your body as you do so. You can also practise eating and walking mindfulness exercises.

The third stage is to gradually, but intentionally, provoke bodily sensations that are associated with anxiety and anxious thoughts. Your aim is to slowly develop the skill of being more accepting and mindful of experiences that you may otherwise avoid.

Engage in this third-stage activity only after you've practised stages one and two several times.

You need to work through a series of steps, as follows:

1. **Decide to be willing to experience a little anxiety throughout the activity (however brief), knowing that being able to do so will help you to live a fuller and more value-consistent life.**

2. **Choose a bodily sensation that you commonly experience when feeling anxious.** Commonly reported sensations include sweating, muscle tension, shortness of breath and trembling or shaking.

3. **Engage in a physical activity that evokes that sensation.** For example, if you've chosen muscular tension, you can start by tensing all of your muscles until they start to shake or you feel tired.

   Provoke the bodily sensation only mildly in the first few sessions.

4. **Take a few minutes to sit in a comfortable position and practise being mindful of the sensations in your muscles (or other relevant bodily sensations).** You may want to repeat Steps 3 and 4, choosing a different bodily sensation this time.

5. **Bring the activity to a close and thank yourself for acting with such resolve and determination.**

6. **Make a record of what you experienced as you worked through Steps 1–5.** You can use a journal or log of some kind.

You may find the format in Table 16-1 useful for recording your experiences.

Table 16-1	Accepting My Anxiety Journal		
Bodily Sensation	*Activity to Induce Sensation*	*Duration*	*My Observations*

Advancing from Avoidance to Action

Unlike many traditional therapeutic approaches, positive outcomes in ACT aren't thought of in terms of symptom reduction. You may experience less anxiety and stress, fewer panic attacks or even more feelings akin to happiness, for example, as the therapeutic process unfolds, but these outcomes aren't what ACT procedures, protocols and activities are actually designed for.

Rather, the aim of ACT is to help you become more accepting of and open to your experiences — positive or negative, pleasurable or unpleasant — so that you can get on with living your life in line with your values.

Imagining an anxiety-free life

Life can be very difficult when you're experiencing many anxious thoughts and feelings. The fact is that being open to and accepting of these experiences isn't easy and that's where having clear values — what matters to you — is essential. Your values give meaning to life's struggles and motivate you to do the things you find hard. Your desire to do the best for your children, for instance, can motivate you to attend school events even though social gatherings may fill you with dread, make you break out in a sweat and cause your heart to race. If someone asks you why you bother when such events make you feel so unwell and distressed, you can affirmatively state 'because this is how I live according to the values that matter to me'.

Sometimes you may find thinking about your values very difficult because your life is dominated by your anxiety. One approach to dealing with that situation is to imagine that your life is free from anxiety and, as a consequence, what you'd do — Table 16-2 provides a few examples.

Table 16-2	If I Were Free from Anxiety . . .
Life Domain	*Value Statement*
Family life	I'd be a kind and caring spouse.
Friendships and social life	I'd be socially outgoing and positive.
Work and professional life	I'd work hard and make a positive contribution to my profession.
Learning and education	I'd be someone who grabbed opportunities to learn and grow in areas of interest.
Physical health	I'd be physically fit and well.
Leisure time	I'd be a charitable, kind person.

Rather than jumping straight to the things that you'd *do* (that is, specific, concrete goals), try to focus on the *personal qualities* that you'd like your actions to represent.

When you've identified your values, you can set some SMART goals that reflect them (SMART goals are specific, measureable, achievable, relevant and time-framed — check out Chapter 5). Pick short-term goals that can be achieved quite quickly to start with so that you can gain a sense of achievement to boost your motivation. You can go on to pick medium- and longer-term goals as you increasingly base your life on the values that represent your goals.

Bringing your anxiety with you

When you set yourself value-based goals, it's highly likely that you'll encounter thoughts and feelings that make you question whether those goals are right for you. Your mind may tell you, 'I should've aimed for something more manageable; starting here is too hard', 'I don't care about achieving this goal as much as I thought I did, so I think I'll do something different instead' or 'I think I'll work on this goal next month instead as I might feel a bit stronger then'.

Having anxious or negative thoughts as you engage in value-based action is almost inevitable. It's also highly likely that there'll be some truth in them. Indeed, thoughts that are well-founded and (at least partially) factually accurate are often the biggest barriers to achieving valued life goals. Consider one of the three examples provided earlier in this section, 'I think I'll work on this goal next month instead as I might feel a bit stronger then'. It may well be true that you'll feel stronger next month. Maybe you'll have less on at work. Your friends may be better able to support you then. Or possibly you're just going through a particularly tricky time at the moment and predicting (fortune telling?) that things will be better in a few weeks.

The problem with buying into these kinds of thoughts is that they can encourage you to engage in experiential avoidance (refer to Chapter 9) and this can interfere with living in line with your values. Rather than allowing such thoughts to control what you do, an alternative approach is to simply take them with you as you move towards achieving your goals.

As you take steps towards your value-based goals, you gradually and inexorably move your life in the directions of the things that matter to you. Using your values to guide your life means you can spend your time living the life you want rather than avoiding the one you're scared of. You may or may not reduce your anxious thoughts and feelings as a result, but at least your daily life is filled with purpose, meaning, vitality and openness. And that's the ultimate aim of ACT.

Chapter 17

Beating Depression with Acceptance and Committed Action

*M*ore than 350 million people around the world have, at one time or another, suffered from depression, and the World Health Organization recognises it as a very serious global problem. While statistics indicate that women are more frequently affected, depression can affect people of all ages, genders and ethnicities.

Common signs of depression include:

- Decline in energy levels
- Loss of appetite
- Loss of interest in life
- Low mood
- Low self-esteem
- Poor sleep
- Short attention span

Diagnosing depression

Although depression is a medical diagnosis, that doesn't mean it's caused by a disease. Rather, depression is indicated by the presence of a number of co-occurring behaviours and emotions. *The Diagnostic and Statistical Manual of Mental Disorders*, Fourth Edition (DSM-IV), for example, states that a diagnosis of depression is appropriate if someone reports five or more of the following difficulties over at least a two-week period:

✔ Depressed mood

✔ Marked loss of interest in daily activities

✔ Significant weight loss or weight gain

✔ Insomnia or hypersomnia nearly every day

✔ Psychomotor agitation or retardation

✔ Fatigue or loss of energy

✔ Feelings of worthlessness or excessive guilt

✔ Diminished ability to think or concentrate

✔ Recurring thoughts about death

In other words, when someone exhibits this particular cluster of behaviours, experiences and feelings, he meets the criteria for a diagnosis of depression. That diagnosis is thus not based on the identification of any underlying disease or disorder. This doesn't mean depression isn't real — far from it. The experiences associated with depression are very real and impact hugely on the individual's life. However, what it means is that depression is more complicated than a biological disease that can be treated medically.

Depression can be experienced on a continuum, ranging from mild to severe. Although depressive episodes can be relatively brief, depression is often experienced as a chronic condition and can last many years. Chronic depression can take the form of a general and sustained low-mood (unipolar depression) or a more manic, up-and-down form (bipolar depression). If you've experienced one period of depression, you're much more likely to face another. Fortunately, a number of effective interventions for depression exist, one of which is Acceptance and Commitment Therapy (ACT).

In this chapter, we explore depression from an ACT perspective and consider some of the central characteristics of ACT-based interventions for people suffering from it. We also describe the positive intervention outcomes resulting from ACT-based approaches for depression.

Depression is a serious condition. Seek help from your GP if you or someone you know is experiencing the symptoms we describe earlier in this chapter.

Keeping Thoughts and Feelings in Their Place

When you're feeling depressed, getting caught up in negative thoughts and feelings can be all too easy. Sometimes you can be so enmeshed that you actually seem to *be* those thoughts and feelings — you, as a person, are inseparable from them. You may have had thoughts such as, 'I'm useless', 'I'm terrible at my job', 'My life is pointless' or 'She'd never go out with me, so why bother asking her?' How do thoughts like these lead you to feel? Are they easy to let go of or do they stubbornly hang around?

In ACT, getting caught up in your thoughts and beliefs is called fusion (refer to Chapter 6 for more on this concept). *Fusion* occurs when you believe the literal content of your thoughts and language to be true. When you believe that your thoughts are correct, they exert a lot of control over what you do, even if they may not actually reflect what you want. (Distancing yourself from your thoughts — surprise, surprise! — is called *defusion*.)

If you're depressed you may often feel quite negatively about yourself, expressed in thoughts such as, 'I'm such a failure' and 'I'm hopeless; nothing I do ever works out'. If you fuse with these thoughts, you may not sign up for a local charity cycle ride because your mind tells you that you can't do it. You may even think, 'No one will sponsor me, so what's the point?' If you believe these thoughts (fuse with them) they're likely to exert a significant influence over what you do. If given free rein, they can quickly lead to a self-reinforcing downward cycle as your negative thoughts discourage you from doing the things you really care about, which in turn leads to lower mood and thus more negative thoughts. You can become trapped in a negative cycle in which your thoughts are calling all the shots. ACT works to break this cycle and put you back in control of your life.

Fusion with your thoughts and language is so automatic that you don't even realise you're doing it. Thoughts just occur and you respond to them accordingly. ACT helps you interrupt this automaticity and see your thoughts (and what you say, hear or read) as simply language you're experiencing. It does so through defusion, which involves coming to see your thoughts as just thoughts, rather than a reflection of reality.

The following exercises help you to notice your automatic thoughts. Give them a go.

Get a pen and paper, then assume a comfortable position, close your eyes and breathe in deeply to centre yourself. When you feel ready, focus your attention on your thoughts. When you notice one, open your eyes and write it down. Don't worry if at first your mind goes blank and no thoughts seem to show up; if you wait long enough, something will eventually come along, even if it's only 'I can't think of anything'. Whatever your thoughts, write them down. When you've experienced and written down three different thoughts, read back over them and try to identify your responses to them. What do you think about them and how do they make you feel? Just notice how you react to them.

Now try a slightly more demanding exercise in which you consciously make contact with some negative thoughts and feelings about yourself. This exercise is more difficult because you naturally shy away from negative experiences, so doing the opposite is more difficult. It's a useful exercise, however, because it helps you begin to notice how you respond to your own experiences.

Take a moment to recall some negative thoughts you've had about yourself. If nothing comes to mind, try to remember occasions on which you've struggled to do something or something went wrong. Write these thoughts on the piece of paper. Now read these thoughts to yourself, maybe even say them out loud, and, as you do so, again notice how you react.

On one level these exercises are very simple, but they're useful nonetheless. Noticing your thoughts is the first step towards stepping back from their literal content (defusing from them). When you do this, you can begin to see them for what they are — just thoughts! — and the power they have over your life diminishes. Similarly, when you make contact with uncomfortable feelings, you come to realise that, while they're not very nice, they needn't control what you do.

Doing What Matters, No Matter What

As well as helping you to defuse from your thoughts, ACT procedures are also designed to help you figure out what's important to you — what you care about most in life — and to help you take action that's consistent with those values. ACT is about helping you behave in ways that reflect how you want to live in the world, even when doing so is hard.

Consider the example of the charity cycle ride used in the preceding section. Maybe someone close to you has recently died and, as a consequence, you want to raise money for a local service or hospice. If you allow your negative thoughts about yourself to dominate your actions, you may end up doing nothing. But when you defuse from these thoughts, you're able to create some space in which to make decisions based on what you really want in life and not on what your thoughts tell you. You can then sign up for that charity cycle ride and do what matters to you.

Considering What Depression Has Cost You

Take a few minutes to reflect on the following questions:

- ✔ What have you missed out on in life because of your depression?
- ✔ What strategies do you use to try to deal with your depression?
- ✔ Do you spend time trying to reduce or avoid unwanted negative thoughts or feelings?
- ✔ Overall how effective have any of these strategies for dealing with your depression been?
- ✔ Can you estimate how much time and energy you typically expend daily on trying to avoid depressive thoughts and feelings?

If what you've been doing to deal with your depression has been working, it makes sense to continue with those strategies. But if not, maybe it's time to try something else. ACT argues that the nature of your thoughts and feelings (see Chapter 11 for details) means that trying to control, change or avoid them is unlikely to be successful. The list of strategies you can employ to avoid unwanted negative thoughts and feelings is huge (for example, distracting yourself with food or activities, taking drugs or trying to think only positive thoughts), but the end result is always the same — failure. At best, control and avoidance will only work for short periods (if they work at all) and often involve considerable effort.

As well as being generally ineffective, trying to control or avoid unwanted negative thoughts and feelings involves another problem — *experiential avoidance* (see Chapter 9 for more on this concept). In an effort to reduce or avoid any activities that might bring about depressive thoughts and feelings, you can end up living a pretty narrow and restricted life. For instance, you can find yourself avoiding activities that you believe may bring about unwanted thoughts and feelings, and consequently find it hard get out of bed in the morning for fear of what might befall you!

The restricted range of activities that stems from engaging in experiential avoidance can interfere with your efforts to do the things in your life that are important to you. For example, you may want to be part of a community of friends. In order to achieve this, you need to place yourself in social situations that give you the chance to develop positive relationships with other people. But what if you worry that you're boring or are scared of rejection or ridicule? While thoughts such as these are in many ways quite natural, if you allow them to dominate what you do, you probably won't go out to meet other people. While this behaviour enables you to avoid difficult thoughts and feelings, it also means that you can't form a close circle of friends, which may well make you feel even more depressed.

Giving Up What Doesn't Work

Carrying on doing things that aren't working will only make your situation worse because they'll get in the way of doing the things that will make your life better. For that reason, ACT encourages you to think about whether what you're doing is really making a difference. Is your life better today than yesterday, last month or last year? If not, then maybe it's time to review what you're doing and ask whether it's working. The following scenario helps you consider that question.

Imagine that you're blind and one day you're taken to live in a field. To help you survive, you're given a tool bag. You're quite happy living in the field, wandering around, eating a bit of grass and so on. But what you don't know is that scattered around the field are a number of deep holes, and eventually you fall into one. That's a bit of a shock at first, but you dust yourself down and feel around to assess the situation. You quickly realise that the hole is too deep to climb out of, so decide to feel inside your tool bag. The only thing you find is a spade so you naturally assume you've been given it to help you in just this kind of situation. You begin to dig, but immediately notice that the soil is just falling back into the hole. 'I must try harder' you conclude and with the extra effort you manage to throw a bit of the soil out of the hole. Great, except now you realise that you're just creating a deeper hole. And the more you dig, the further down you are. You realise that digging isn't getting you out of the hole, so what do you need to do? Well, before you do anything else you need to put down the spade! (See Figure 17-1 for a visual representation of this scenario.)

Unfortunately, despite your best efforts, you cannot rid yourself of depression by attempting to control unwanted negative thoughts and feelings. The research evidence is quite clear — the more you try to control internal experiences, the more they persist. Your efforts to control your internal world are part of the problem, not part of the solution.

It's easy to see why you may think you can change or control negative or unwanted thoughts. This strategy works pretty well in the world outside of your skin. If you run out of washing-up liquid, you can go to the supermarket and buy a new bottle. When your hair flops in your eyes, you can brush it away. But you can't do the same with your depressive thoughts and feelings because you just don't have enough control over them. This doesn't mean you're powerless in the face of your depression; rather, it means that, instead of trying to control or avoid the negative symptoms that come with it, you're better off trying something else. The following sections describe some different strategies you can try.

Figure 17-1:
Digging
your way
out of a
hole: a
fruitless
task?

Trying acceptance rather than avoidance

If trying to control your depressive thoughts and feelings isn't the solution, what is? ACT proposes that your best option when faced with things that can't be changed is to accept them. Although this may seem an unattractive strategy at first glance, it actually has a lot of merit. In particular, it frees you from a fruitless struggle to avoid, change or control experiences that can't easily be avoided, changed or controlled (if at all). Instead of fighting against depressive thoughts and feelings, you just observe them — you allow them to come when they come, be with you for as long as they're with you and to go when they naturally fade away of their own accord. In other words, you give up actively trying to avoid or manage your thoughts and feelings and just let them be.

Of course, accepting unwanted, negative thoughts and feelings isn't easy. Who, after all, wants to experience critical or unkind thoughts or feelings that eat them up on the inside? No one does. But what's the alternative? To continually struggle trying to control and avoid thoughts and feelings that can't be controlled? Or to find a way to accept and live with them so that you can use your energy to get on with the life you want to be living.

Mindfulness exercises are a useful way to notice your thoughts and feelings without doing anything about them. This is what's meant by acceptance — being aware of, and open to, all of your experiences, without defence or avoidance. The following exercise helps you practise making contact with the present moment.

Find a nice comfortable position in which to sit, either on a chair or cushion on the floor. Make sure that you maintain an upright posture. Now follow these steps:

1. **Place one hand on your belly and one on your chest.** Take a deep breath and slowly allow your eyelids to rest down over your eyes.

2. **For the next minute or so, gently begin to establish a rhythm in your breathing.** Make sure that the hand on your belly is moving in and out; that is, you're breathing low down and not shallowly into your chest.

3. **When you've established a gentle rhythm in your breathing, allow your hands to drop down.** Let them fall either into your lap one on top of the other or, if more comfortable, onto your knees, palms down.

4. **Maintain awareness of your breathing over the next three to five minutes and, at the same time, notice any thoughts, feelings and bodily sensations that you experience.** Just notice them, let them come, let them be and, when they naturally do so, let them go.

5. **When you notice that your mind has wandered (and it will, probably more than once!), just note what you were thinking about and gently bring yourself back to the exercise.**

6. **After a few minutes, when you feel ready, gently begin to open your eyes and bring the activity to a close.** Flex your neck and shoulders a bit and take a deep breath as you do so.

How did you get on? Did your attention stay focused for the whole exercise or did it move around? Being able to maintain concentration throughout even a short exercise like this one is extremely unusual. Fortunately, that's not the point! In fact, it's important not to see that as the point of this exercise because doing so can lead to fusion with thoughts such as, 'I'm no good at this' and 'This is too difficult'. What's important is practising noticing your thoughts and feelings as they arise and pass, being aware of your ever-changing present-moment experience.

Contact with the present moment — which you're aiming to achieve through mindfulness exercises such as this — is one of the core therapeutic processes used in ACT-based interventions (see Chapter 3 for details).

Exploring your values

Helping you do the things that matter to you so that your life can be filled with meaning and purpose is the ultimate aim of ACT. Life's short and you have little to gain from spending it avoiding the things you don't like. And rather than chasing the tail of the dog called Happiness, you can live a life directed by your *values*. Your values reflect how you want to behave in the world and the sort of person you want to be. They're the personal qualities that you want to define your life and represent what you care about most deeply. Values are qualities such as kindness, creativity, fairness, honesty, respect, friendship, love and endeavour. Chapter 4 covers values in more detail and provides some exercises that can help you identify what they are.

Have a go at the following exercise to get a sense of what values are and how they can be used to guide you as you live your life.

Imagine that you've lived a long life and are sitting in a chair enjoying a spot of quiet reflection. You look back over the years and remember your actions and experiences. Now complete the following statements:

I'm glad I spent time _____

I wish I'd spent more time _____

I'm glad I didn't waste too much time _____

I wish I'd spent less time _____

One thing I'm very happy I did is _____

One thing I regret is _____

Your responses to these statements can help you identify your values — the things that you do that you care most about. Rather than pondering on these points in your dotage, you can actually do something about them now — you still have time to be the person you most want to be.

Distinguishing values from goals

Use the Values Bull's Eye in Figure 17-2 (developed by Swedish ACT therapist, Tobias Lundgren) to explore how closely you're living your life in accordance with your values at this moment.

It divides your life into four domains:

- **Work and education:** What you want from your work or career — your desire to learn new things or courses you'd like to go on.

✓ **Leisure:** How you like to spend your free time — how you enjoy yourself, your hobbies or other activities that you like doing.

✓ **Relationships:** The important relationships in your life — with family, friends, children or people in your local community.

✓ **Personal growth and health:** Your health, community and spiritual life.

Consider each of the domains in the Values Bull's Eye in Figure 17-2, and what you really want to achieve in each one. Try to identify specific values in each domain. Remember, values are ongoing actions and reflect what you want your life to stand for and represent. For example, you may value being a supportive son to your frail elderly parents or a trusted mentor to your apprentice. When you know what you want to be doing in your life, you can set specific goals in relation to your values. You may set yourself the goal of taking your parents to do their food shopping each week or sitting down over a cup of tea with your apprentice to ask how he's getting on.

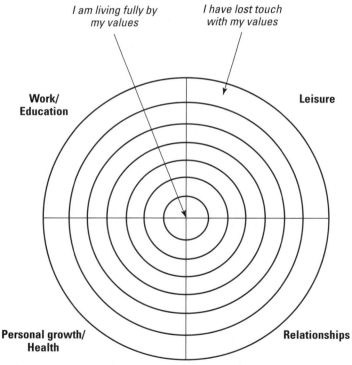

Figure 17-2:
The Values
Bull's Eye.

Now work out where on the Values Bull's Eye you'd place crosses indicating how closely you feel you're living in line with your values in each domain. The closer you place a cross to the centre, the more strongly you feel you're living up to that value. Take a moment to reflect on where you've positioned each cross and why.

You may want to address the values farther from the centre, as you've identified that those values are important to you but you're not acting on them currently.

Setting SMART goals

When you've identified your values — the things that are deeply important to you — the next step is to start *doing* things that reflect them. Setting SMART goals is the best way to do so. SMART stands for:

Specific: Clearly define what you're going to do

Measurable: Gather clear evidence of what you've achieved

Achievable: Make your goal stretch you but not to such a degree that it's impossible

Realistic: State a clear value-based outcome that you're both willing and able to achieve

Time-framed: Specify the time frame within which you'll achieve your goal(s)

Set yourself some value-based SMART goals by considering your responses to the Values Bull's Eye in Figure 17-2. What do you need to do to enable you to place the crosses a little closer to the centre?

Turning goals into actions

Even when you use the SMART goals approach described in the preceding section, achieving a goal can sometimes feel completely beyond you. This can be especially the case when you're feeling depressed and have spent a lot of time and energy battling to control negative thoughts, feelings and beliefs about yourself and what you're able to achieve.

When you feel daunted by a goal, consider breaking it into smaller SMART targets. Keep doing so until eventually you reach a task that you can complete in the next 60 seconds. For example, if you set yourself a value-based goal of writing a novel, you may feel uncertain about where to start. If so, you can break it down into smaller goals, such as writing a short outline of the plot and describing the main characters. And if that feels too big a task, you can set yourself the goal of coming up with the title. And a 60-second goal can be deciding on the geographical location of your story. These goals are still a long way from writing the book, of course, but they're a start. Often it's getting started that's difficult, so beginning with something small can get the ball rolling. Remember that every journey starts with a single step and this is just the beginning. Your next sets of goals can be gradually more challenging and ambitious.

When you set yourself goals, you also need to be willing to experience some difficulties along the way (see Chapter 5 on committing to action). Life will always deliver challenges and the bigger the task you set yourself, the more challenges you're likely to face. If you aren't willing to have them, these challenges will stop you in your tracks. That's why willingness is so important: it enables you to persevere in pursuit of your goals when the going gets tough.

While you may need to overcome external problems and challenges as you engage in value-based actions, you're also likely to experience internal barriers, such as doubts, worries and negative feelings. If you fuse with a thought such as 'I just can't do it', it's likely to dominate your actions and you'll struggle to complete the task at hand. The following exercise helps you identify internal barriers and challenges you may face as you embark on your goals. By spending a bit of time identifying what they are and how you can respond to them, you can be more prepared when they show up and hence more likely to succeed in achieving those goals.

Complete the following sentences (write them down on a piece of paper if you want):

The value I want to work on is

_____

My value-based SMART goal is

_____

The things I will do to achieve this goal are

_____

_____

The thoughts, feelings, memories or sensations that I'm willing to experience as I strive to achieve my goal are:

Thoughts: _____

_____

Feelings: _____

_____

Memories: _____

_____

Sensations: _____

_____

When things are difficult, it would be useful to remind myself that:

_____

_____

Putting the Horse before the Cart

A popular misconception in Western culture is that your thoughts and feelings control how you behave. This belief is so universal and pervasive that it's taken for granted by most people. Actually, however, it isn't true. It's quite possible to feel jealous and behave generously (and vice versa) and to think or say one thing and yet do the opposite. Try this: think or say aloud several times 'I must keep my toes still' and at the same time wiggle them up and down. Simple, eh? But how is this possible if words control what you do? Here's the truth of the matter: while your thoughts and feelings are important and can influence what you do, they don't actually control your actions.

One consequence of believing that your thoughts and emotions control how you behave is that it seems quite logical to conclude that you have to feel okay or ready before you can do the things you want to do. Similarly, you may think that you have to believe you can do something before you can do it. In short, your thoughts and feelings need to be positive before you can behave positively; for example, you may think, 'If I could just feel more confident, I could behave more confidently' or 'If I didn't have these negative thoughts, I could go out with my friends'. As a consequence people can spend a lot of time and effort trying to control their thoughts and feelings so they are positive and aligned with what they want to do. The problem is that you just don't have enough control over what you think and feel to make this a workable strategy. After all, if you could change your thoughts and feelings at will, you need never be unhappy again!

ACT asks you to do something different. Rather than waiting until you feel better or ready to do something, instead just do it and see how it feels. From an ACT perspective, how you feel and what you think depends largely on what you've done and whom you've interacted with. Thus, to feel more positive and have more positive thoughts about life, you have to *do* positive things. Where your actions go, your thoughts and feelings will follow. But remember, the primary aim of ACT is to live a life with meaning and purpose, and not to feel fulfilled or to think positively. Chasing around after one feeling or another or trying to control your thoughts is the problem, not the solution.

Although jumping in and taking action can be difficult initially, the more you do the things that matter to you, the easier it becomes. It is possible to think and feel one way and yet act differently. For example, you can put on a brave face and smile when you're feeling depressed or not raise your voice when you're angry. Similarly, you can think or say, 'I can't go out tonight' and nonetheless still go out to meet friends.

Think or say out loud, 'Raise your left arm' and keep your arm by your side. You can do it because your thoughts and feelings don't actually cause your behaviour. Instead, let your values guide how you behave and be the basis of the goals you set in life.

The constant negative chatter of your mind makes it all too easy to lose sight of the fact that you have a choice about how you act. Big things — such as overcoming depression — are achieved by slowly putting one foot in front of the other and doing the things that are important to you. Approaching each day in this way will loosen depression's grip and allow you to reclaim your life — whatever your mind may be telling you!

Chapter 18

Dealing with Addiction

In This Chapter

▶ Looking at addiction from an ACT perspective

▶ Establishing goals based on your values, in the face of addiction

▶ Believing that you can lead a different life

*A*ddiction is a major problem. While most commonly associated with drug and alcohol misuse, the term actually applies to any excessive behaviour that leads to harmful consequences for the individual and those around her. For example, people can become addicted to gambling, sex, shopping and food.

Because addiction occurs in almost every area of human life, capturing its full costs and implications is difficult. However, the data on drug and alcohol addiction makes for depressing reading. A 2013 report by the Centre for Social Justice, for instance, estimated that drug and alcohol misuse costs the UK £36 billion annually and has a hugely negative effect on certain sections of society. The report points out that, as well as damaging the health of individuals, drug and alcohol misuse can lead to poverty, deprivation, family breakdown, child neglect, homelessness, crime, debt and long-term unemployment.

Meeting the challenge of addiction is a huge task. However, over the past two decades ACT-based interventions have proven to be effective for a range of addictions.

The term 'addiction' covers a vast range of behaviours and, as such, finding a single definition for it is difficult. Generally, *addiction* refers to excessive and harmful behaviours. If you do something excessively, but it doesn't hurt you or anyone else, it's just a hobby or an obsession. It only becomes an addiction when the consequences are harmful.

One way or another, addiction affects everyone. Perhaps you are, or have been, an addict yourself. Maybe you have a friend or close colleague who has an addiction. You may have been a victim of a crime committed by an addict.

At the very least, some of your taxes will go towards funding the legal, health and social systems supporting people with addiction.

In this chapter, we describe how ACT sees addictive behaviour and explain what can be done to support a more positive lifestyle.

Seeing Addiction through an ACT Lens

When people with addiction talk about their difficulties, they frequently refer to very strong or uncontrollable urges, desires, compulsions and cravings as the cause of their behaviour. They talk about unpleasant physiological experiences associated with drug dependency and withdrawal.

Emotional and physical symptoms of withdrawal can include:

- ✔ Anxiety
- ✔ Headaches
- ✔ Insomnia
- ✔ Irritability
- ✔ Jumpiness
- ✔ Low mood
- ✔ Muscle tension
- ✔ Nausea or diarrhoea
- ✔ Palpitations
- ✔ Poor concentration
- ✔ Racing heart
- ✔ Sweating

These are all unpleasant physical experiences and the next 'hit' alleviates them — but only temporarily. In addition to the physiological effects of withdrawal, people with addictions often experience thoughts encouraging them to engage in them, such as:

- ✔ I need a drink.
- ✔ I can't fight this any longer.
- ✔ I have to smoke.
- ✔ I can't sleep without it.
- ✔ Just one joint will calm my nerves.

Wine o'clock addiction

Many people have issues with alcohol without even realising it. Having a drink to relax after work isn't unusual and in fact it does relieve stress because alcohol is a sedative. However, drinking regularly in this way can easily lead to addiction. Research into attitudes toward drinking revealed that many people thought problem drinking is something that happens to 'other' people, such as binge drinkers on a night out; drinking at home is a normal and acceptable form of relaxation; and alcohol consumption that doesn't affect daily functioning (either at home or work) is acceptable and harm-free. Unfortunately, many people who drink regularly and believe it's merely a social habit may actually have an alcohol dependency.

Thoughts such as these can be very insistent and when you believe them to be true they can exert a strong influence over your behaviour. People with an addiction know their thoughts can be hard to resist and generally try to avoid them — or situations that may set them off.

Acknowledging the illusory power of thoughts and feelings

While initially it may make sense to try to control or manage difficult urges, desires and thoughts related to an addiction, ACT takes a different line and focuses on building awareness and acceptance of these experiences instead — and for a pragmatic reason. Gaining enough control over what you feel and your urges, desires and thoughts in order to make this strategy effective just isn't possible.

For a start, how you feel depends on your history and what's happened to you. You feel hungry or tired when you haven't eaten or slept, for example. Likewise, you feel the urge to drink alcohol, use drugs or gamble in response to events that have happened in the past or are happening now. For example, you may be experiencing the symptoms of withdrawal because you haven't used heroin or had an alcoholic drink for 24 hours. Maybe you've just walked past a betting shop or heard mention of a horse race on the radio. What you need to bear in mind about these events is that they're *historic* and therefore can't be changed (not until a time machine is invented anyway).

As for changing or controlling your thoughts and wishes, the bad news is that it's very hard to do. What you think — and language in general — can be triggered by quite arbitrary events happening around you. Language works by linking things together via arbitrary and reversible relationships.

For instance, if someone with a history of gambling visits a friend and is offered a muffin with his coffee, this small event can trigger the thought, 'Muffin the Mule' and an image of that animal can appear in his mind. Mules look like horses and this thought inspires memories of his gambling addiction and what the urge felt like. Although this scenario appears silly, word and thought associations happen just like that. Seemingly innocuous situations or statements can re-establish addiction behaviours in an instant. Trying to suppress or avoid thoughts that trigger or lead to addiction behaviours may seem a good solution — unfortunately, the opposite happens: those thoughts just won't go away!

Although you can't avoid or control your cognitive and emotional content (your thoughts) sufficiently (if at all) to make efforts to do so effective, don't give up hope. You just need to find another way of responding to it.

Instead of trying to change your thoughts, feelings, urges or cravings, the therapeutic goals of ACT for addiction focus on:

- ✔ Increasing awareness of difficult thoughts and feelings
- ✔ Acknowledging the impossibility of controlling these thoughts and feelings
- ✔ Creating some distance from difficult thoughts and feelings by accepting them and letting them be
- ✔ Developing empathy, self-compassion and self-acceptance
- ✔ Gaining clarity about what's really important (values)
- ✔ Acting in a way that's consistent with those values

ACT thus helps people respond to addictions in a different way. Later in this chapter, we provide some exercises to work through that can help you to do this.

Reconsidering your strategies

People with addictions usually know that they have a problem. They've probably tried repeatedly to do something about it, such as attempting to stop or reduce the problem behaviour, but with little or no success. Almost universally, such people have long histories of trying and failing to change. Often their perseverance is inspiring: they keep trying even though they always fail. And here's where ACT steps in.

Failure and learned helplessness

Stopping doing what isn't working is a good thing because it saves wasting time and energy on things that give little or no return. When you experience multiple failures in multiple settings over a sustained period of time, however, you can be tempted to give up trying altogether. For example, you may have tried on several occasions to give up drinking or using cocaine by isolating yourself from the people with whom you engage in this behaviour and thus avoid peer pressure. However, trying to quit on your own is likely to create a sense of loneliness and isolation, thus eventually leading to your using again, and again. Alongside this behaviour you may develop a sense that you can't do anything to break this cycle and a gradually mounting concept of yourself as a failure. After all, if every past effort came to nothing, why bother trying again? This cyclical scenario is called *learned helplessness* and is associated with feelings of resignation, low self-esteem and, in the worst cases, depression.

When people with addictions fail to change, they're often seen as weak, lacking in willpower or simply not smart enough to do so. They look around and see other people managing their lives and view their own failures as evidence that there's something wrong with them — that they're fundamentally broken or flawed in some way. Their self-critical mind can really get to work and flatten their self-esteem and self-worth.

ACT doesn't see the individuals as broken; rather, what they're *doing* is what isn't working. The task is to find another way to address your problems and the first step is stopping what you're currently doing so that you can make space to do something different. Doing so is harder than you may think because cultural expectations emphasise that you just need to control or manage your impulses, desires, thoughts and cravings in order to be able to change. But that attitude is fruitless.

The *control agenda* (that is, trying to change your thoughts and feelings) is flawed but the person engaging in such control strategies is not!

ACT employs a range of exercises and metaphors to help you recognise the futility of your control agenda. It aims to reveal the unworkability of what you've been doing so that you can create some space to do something different next time. For example, reviewing the success of your past efforts can help you see the ineffectiveness of past control strategies. Such strategies may include:

- Distracting yourself by doing something else
- Avoiding situations or people that increase your urges
- Challenging or denying your thoughts or urges

On a piece of paper, write a list of the strategies you've used to address your addiction and rate their success over the long term on a scale of 1–10. Be as specific as possible. For example, you may write, 'In order to reduce my alcohol consumption, I've tried to stop going to the pub. I've used this strategy 5 times over the last 12 months and, on average, it's lasted for about 2 weeks. For that reason, I'd rate it 3/10'.

What conclusions do you reach? Are your current strategies successful? If so, continue with them. If not, you need to ask why. Possibly you're trying to control or avoid problematic thoughts and feelings in some way.

Learning to lean in

Your default response when faced with painful events is to try to figure out a way to get rid of them. This approach can be effective for the world outside of your skin, but it just doesn't work when it comes to what's going on inside your head. ACT argues that when things can't be avoided or controlled, simply accepting them is the best thing to do. Initially, the idea that you have no (or very little) control over unwanted inner experiences can be very difficult to accept; however, you actually have no choice.

ACT aims to challenge and undermine your commitment to unworkable efforts to control and avoid internal experiences by evaluating for yourself the effectiveness of your strategies. Only when you review the workability of your actions can you make a judgement about whether or not to continue with them. Making such judgements is important because when you stop trying to control your internal psychological content you can create time to do other things.

The ACT alternative is to simply accept internal experiences — to lean into rather than away from them. The nearby sidebar 'The Chinese finger trap metaphor' provides a useful illustration of this concept.

The Chinese finger trap metaphor

ACT uses the metaphor of a Chinese finger trap to illustrate how you sometimes need to move towards the thing you're trying to avoid. It's a simple puzzle that traps the victim's fingers in both ends of a small cylinder woven from bamboo; when she tries to pull her fingers out, the tighter the trap becomes. Only by doing the opposite to what instinct tells you and pushing your fingers further into the trap are you able to free yourself. Likewise, only when you move closer to your difficult thoughts and feelings and accept them can you free yourself of the trap of trying to avoid them.

Accepting Yourself

Becoming more accepting of painful thoughts and feelings is a skill and, like all skills, getting better at it takes practice. A first step towards cultivating acceptance is to notice your experiences without doing anything about them. This practice is at the heart of mindfulness (Chapter 7 covers mindfulness in detail), which involves observing events taking place inside and outside your body and just letting them be.

Dispassionate observation of non-challenging experiences, such as the sound of birdsong or a thought about someone you love, is relatively straightforward. However, when your attention focuses on a distressing physical pain, a disturbing memory or a strong urge to smoke or drink, it's much harder. While the 'noticing' task remains the same, the level of difficulty you experience is significantly greater. Rather like jumping from a high or low diving board, the 'jump' is the same but the level of difficulty is quite different.

As with all new skills, here you need to attempt observing easier events and experiences and gradually move to more challenging ones as you get better at doing so. The following mindfulness exercise helps you to focus on your thoughts and just let them be.

Find a nice comfortable position in which to sit, either on a chair or on a cushion on the floor. Make sure that your posture is upright. If sitting on the floor, you may want to have small cushions under your knees. When you're comfortable, close your eyes. Take a deep breath and just sit there. Sit and wait. Before long, you'll notice a thought, feeling or bodily sensation. When this happens, take a moment to really notice and focus on the experience. Then silently ask yourself:

- ✔ For a thought: 'To whom is this thought coming?'

- ✔ For a feeling: 'Who is feeling this feeling?'

- ✔ For a bodily sensation: 'Who is noticing this sensation?'

Try to notice who is doing the noticing. Gradually, you'll start to identify the distinction between the transient event (the thought, feeling or bodily sensation) and your observing self, noticing these transient events as they show up and eventually fade away. This is your self as context, constantly at the centre of an ever-changing process of psychological experience. Whatever the thought, feeling or bodily sensation you experience, positive or negative, pleasurable or painful, just let it be. Eventually, maybe even quite quickly, it will pass and be replaced by something else as your attention focuses on another thought, feeling or sensation. When this happens, repeat this exercise and ask who is noticing.

Continue this process for five minutes (or even longer if you want to). When you feel that you've had enough, take a slow, deep breath and gradually open your eyes.

Gaining some distance from your thoughts

If you really believe something, does that make it true? Like most people, you'll answer a resounding 'no' to that question because coming up with examples that contradict it is easy. The moon isn't made of cheese no matter how convinced you are that it is.

Interestingly, however, when you believe your thoughts you can act on them as though they're true. If you believe thoughts such as 'Just one more won't hurt', 'I'm a failure' or 'I need it', they can influence how you behave — and become practically true, even though they're not literally true.

ACT calls the process of believing your thoughts *fusion* (Chapter 6 has more on this concept). Fusing with your thoughts is problematic because they can be just plain wrong. And even when they're true, they aren't always useful in relation to living a life based on your values. For instance, thinking 'It will be very hard to change' may be true, but it's hardly supportive or motivating.

ACT aims to increase your *psychological flexibility*, which means doing more and more of the things that matter to you while being open to and accepting of all your experiences along the way. Being psychologically flexible means that you can make your life about the things that matter to you — a life defined by your values.

Gaining some distance from your thoughts can be helpful. Rather than looking at the world *from* your thoughts, you can look *at* your thoughts instead. When you do so you come to see your thoughts for what they actually are — just thoughts. Bits of private language going through your head.

You reduce the fusion with your thoughts by relating to them in different ways. One quick and easy way to do this is to add 'I'm having the thought that' to things you say to yourself, for example:

- ✔ *I'll always be an addict* becomes *I'm having the thought that I'll always be an addict.*

- ✔ *I can't change* becomes *I'm having the thought that I can't change.*

- ✔ *I don't deserve to be happy after the things I've done* becomes *I'm having the thought that I don't deserve to be happy after the things I've done.*

These sentences make it clear that such observations are merely negative thoughts — not statements on reality. Depending upon how you relate to them, they need not exert an influence on how you choose to act.

Identifying your values

Being clear about your values — the things you care most about — is an essential part of ACT. You can think of your values as a compass to guide your behaviour to ensure that what you do maximises your chance of achieving, and investing in, what's most important to you. Living life without a clear sense of your values resembles trekking without a path or compass to point you in the right direction. Without those values, chopping and changing direction, and trying to avoid short-term negatives and encounter short-term positives, is all too easy.

Rather than being things, goals or actions that you can achieve in the direct sense of the word, values are best thought of as areas, or domains, of life that you care about, which can motivate you to engage in behaviours that are in your long-term best interest. For example, you probably hold values relating to your relationships, health, leisure activities and profession. Although you can't actually achieve your values (you can't arrive in a place called 'North'), being clear about them enables you to identify goals that move you in that general direction — *value-based goals*.

Values help you stay the course when you may otherwise be diverted by cravings, impulses or thoughts that encourage you to do other things. For example, consider a person with a drug addiction who identifies 'being there for my children' as an important personal value. When she feels the desire to use drugs, the value that she wants to define her life can motivate her to focus on her value-based goals. And when she does so, she'll also abstain from doing the things that she knows will impair her parenting ability. She won't find the process easy and it will probably require her to accept difficult emotions, maybe even withdrawal symptoms, and to defuse (dissociate) from tricky thoughts. But the prize is now clear to her — she can be the parent she wants to be.

To help you think about your values, try organising them into domains, like those in the chart in the following exercise. Obviously a far greater range of domains, and sub-domains, exists, so amend the chart as you wish. The aim of this exercise is to think carefully about what matters to you so you can then prioritise what you want to work on.

Rate each of the life domains on the chart according to its importance right now (possibly not all of these domains will be relevant to you). Then rate how consistently you're living in line with each value. For instance, you may rate spirituality as important, say, 8/10, but feel that you're only living as spiritually as you want to at, say, 5/10. Mismatches between the importance you attribute to a particular domain and the degree to which you're living in accordance with it clearly need addressing.

Life Domain	*Importance (1 = low, 10 = high)*	*Degree to Which Living in Line with This Value (1 = low, 10 = high)*
Intimate relationships		
Parenting		
Other family relationships		
Friendships		
Employment		
Education/ training		
Recreation		
Spirituality		
Health		
Community		

Setting Value-Based Goals

When you're clear about which values you want to define your life, the next step is to set specific goals based on them. If your values represent the direction in which you want your life to be moving, the goals are those things you achieve along the way. An important distinction between values and goals is that, while values can never be achieved, goals can.

Set *SMART goals*, that is, those that are specific, measureable, achievable, relevant and time-framed (Chapter 5 covers SMART goals in detail). Thinking of goals in terms of the short, medium and long term can also be helpful, so that you always feel as though you're making progress. Use the following exercise to set your own value-based goals.

For each of your chosen domains, draw up a set of statements identifying your value-based SMART goal and identify the barriers you need to overcome, for example:

Domain: Health.

Value: Physical wellbeing.

The SMART goal I will set is: To go for a one-mile run three times in the next two weeks.

The barriers (thoughts and feelings) I need to overcome to achieve this goal are: Thoughts such as 'I'm too busy', 'It's raining', 'I think I'll just do it tomorrow' and 'This isn't going to make any real difference in my life, so what's the point?'

What I can do to overcome these barriers: I can notice and defuse from my thoughts by practising a brief mindfulness exercise when I notice one of these barriers showing up.

Set positive goals. When asked what they want to achieve, most people with an addiction simply say they want to stop engaging in their addictive behaviour. While this is quite understandable, framing goals negatively isn't a good idea because they don't tell you what to do instead. If you ask someone for directions and she tells you where *not* to go, you're none the wiser about how to reach your destination. Negative goals are the same.

Goals are most effective when they describe actions you can take. For example, rather than setting a negative goal of not taking a prescription drug when she feels emotionally vulnerable, the person with an addiction can aim to work through a defusion exercise and then to continue with what she wants to do that day. As a result of setting positive goals, your life is defined by moving towards something good and not simply avoiding the bad.

Moving on from Addiction and Living a Valued Life

A person with an addiction is in a hard place. Changing her life so that she does more of the things that matter and simultaneously engages less in her addictive behaviour won't be easy. But it is possible and ACT is one way to achieve it. By abandoning ineffectual efforts to control or avoid negative or unwanted psychological content (using acceptance and defusion), you create the space to engage in value-based living.

Define your life positively by what matters to you, rather than by the avoidance of your fears, pains or tricky thoughts. As a consequence, you can set your life on a different path into the future — a positive future you really, truly, deeply want, not a negative future you really, truly, deeply want to avoid.

Chapter 19

Recovering from Psychosis

. . . .

In This Chapter

▶ Exploring what psychosis means

▶ Defusing from psychotic thoughts

▶ Discovering how to accept the symptoms

. . . .

*I*magine thinking that people in your street are spying on you and telling the police about everything you do. When you meet them they take notes and pass them to the authorities. You don't understand why they're behaving in this way because you don't think you're doing anything wrong. It feels like everyone's out to get you. Alternatively, you may hear voices in your head telling you to do things or saying nasty stuff about you or other people. No matter what you do, those voices are always with you, relentlessly dominating your thoughts.

If these things were happening to you, you'd probably find the world a scary and difficult place. These types of experience are the basis of psychosis and they can make the world seem very dark and disorientating indeed.

This chapter outlines the experience of psychosis from an Acceptance and Commitment Therapy (ACT) perspective and describes what can be done to support people struggling with it.

While we do present some proactive ideas and options, these shouldn't be seen as an actual intervention programme for someone experiencing psychosis. If you need to access such a programme, seek advice from your GP.

Understanding Psychosis

Psychosis describes a condition involving three related experiences:

- ✔ **Delusions:** You believe something to be true when it's actually false or highly unlikely. For example, believing your neighbour is conspiring to hurt you or MI5 is monitoring your phone calls.

- ✔ **Hallucinations:** You see or hear things that aren't there. For example, seeing fairies at the bottom of the garden or hearing Napoleon talking to you.

- ✔ **General confused and disturbed thinking:** You're unable to function because your thoughts are so jumbled up that nothing makes sense. These symptoms mean that psychosis can be a very frightening experience. You may feel very threatened when you're experiencing psychosis, which can make you behave in bizarre and even dangerous ways.

Seek immediate specialist help if you or someone you know experiences these symptoms.

The UK National Institute for Health and Care Excellence (NICE) estimates that 1 per cent of the adult population will experience psychosis at some point in their lifetime. This may appear a small percentage, but it represents a great many people in distress. For approximately 20 per cent of people it will be a one-off event, a moment of crisis that they recover from. For others, psychosis can become a recurring pattern in their life. Evidence shows that specialist support after the first episode reduces the likelihood of future re-occurrence. To support these efforts, NICE has issued best practice guidance on how to respond to first- and multiple-episode psychosis (see clinical guideline 178 at www.nice.org.uk/guidance/cg178 for advice).

Psychosis and comedy: Natural bedfellows?

A recent study involving 523 comedians found that they scored more highly on four measures of psychosis than people working in non-creative professions. They reported a greater number of unusual experiences (such as supernatural events), mental disorganisation and distractibility, impulsive non-conformity (including antisocial behaviour) and a reduced ability to feel social and physical pleasure (including emotional intimacy). The researchers concluded that the characteristics that make comedians funny are remarkably similar to those of people experiencing psychosis. Being a little on the edge of mainstream thinking appears to be a good thing for comedians, giving them an idiosyncratic, outsider view of the world and a greater creative sharpness.

Psychosis is a complex condition and the specific processes and mechanisms that underpin it are still mostly unknown. That said, two broad sets of circumstances are associated with an initial psychotic episode:

- **Illnesses and health conditions:** People can experience psychosis as a result of a stroke, a brain tumour, dementia or nutritional deficiencies, for example. Postpartum psychosis can also occur in women after childbirth.

- **Environmental factors:** Drug and alcohol use is a common precursor to psychosis. In addition, psychosis can occur after a traumatic event, such as a physical assault or the death of a loved one.

In many ways, the ACT model is well-matched to the challenge of psychosis. People with psychosis typically experience disturbing thoughts and feelings that can impair their functioning and everyday living. And ACT specifically targets disturbing thoughts and feelings to facilitate more meaningful and positive lifestyles. ACT works on the specific mental distress that people with psychosis experience by helping them develop *psychological flexibility* (Chapter 3 gives you all the details).

Psychological flexibility means being open to and accepting of unwanted negative internal events (such as thoughts, feelings and sensations) while continuing to engage in behaviour that reflects your values (that is, how you want to behave in life, such as being a kind person or raising your children with respect and compassion). When you're more psychologically flexible, you're more connected with the world and more able to do the things that matter to you. And this seems to be the key problem for people with psychosis — their troubling negative thoughts and emotions overwhelm them to such an extent that they become disconnected from the world.

Many traditional pharmacological or psychotherapeutic interventions for psychosis target symptom reduction as their primary goal. The rationale is that because people are disturbed by their delusional thoughts and difficult emotions, removing or reducing these thoughts and emotions will end the disturbance. This is the medical model approach to psychosis: remove the negative symptoms and you're once again healthy.

Instead of trying to control and reduce negative cognitions, memories or emotions, ACT focuses instead on changing your relationship with these events. As we discuss in Chapters 9 and 11, the nature of your thoughts and feelings means that trying to control them is doomed to failure. But that doesn't mean you're powerless in the face of disturbing psychological content. While you have little direct control over what you think and feel, you can change how you relate to those experiences and therefore what they mean to you (check out the nearby sidebar, 'Decentring negative events' for examples). ACT defusion and mindfulness processes are designed to help you do just that.

Decentring negative events

If you experience a frightening auditory hallucination, you may try (indeed you may be encouraged by professionals) to ignore it, not hear it or even talk back to it. These are all attempts to reduce, control or minimise the unpleasant experience of that voice in your head. While these may seem sensible responses to unpleasant thoughts and feelings, focusing your energy on trying to influence or regulate the hallucination means that it now takes up a prominent position in your life and is much more likely to impact on how you behave.

In contrast, ACT helps you respond to such experiences in ways that aren't avoidant or controlling. ACT processes aim to build a different relationship with these events such that you come to accept them as experiences (albeit not very nice ones) you're having rather than a necessarily accurate reflection of reality. As a result the hallucinatory experience can move from the centre of your life to the periphery. It's still there, but is no longer controlling what you do to the same extent.

Applying an Acceptance-Based Intervention

Instead of trying to reduce unpleasant cognitions and psychotic symptoms, ACT works to build openness to and awareness of these experiences so that you can engage in value-based actions. There are good reasons for this. First, you can't easily change these experiences and, second, it's well-documented that the presence of psychotic symptoms doesn't always lead to distress or disturbed behaviour. Psychotic-type thinking is actually quite common, but people don't tend to talk about it. When surveyed, however, lots of people state that they believe in telepathy, ghosts and telekinesis (moving objects through the power of your mind), for example. Indeed, a survey conducted in the Netherlands found that 4 per cent of respondents regularly hear voices.

ACT uses a range of experiential exercises that help you develop a different relationship with your thoughts and feelings. Through these exercises you come to understand that your thoughts and feelings aren't always what they seem. You discover that you don't have to change or get rid of them to live your life. You can live *with* them rather than live *in* them. When you reduce the believability of your thoughts and the insistence of your feelings, you can begin to ask what you want to be doing with your life and to set value-based goals to steer you in the right direction.

Two of the key focus areas for ACT-based interventions for psychosis are defusion and acceptance.

Defusing from your thoughts

Nowhere is the idea of defusing thoughts more appropriate than in psychosis. People can experience truly explosive thoughts, and if these are allowed to 'go off' they can (and do) blow their lives apart. If you're sitting with lots of little bombs in your head, defusing them is clearly a good idea.

Thoughts aren't dangerous on their own, however; they need a detonator to make them explode. And that detonator is their believability — check out Figure 19-1. When you believe your thoughts, you provide the detonation that allows them to explode. In contrast, when you take away the detonator of believability, they remain just thoughts — bits of language that float through your head from time to time.

Figure 19-1:
Don't give
your
thoughts the
power to
explode.

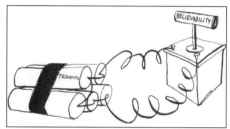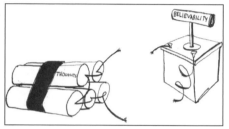

Illustrations by Joe Munro

People who experience psychotic-type events typically focus more strongly than normal on their internal world and are more aware of what they're thinking. When you believe your thoughts to be literally true and to reflect the world as it really is, you're fused with them. Fusing with your thoughts means you're more likely to be influenced by their content (Chapter 6 covers fusion in detail). For example, if you fuse with the thought, 'They're trying to get me', you may run away from people or attack them because you feel you really are at risk.

In contrast, if you're able to defuse from your thoughts, you may simply think, 'I'm having that thought again, that they're trying to get me'. The meaning of the thought has now changed from being a supposedly accurate representation of the world to being just a thought. Having a defused relationship with your thoughts creates a small amount of space in which you can decide how you want to respond to them. This little bit of wriggle room is all you need. It creates just enough time to notice your thoughts and in that moment reduce their believability and avoid detonation.

Try the following exercise to experience directly noticing your thoughts and changing their meaning as a result of doing so.

Picture your mind as a bully who wants to be in charge. The more you struggle and push it away, the more it pushes back and tries to dominate you. This process is exhausting and even though you've tried so very hard to get rid of it over the years, it just won't go. You've also tried a different approach: doing what it tells you and believing everything it says. However, while not fighting against it provides some relief, doing what it says can get you into serious trouble. You can find yourself doing things that you don't really want to do and not doing things you actually do want to do.

You can get so caught up trying to avoid, resist or fight against the content of your mind that you don't notice what these experiences actually are — merely thoughts and images going through your head. Stop and take a closer look. The mind is like a monster containing speech and thought bubbles. As a whole, the bubble monster appears scary — but really it's just a collection of words.

Take a look at your own bubble monster. Consider what words you'd write in Figure 19-2; we've filled in one bubble as an example.

Figure 19-2:
The evil bubble monster wants to demoralise and control you.

Illustration by Joe Munro

How does looking at your bubble monster, who likes to bully you and push you around, make you feel? Do any thoughts come into your head? Are they the bubble monster's thoughts or yours?

Now that you recognise that your mind is just a collection of words and phrases, sometimes saying nasty or strange things, you have a choice. You can do what you did before and go back to fighting and listening to it. Or you can simply let it be. You can't actually get rid of your mind — and it's often very useful! — but letting it be means you can now get on with doing what you want to do with your life.

This exercise enables you to no longer see thoughts, hallucinations and delusions as factual or real but instead as just language produced by your mind. Your mind will go on 'talking' (that is, thinking, evaluating, criticising and so on) because that's what your mind does, but you can now choose whether or not to respond to the content of what's said.

Being able to distance yourself from your own verbal content becomes an alternative to trying to stop, escape from or avoid it. As a result you can behave more flexibly in the presence of distressing thoughts, hallucinations and delusions, and spend your time getting on with value-based living.

Accepting your feelings

Psychosis can also involve experiencing difficult feelings in your body or disturbing mental images and memories. The nature of these events means it's quite natural that you want to avoid them. But being unwilling to remain in contact with unwanted internal events (memories, feelings and mental images) can lead to ultimately futile efforts to change or avoid them. That unwillingness is the basis of experiential avoidance, which we cover in Chapter 9.

Trying to avoid your thoughts, feelings, memories or bodily sensations is a waste of your time and energy because you don't have enough control over them to make this strategy successful in the longer term. How you feel depends on your past, which means that you can't change your emotional experience in the here and now. All you can do is give yourself new experiences so that you can feel differently in the future.

The situation is similar for your memories and thoughts. These are linked via arbitrary relationships to things all around you over which you have little or no control, which means that your memories or mental images can be pulled into your consciousness at almost any time. Everyone's experienced moments when things just pop into his mind. Sometimes you notice the event that led to it, but often not. When you notice the event that prompted a memory or thought, you may then want to avoid similar events in future. Unfortunately, you can't shut out the world completely and memories, thoughts or images will always find a way to emerge in your life.

Sadly, even though we can't avoid our internal psychological content, that doesn't stop us from trying. We're so culturally conditioned to believe that we can control how we think and feel that we battle on trying to do so even when we can see it isn't working. When we fail to exert control we see it as something else we're bad at and criticise ourselves for not being clever or strong-willed enough.

Not only is experiential avoidance ineffective, it actually makes things worse for two related reasons:

- ✔ Research indicates that the more you try to control your emotions and internal experiences, the more you focus on them and the more dominating they become.

- ✔ Every second that you spend trying to control your emotional and internal experiences can't instead be used for doing the things you care about.

Rather than avoiding or rejecting what you feel and sense, ACT shows you how to accept these experiences. Not because you want to, but because when you're willing to have them you're no longer wasting time in a futile battle to be rid of them. In the same way that you can discover how to accept your thoughts, you can also develop the skill of remaining in contact with unwanted, negative and/or distressing emotions and sensations.

ACT uses a range of experiential and mindfulness exercises to help you develop this skill. Doing so isn't easy, but evidence does show that it's possible. Research conducted by Patty Bach at the University of Central Florida, for example, demonstrated a 50 per cent reduction in hospital readmissions for people with psychosis following engagement in an ACT programme. Even people with multiple, complex histories of psychosis can develop these skills so that they can come to relate differently to their thoughts and other internal experiences.

Try the following short mindfulness exercise to practise being present with difficult thoughts and feelings. Your task is to notice what you're experiencing without trying to control or alter it in any way. While a simple idea, it can seem quite radical if you have a long history of trying to control or minimise unwanted cognitions and emotions. Remember that the ability to be present with your experiences is a skill that you need to practise in order to be good at. And the more you practise, the better you get.

This exercise takes about ten minutes, but you can speed it up or slow it down depending on how much time you have. Follow these steps:

1. **Find a quiet place to sit or lie down in a comfortable position, making sure that you're not restricted by your clothing.**

2. **Take a few deep breaths and, when you're ready, close your eyes.**

3. **Focusing on your feet, pay attention to any physical feelings you notice.** Are you aware of pain, discomfort, coolness, warmth, tension, tightness, for example? Simply pay attention to what you can feel and any sensations you have.

4. **Be aware of your mind making judgements about how you're doing, but don't respond to them.**

5. **Repeat this process for the rest of your body, moving slowly upwards through your thighs, stomach, back and so on until you reach your forehead.**

6. **When you've finished concentrating on your forehead, work back down your body in reverse, noticing the sensations you experience and the judgements your mind makes until your awareness finally settles back on your feet.**

How did you get on with this mindfulness exercise? Were you able to be present with your body and the sensations that arose within it? Did you find yourself struggling with them or being open and accepting of them?

Exercises like this help you notice and accept your experiences for what they are. They may not be pleasant and you may not want them, but they exist nonetheless. When you're willing to accept all experiences, positive and negative, however, they're no longer the basis for struggle and distress.

Psychosis is a serious and frightening experience for individuals *and* their friends and family. ACT can support people experiencing delusions, hallucinations and confused thoughts by showing them how to defuse from them. It also helps them to accept difficult feelings so that they exert less influence over their behaviour.

Part V
The Part of Tens

For ten easy things you can do to live a better life, head to www.dummies.com/extras/acceptanceandcommitmenttherapy.

In this part . . .

- ✔ Explore new ways to live a meaningful life, even in the presence of anxiety.

- ✔ Discover some simple exercises for identifying your core values and setting you on the path to behaving consistently with them.

- ✔ Try out ten brief exercises to practise your defusion and acceptance skills.

Chapter 20

Ten Brief Exercises to Help You Live More Mindfully

In This Chapter

▶ Integrating mindfulness into your everyday life

▶ Eating supper, drinking tea and listening to music in a mindful manner

*M*indfulness involves being consciously aware of and open to your experiences in the present moment. While mindfulness is a very simple idea, doing it in practice can be difficult because of your tendency to drift off into the content of your thoughts. Mindfulness is a cyclical process of continually disengaging from your thoughts and reconnecting with your present moment experience before drifting off into your thoughts again.

You can gain numerous benefits from practising mindfulness. It enables you to slow down and really connect with the world. Spending too much time with your thoughts or memories reduces your ability to make contact with the events occurring around you. As a consequence, you can become insensitive and unresponsive to the world in which you live, which makes living in line with your values harder. Mindfulness also helps you defuse from your language — believe less in its literal content — and become more accepting of your experiences.

This chapter looks at some different ways in which you can practise mindfulness and make it part of your everyday life. To get the most out of the exercises, you need to try them out for a while. Mindfulness is a skill like any other: the more you practise, the better you get. If you find yourself judging how you're doing, simply notice those judgements, thank your mind for offering them and continue with the exercises.

Slowing Down and Connecting

Being fully present in the world is difficult if you're continually hurrying through it. Although life is often very busy, which naturally gives you a sense of urgency, rushing is rarely a good idea. As Kelly Wilson, one of the pioneers of ACT, often says on training courses, 'We've got a lot to get through, so we best go slowly'. The Romans even had a phrase for making haste slowly: *Festina lente.*

Rushing may also be a form of avoidance because it can stop you really connecting with the world around you. Have you ever sped through a conversation because you felt anxious about what the other person may or may not say? While this tactic may reduce your initial sense of stress, it also means you can't be fully present in the moment. And this can be problematic because if you can't fully connect with the world, you can't be fully effective.

Rather than zooming through your daily experiences, consciously slow down everything you do and really connect with what's happening. You can do it right this minute by following these steps:

1. **Take two slow and deep breaths.**

2. **Slow down your reading and really focus on each word.**

3. **Feel the sensation of the book or tablet in your hands.**

4. **Observe what you smell or hear in your immediate environment.**

Greeting the Day

Start each day with a burst of mindfulness! Even if you're woken abruptly by an alarm clock or children, before jumping into action take a brief moment to be present with yourself. In those first few seconds:

1. **Close your eyes.**

2. **Breathe in deeply, twice.**

3. **Scan your body from your feet to your head, noticing the sensations you experience.**

4. **Notice any thoughts popping into your head and welcome them.**

5. **Open your eyes and start the day.**

Celebrating Your Wandering Mind

No matter what you do, your mind will wander from one topic to another. Remaining totally focused on one thing is impossible; your attention always drifts onto something else. While this can be irritating, you can also celebrate your mind's ability to flit about. You can follow your attention as it moves from topic to topic:

1. **Find a quiet spot and close your eyes.**

2. **Take a moment to notice your thoughts.**

3. **Follow your thoughts wherever they go — maybe you briefly consider what to eat for lunch, how much money is in your purse, where you bought that purse, how much you like the little dog on the purse, what sort of dog you'd like to own, whether you fancy a cheese sandwich and so on.**

4. **When you become embroiled in a particular thought, such as considering various breeds of dog — and you will! — gently bring yourself back to the task of simply noticing your thoughts and seeing where they go. Observe yourself and note, 'Oh, I'm thinking about dogs now'.**

5. **When you've had enough of following your thoughts around, thank your mind for taking you on a journey and open your eyes.**

Appreciating Your Food

Most people will have eaten food without really tasting it. What a waste! Food is one of life's great pleasures. You can adopt a mindful approach to eating so that you savour the experience. Follow these steps at your next meal:

1. **Look at the food you're about to eat and observe its shapes, colours and textures.**

2. **Bring the food to your nose and notice what you can smell.**

3. **Bring a forkful of food deliberately to your lips and pass it slowly into your mouth.**

4. **Before you chew, notice the sensations in your mouth for a moment.**

5. **Slowly begin to chew, and notice the tastes you encounter.**

6. **Chew for longer than you normally would, and relish the textures and tastes you experience.**

7. **Swallow that mouthful and repeat Steps 1–6 until the meal is finished.**

Getting to Know Your Hands

Your hands are amazing tools but you often take them for granted. Consider for a moment that each one contains 27 bones plus skin, muscles and blood vessels.

Your hands are truly a wonder of evolution. Not only do they enable you to do all sorts of things but, because they're always present, they're also perfect for practising mindfulness, wherever you happen to be. Use the following steps to mindfully appreciate your hands:

1. **Take a moment to look at your hands.**

2. **Notice the sensations you experience in your hands: perhaps they're warm and soft; maybe they're cold, sore or itchy.**

3. **Examine the lines and creases on your palms; trace along them with your eyes.**

4. **Study any marks or scars on your hands.**

5. **If you have a ring on your finger, be aware of how it looks and feels.**

6. **Notice the veins and tiny hairs on the backs of your hands.**

7. **Marvel at the work your hands can do and how they help you live your life.**

8. **Mindfully thank your hands and return to what you were doing.**

Savouring a Cup of Tea

You may have a chance to work through this exercise several times a day! Follow these steps the next time you pause for a cuppa:

1. **Choose a cup, hold it in your hands and notice its shape, texture, colour and temperature.**

2. **Pick up a tea bag and look at it closely. Observe its shape, perforations and aroma. Place the tea bag in the cup.**

3. **Fill a kettle with water and listen to the sound of it heating up.** Hear the bubbling and notice the steam rising from the kettle and disappearing into the air.

4. **Carefully pour the hot water into the cup, observing the sound it makes.**

5. **If you take milk, pour it slowly and watch how the tea changes colour.**

6. **If you take sugar, slowly tip a spoonful into the tea and watch the granules melt.**

7. **Pick up the cup and take a sip of tea. Notice its smell, temperature and taste.** Hold the tea in your mouth for a moment before swallowing it. Feel the muscles in your neck move as you swallow.

8. **Continue drinking the tea slowly and mindfully until it's finished. When your cup is empty, carefully put it down.**

9. **Take a moment to breathe deeply and reflect on the moments you shared with your cup of tea.**

Finding Your Balance

This exercise, which focuses on your sense of balance, is fun but a little tricky. Find a place where you can safely stand for a minute or so without being in anyone's way or interrupted, and then work through these steps:

1. **Stand up straight and let your arms fall to your sides. Breathe in deeply three times and, when you're ready, close your eyes.** Keep your attention focused on your breath.

2. **Move your attention to your posture and notice how you gently sway back and forth.** Your body is in constant motion to keep you still. It's forever finding and losing and finding its balance. Take a moment to notice how your body effortlessly and automatically does this.

3. **If your mind wanders and you find you've drifted off into your thoughts, simply be aware of this fact and gently bring your attention back to your balance.**

4. **After a minute or so, open your eyes and thank your body for its ongoing and continual ability to sustain your balance.**

Hearing the World

The world is full of sounds but you often miss them! This simple exercise involves listening to what's going on around you.

1. **Find a spot where you can safely close your eyes without being disturbed for five minutes or so.**

2. **Take two deep breaths and then close your eyes.**

3. **Focus your attention on your breathing for two or three breaths.**

4. **Now start listening to the sounds around you.** If your mind labels the sounds or evaluates them, that's fine, just notice that this has happened and keep listening. Sounds will come and go. Just be aware of the sound in your world.

5. **After five minutes open your eyes and reconnect visually with the world around you.**

Feeling Gravity

Gravity is the second-most powerful force in the universe (after love, of course!) and it influences everything on this planet and beyond. As with so many things, however, it's easy to miss or forget about. Use this exercise to experience the pull of gravity.

1. **Find a place where you can safely close your eyes for 5–10 minutes.** You can do this exercise standing, sitting or lying down, but for the sake of simplicity we assume you're standing.

2. **Slowly take two or three deep breaths and allow your body to relax a little.** Feel the air flow in through your nostrils and fill your lungs. Notice how your chest rises and falls with each breath.

3. **Now close your eyes and focus your attention on your feet on the ground.** Feel their weight. They feel very heavy, right at the point where they touch the ground, as though they're magnetic and you're stuck to a steel planet. Become aware of the solid connection you have with the ground. Feel gravity pulling you downwards, through your feet. The earth is huge beneath you and its mass is drawing you down.

4. **When your mind wanders — inevitably! — gently bring it back to noticing your experience of gravity pulling you downwards.**

5. **When you've had enough of sensing your gravitational attraction to the planet, open your eyes and come back into the room.**

Listening to Music

Music is a very effective means of practising mindfulness because it can hold your attention in the present moment as you follow it. Any music will work, but you might like to try an instrumental piece for this exercise, without lyrics, so that your mind doesn't focus on the words and try to analyse or judge them:

1. **Find a place where you can safely close your eyes and listen to a piece of music.**

2. **Close your eyes and focus your attention on the melody, individual instruments and repeated refrains.**

3. **When your attention wanders, gently return it to the music.**

4. **When the piece comes to an end, open your eyes.**

Chapter 21

Ten Tips for Value-Based Living

In This Chapter
▶ Identifying and putting your values into practice
▶ Following some central ACT concepts

*V*alues are a central feature of Acceptance and Commitment Therapy (ACT). They're verbal statements about the behaviour you want to engage in so that you can achieve certain outcomes. They describe what's important to you and how you want to behave on an ongoing basis. Values define what you want your life to stand for and mean, and as such they dignify your struggles as you strive to behave consistently with them.

To make your values as clear as possible, consider writing them down. Remember: you don't need to justify or explain your values, just as you don't need to justify why you prefer vanilla to chocolate ice-cream. You do, however, need to prioritise your values because it's hard to focus on several different life directions all at once.

In this chapter, we provide tips to help you identify and prioritise your values so that you can create a life that represents them.

Dedicate Time to Defining Your Values

Working out what your values are takes time and a bit of thinking. Rushing through this important stage won't help you in the long run. You need to set aside some time to give yourself the chance to really think through what matters. You may even need several thinking sessions to clearly define your values.

Choose a specific time and place, turn off your phone and sit down to engage in the process. Consider working through a brief mindfulness exercise (such as mindful breathing, the body scan, described in Chapter 8, or mindful walking, covered in Chapter 3) to bring yourself to the present moment before you begin.

Consider a Time When You Were Very Happy

Experiences of genuine happiness can tell you a lot about what matters to you. During these moments you can feel at your most fulfilled and purposeful, which means these moments are important. When you can work out *why* they're important, you can use that information to inform your values.

Think about a time when you were very happy and life was going really well. Now ask yourself:

- ✔ What was I doing?
- ✔ What were the effects of my actions?
- ✔ What values were represented in my actions?

For example, you may have been studying at the time; the effect of your actions — working hard at your essays, revising for exams — was to gain a good degree; and your behaviour represented your future career as a teacher.

Your answers to these questions represent the ongoing actions — your values — that you identify as important. Maybe you now feel aimless at work and that you need to concentrate on furthering your career. Focusing on your values can help you to identify the direction in which you want your life to be heading and to set goals based on that value.

Focus on a Period When You Were Really Sad

Although it's not always immediately obvious, those times when you feel sad, vulnerable or distressed can also tell you a great deal about what matters. It can be harder to spot the values your vulnerability and pain reveal, but they're there nonetheless. If you didn't care about something it wouldn't upset you. For example, if an incident made you feel unjustly treated, you can take that as a sign that justice is important to you. If you felt despondent because you were wasting your time, you recognise that being productive holds value for you.

Now, in addition to the three questions you asked yourself in the preceding section, also consider:

✔ What would I choose not to care about in future?

✔ How do I wish I'd behaved at the time I experienced the difficult issue?

Use your responses to these questions to identify your values. For example, you may want to ensure that you always treat people justly and give them a fair hearing.

Prioritise Your Values

Focusing on two or more values at the same time can be very difficult, and sometimes impossible. For example, you may value being a loving partner and also being a supportive colleague. If a colleague wants to meet with you after work one day to discuss his problems with the boss, you'll be unable to get home in time to share a meal with your partner.

This scenario draws your attention to a key point about values — they have to be *prioritised*. Not only will different values be important at different times, but they can also change over time.

Check in on your values now and then to make sure that they still really matter and are relevant.

Identify Characteristics You Value

You can use behavioural characteristics to identify your values. The way you behave reflects what's important to you. If someone describes you as a compassionate person, you clearly value treating others kindly.

Check out the following adjectives and identify the six most important to you — those characteristics that you respect in others and would like to demonstrate yourself.

Adventurous	Empathetic	Independent
Assertive	Exciting	Intimate
Authentic	Fair	Kind
Beautiful	Fit	Loving
Bold	Flexible	Open
Caring	Free	Patient
Charming	Friendly	Persistent
Compassionate	Forgiving	Political
Competitive	Fun	Powerful
Conforming	Generous	Respectable
Connected	Genuine	Responsible
Considerate	Grateful	Romantic
Co-operative	Hard-working	Self-controlling
Courageous	Healthy	Sexual
Creative	Honest	Spiritual
Curious	Humble	Steady
Dangerous	Humorous	Successful
Dominant	Imaginative	Trustworthy

Use those six characteristics to guide your actions — that is, to live according to your values.

Act on Your Values

When you've identified a particular value, you then need to establish specific goals to enact it. Ensuring that your goals are SMART (specific, measurable, achievable, relevant and time-framed; Chapter 5 covers SMART goals in detail) means you'll have a better chance of achieving them. Also consider setting short-, medium- and long-term goals. For example, a long-term goal may be to apply for a promotion at work; a related medium-term goal is to research what the management role involves; and the short-term goal is to complete and submit the application form.

Make Your Goals Public

Telling other people about your goals means you're more likely to achieve them. If you say you're going on a diet because you value being more healthy, you don't want to still be struggling into elasticated trousers six months later — doing so would be embarrassing. Bringing social dynamics and peer pressure into play increases the likelihood that you'll follow through on your goals. Obviously you'll feel an extra sense of pressure, but that's the point.

Valuing and reinforcing behaving consistently with what you say is a social norm. It means other people will notice and judge your behaviour in relation to what you said you'd do. If you don't feel you want this extra social pressure, there's no need to publicise your goals. But if you want a bit of extra motivation, do share them with people whose opinions you care about.

Be Willing

Even when you really want something, you can still struggle to make it happen. One reason for this can be your unwillingness to experience difficult and unwanted emotions that arise along the way. As you begin to work on goals to help you create a life based on your values — trying to be more assertive at work, for example — you may feel anxious and uncertain. When you stop trying to behave more assertively, those feelings may subside. If you aren't willing to experience these (or similar) feelings, they'll act as a barrier to living according to your values.

That problem can be resolved by setting your willingness 'high'. While you can't control how you feel when you engage in value-based actions, you can control your willingness. Willingness is a choice: you can choose to experience all that life brings, good and bad. As a payoff, you can then do the things that matter in life.

You can increase your willingness with practice. Check out the exercises in Chapter 5.

Defuse from Your Thoughts

Fusing with your thoughts — believing them as the literal truth — is another barrier to action, alongside being unwilling to experience difficult emotions (as described in the preceding section). You need to be particularly aware of the reasons that you give to yourself or other people to explain your actions. While they can seem quite reasonable or accurate, it's important to remember that they're just bits of language.

Thoughts are just thoughts; reasons are just words.

You need to ask yourself whether your thoughts or reasons are useful in terms of achieving your value-based goals. If they're not, simply thank your mind for them, remind yourself of your values and continue with your actions. For example, if your value-based goal is to clean the kitchen this evening, when thoughts such as, 'I'm too tired, so I'll do it tomorrow' or 'I need to check my e-mails first' pop into your head, just notice that your mind is coming up with reasons to avoid doing something that you actually do want to do. You can then make a decision about how you want to behave. Maybe you do indeed postpone cleaning the kitchen, but at least you've made a decision about what actually matters, rather than allowed your thoughts to control what you do.

Remember Some Key Tenets of ACT

This section is based on Steve Hayes's *ACT Therapeutic Posture* (available on the Association for Contextual Behavioral Science (ACBS) website: https://contextualscience.org/acbs; see the Appendix for more details about this organisation). Bear these notions in mind as you engage in ACT:

- ✔ **Your experiences aren't your enemy.** It's your fight against your own experiences that's harmful and leads to suffering.

- ✔ **Only you can rescue you from the situation you're in.** Other people can help, but ultimately it's down to you to bring change into your life.

- ✔ **Beware the reasons you give yourself to explain why you behave as you do.** Even if they're correct or reasonable, the real issue is whether they help you live a valued life.

- ✔ **How you think and feel aren't barriers, but opportunities to help you address what needs to be worked on.** If you feel sad or think 'I can't do it', you can address these psychological events.

- ✔ **Rest assured that you're not alone — everyone struggles with the same underlying language processes that can lead to suffering.** While the details of people's lives are different (including their thoughts, memories and histories), every language-able human faces the same struggle with language to some degree.

✔ **Assuming that you can think or talk yourself into a better life is a mistake.** Rather than relying upon some rare and special wisdom to turn your life around, change occurs as a result of *doing* new things.

✔ **The most important thing to ask is what does your behaviour *do*; what is it in the service of?** It doesn't matter what your behaviour looks like or how frequently it occurs: if it helps you live according to your values, carry on behaving in the same way. But if your actions don't match your values it's time to try something else.

Chapter 22

Ten Ways to Overcome Fusion and Experiential Avoidance

In This Chapter

▶ Singing your thoughts and other defusion tactics

▶ Practising accepting your difficult thoughts and emotions

A s sure as night follows day, as you live your life you'll encounter difficulties along the way. These difficulties can become barriers to living in line with your values if you don't respond to them in effective ways. This chapter looks at the two types of difficulty you face — fusion and experiential avoidance — and describes some ways in which you can overcome them.

Fusion occurs when you believe the content of your thoughts and respond to them as though they were a true or accurate reflection of the world (refer to Chapter 6 for more on fusion and its opposite, defusion). Fusion is problematic because when you believe your thoughts they can influence what you do in unhelpful ways and you become less connected with the world around you. Add to this the fact that your thoughts are often negative evaluations about yourself and the world in which you live and it's clear that spending too much time in your head can be a demoralising and unproductive experience. *Defusion* is the most effective response to fusion: the process whereby you learn to step back from the literal content of your psychological content and relate to it differently. It is the process by which you come to recognise your thoughts, statements and the reasons that you give to explain your actions for what they are — just bits of language rather than the actual truth.

Experiential avoidance refers to your unwillingness to remain in contact with unwanted negative thoughts and feelings, which leads to counterproductive efforts to avoid them (Chapter 9 covers experiential avoidance in detail). Trying to change or avoid your own psychological experiences is counterproductive because you don't have enough control over them to make this an effective strategy. This means that you can waste a lot of time and energy trying to control or avoid experiences that can't be controlled or avoided!

The answer to experiential avoidance is to open up, stop struggling and be willing to experience emotionally challenging events — the acceptance part of Acceptance and Commitment Therapy (ACT).

The first five exercises in this chapter focus on defusion, and the remaining five exercises focus on willingness and acceptance.

Sounding Out Your Thoughts

The aim of this exercise is to really hear your thoughts so that you can recognise them for what they are — just bits of language going around in your head. It involves saying your thoughts out loud and noticing what you hear. That's it. It's a simple approach but it's very effective in helping you relate to your thoughts in new ways.

Try these three different methods:

✔ Write down some troublesome thoughts that keep popping into your head. Now, very slowly, say them out loud. Now say them again, but very, very slowly. And now say them again but very, very, very slowly. Repeat this process for a minute or so and then stop and reflect on the words you've just spoken.

✔ Write down some troublesome thoughts that keep popping into your head. Now sing them out loud. Don't worry if you can't sing in tune, just do it anyway. If you find it useful, sing the words to a tune such as *Happy Birthday* or *Three Blind Mice*.

✔ Write down some troublesome thoughts that keep popping into your head. Now say them in different silly voices or regional accents. For example, try Homer Simpson's voice or a Scottish accent.

Do one — or all, if you're particularly enthusiastic! — of these exercises regularly throughout the day and notice how the meaning of the words changes and sometimes disappears completely as they simply become nonsense sounds.

Taking Your Mind for a Walk

To get the most out of this exercise you need two people. Find someone with a sense of fun to do it with you.

Begin by noticing who's in the room. The room actually contains four of you: you and your mind, and the person you've chosen to do the exercise with — we'll call her Sheena — and her mind. You generally don't notice that your mind is always with you, chattering away in your thoughts.

To help you become more aware of your mind, you take the role of the Person and Sheena takes the role of the Mind. (You swap places in a moment so it doesn't actually matter who starts as what.)

Now you (the Person) go outside for a walk with the Mind (Sheena). The Person can go where she likes and the Mind follows close behind. As you walk, the Mind constantly comments on what it sees and notices. It evaluates, passes judgement, compares, predicts, jokes, criticises, describes and so on — basically, it does everything your mind normally does. While the Mind is constantly talking, the Person mustn't reply, but just keep on walking. If the Person tries to communicate with the Mind, the mind replies, 'Never mind your mind' and carries on with its running commentary.

After five minutes (monitored by the Mind), the Mind and Person swap roles and repeat the exercise. At the end of the second five minutes, you and Sheena set off in different directions and continue wandering about; this time, however, you notice how your own mind is with you. Be aware that your mind is evaluating, passing judgement and so on, just like the other Mind did.

This exercise highlights the similarity between your own thoughts and the words spoken by somebody else. And words — whether thought or spoken by another person — are just words. This exercise also helps you practise hearing your mind's chatter and still choosing to do something else. It demonstrates how you can be in control of what you do irrespective of what thoughts are going through your mind.

Giving Reasons for Your Behaviour

Giving reasons for your behaviour is something your mind regularly does, but doing so can be problematic if you fuse with them. Reasons can appear to explain why you behave as you do, but actually they're just words that purport to describe events and processes that may or may not have led to your behaviour. And that's true even when your verbal reasons are accurate, they're still just words.

Think of something you did recently about which you're unhappy; for example, maybe you missed a GP appointment, told a white lie, shouted at someone or drank too much. Now write down a list of reasons why you did that.

This exercise works best if you can come up with at least three or four reasons. Here's an example: I shouted at my daughter because . . .

- I was angry.
- She really wound me up.
- I've got a short temper.
- She won't listen to me if I don't.

Beneath this list, now write another list of reasons why you shouldn't have done what you did; for example, I shouldn't shout at my daughter because . . .

- It upsets her.
- I'm tired.
- She's just a child and I'm the adult.
- She won't respect me if I lose control.

When you now look at this list of reasons for doing and not doing a particular action, you may conclude that you behaved as you did because one set of reasons outweighed the other. But is this actually the case? Isn't it true that you could write a long list of reasons to do something and still not do it? And vice versa? How is this possible if reasons cause your behaviour? Reasons are just words. They may seem convincing, but they're just words nonetheless. Here's a little experiment: say out loud 'I can't wriggle my toes' and then wriggle them. How is this possible if words control what you do?

You don't have to act on what your mind tells you!

Sitting on a Description

Language can so dominate your mind that it can appear to actually be a true representation of the physical world in which you live. But language is just words and symbols. Bear in mind that 'the map is not the country' — a map isn't the same as the land it describes.

Get a pen and paper and describe a chair in as much detail as possible. When you're finished, take that description and sit on the chair that you've described. Can you do it? Of course not. The best you can do is sit on the list of words you've written as no physical chair exists.

Words are just words, not the things or processes they describe.

Thinking and Observing

It's all too easy to be wrapped up in your thoughts so being able to observe them without being drawn into their content is useful. This exercise helps you notice the difference between thinking and observing.

This exercise takes about five minutes. Find somewhere quiet and sit down. Focus your attention on your breathing and follow your breaths in and out. When you feel comfortable, close your eyes, or focus on a fixed point in the room if you prefer. Maintain your attention on your breathing and breathe in deeply and regularly for five breaths.

Now notice any thoughts you're experiencing. Try to locate their position in your head. Are they at the front, in the middle or at the back? Maybe they're floating outside your head? Notice where they are and watch them come and go. From time to time you'll drift off into your thoughts as you fuse with them. When this happens (and it will), gently let go of the thoughts and bring yourself back to noticing the process of them coming in and out of your awareness.

As you undertake this exercise, see if you can also become aware of two parallel processes — a thinking process and an observing process. Try to notice that you're both thinking and observing your thinking.

As you become aware of your thoughts, notice also that a 'you' is observing these thoughts. Part of you is thinking and part of you is observing your thinking.

Noticing your thoughts rather than being inside them distances you from their content so that they exert a little less control over how you behave. When you step back from the content of your thoughts, you're more able to be guided by your values than what your thoughts are telling you.

The next five exercises help you work on willingness and acceptance.

Getting Closer to Your Past

This exercise helps you practise willingness. Through recalling a difficult or painful memory from the past, you can practise allowing this experience to be present in your life without trying to get rid of or change it. The memory you recall will no doubt be accompanied by some difficult sensations, and that's the point. You can practise being willing to experience those sensations even though you don't want them.

Close your eyes and take a moment to recall a difficult memory; nothing too challenging, just something that makes you feel a little uneasy, for example. Remember: you can decide how challenging this exercise will be by choosing a more or less difficult memory to practise with. This memory is from your past and what happened cannot be changed. This experience is part of your life, even though you probably wish it wasn't. Allow the memory to remain in your awareness without trying to change or escape from it. Notice that you aren't struggling against it, but are just allowing it to be present. You're willing to have this experience because it's part of who you are. After a minute or so, open your eyes and reflect on what you're feeling.

By making contact with a difficult memory you can practise willingness and acceptance, which will help you learn how it's possible to have unwanted and negative memories without being controlled by them.

Using Argyle Socks to Recognise Why Feelings Aren't Causes

This exercise helps you consider whether what you feel controls how you behave. Do you know what Argyle socks are? Don't worry if not; most people don't and that's the point. (For your information, Argyle socks have a distinctive diamond pattern.)

Now imagine that you care very deeply about Argyle socks, so much so that you feel everybody should be wearing them. Even though you probably don't feel this way, the question here is whether you can behave as though you do. Consider for a moment what you can do to demonstrate to others your passion for Argyle socks.

What did you think of? Maybe you considered wearing Argyle socks every day or T-shirts extolling their virtues, giving them as birthday and wedding presents, setting up a fan club, developing a website, blogging on a daily basis or writing to your MP asking her to support your campaign to make everyone wear them. Or you may think that walking up and down the high street with a billboard stating 'The end of the world is nigh; make sure you're wearing Argyle socks!' is a good idea.

The list of possibilities is endless, but the point here is whether or not you could do those (or similar) things. Yes or no? Even though you may be indifferent to Argyle socks, of course you could still carry out the actions you thought of so that people would think you cared. Now ask yourself: what does this tell you about the causes of your behaviour? How much does what you feel actually influence what you do? Is it possible to think and feel one thing and yet do the opposite? The answer is yes!

Making Your Emotions Physical

If you avoid difficult or unwanted thoughts and feelings, you'll never find out what those experiences are actually like.

Take a moment to think about a difficult emotion that you try hard to avoid. When you identify that emotion, close your eyes and imagine where inside your body it's located. Picture its size, colour, texture and temperature. Does it make a sound?

Now imagine taking this emotion out of your body and holding it in your hands. What do you feel as you look at it? What thoughts do you have? What would you like to do with it? Maybe you'd like to throw it away or stamp on it. Maybe you puzzle over how this little hot prickly thing can cause you so much distress.

When you're ready, let the emotion leave your hands and return to its place inside you. How does this feel?

Now open your eyes and reflect on your experience. Did you notice any change in the emotion as you looked at it? Did the emotion feel different after you finished the exercise?

This is another exercise that gives you some exposure to a troubling or painful emotional experience and allows you to develop a new way to relate to it that doesn't involve trying to change or get rid of it.

Controlling Thoughts about Jam Doughnuts

This exercise demonstrates how difficult it is to control your thoughts — even when you work really hard at doing so!

Try really hard to not think about warm jam doughnuts. Seriously, don't think about them! Stop thinking about them right now. Stop thinking about how they smell when they first come out of the fryer. Stop thinking about that RIGHT NOW! Don't think about the delicious taste of the jam as you sink your teeth into the doughnut. Don't imagine it squirting hotly into your mouth.

Stop thinking about the sugary texture against your lips. Just stop thinking about anything related to lovely warm jam doughnuts!

You found that very difficult, didn't you! Did it help you accept that you don't have anything like as much control over your thoughts as you'd like to believe?

Stop trying to fight distressing thoughts and emotions because doing so is fruitless. Preserve your time and energy for doing things that matter to you instead.

Being Still

This exercise aims to strengthen your willingness to accept uncomfortable sensations. If you can simply accept feeling physically uncomfortable, you can also accept difficult thoughts and emotions and just let them go. Acceptance is a skill and practising will improve your ability to do it — even in your head.

Find a quiet place to sit where you won't be disturbed. Get comfortable and focus your attention on your breathing. Just follow each breath in and then out. Notice how your shoulders and chest rise and fall with each breath. Continue for ten minutes and notice the different sensations that you experience from time to time. Maybe you notice an itch, a thought about how you're doing or some mild discomfort. If so, your task is to just notice these events and keep still, simply breathing in and out. Don't scratch an itch, don't interpret your thoughts and don't shift your position to relieve any discomfort. Instead, merely notice these things and be willing to experience them for the brief period of the exercise.

From time to time you'll drift off into your thoughts and stop noticing your breathing. When this happens, gently and without judgement bring your attention back to your breathing.

After ten minutes, open your eyes and look around the room.

Willingness is a choice you make about how to respond to your experiences. It involves being open to and accepting of what you think, feel and remember, rather than trying to avoid these experiences. And you do so because you then have more time and energy for pursuing your value-based goals.

Appendix

Further Sources

· ·

Books

You can find loads of great books about Acceptance and Commitment Therapy (ACT) out there. Here are a few recommendations:

- *Acceptance and Commitment Therapy: An Experiential Approach to Behavior Change* (Guilford Press, 1999), by Steven C. Hayes, Kirk D. Strosahl and Kelly G. Wilson.

    The core ACT text! Not only does it describe how ACT is applied across a range of needs, it also covers the underlying philosophy and Relational Frame Theory (RFT).

- *ACTivate your Life: Using Acceptance and Mindfulness to Build a Life that Is Rich, Fulfilling and Fun* (Robinson, 2015), by Joe Oliver, Jon Hill and Eric Morris.

    An excellent book for clinicians and those who want to understand and change their own behaviour.

- *Brief Interventions for Radical Change: Principles and Practice of Focused Acceptance and Commitment Therapy* (New Harbinger Publications, 2012), by Kirk D. Strosahl, Patricia Robinson and Thomas Gustavsson.

    A wonderful book showing how you can change your life profoundly *and* quickly.

- *The Research Journey of Acceptance and Commitment Therapy (ACT)* (Palgrave Schol, 2015), by Nic Hooper and Andreas Larsson.

    If you're interested in learning about the research base underpinning ACT, this is the book for you. A comprehensive and accessible summary guide to ACT published research.

You can also find lots of useful self-help books, including:

- ✔ *Get Out of Your Mind and into Your Life: The New Acceptance and Commitment Therapy* (New Harbinger Publications, 2005), by Steven C. Hayes and Spencer Smith.

  This fantastic book provides lots of great exercises and ways to engage in ACT.

- ✔ *Get the Life You Want: Finding Meaning and Purpose through Acceptance and Commitment Therapy* (Watkins Publishing, 2013), by Freddy Jackson Brown.

  An easy-to-read book if you want a straightforward introduction on how to use ACT to create a value-based life.

- ✔ *The Happiness Trap: Stop Struggling, Start Living* (Little, Brown, 2008), by Russ Harris.

  The original ACT self-help book, it offers lots of mindfulness techniques to help you manage the things that make your existence difficult, such as stress, doubt and insecurity, and simultaneously create a meaningful and enjoyable life.

Courses and Training

Lots of opportunities exist to train in ACT, from short courses to courses within broader degree programmes. Check out:

- ✔ The training page on the Association for Contextual Behavioral Science's (ACBS) website, which is one of the best places to look for training events near you — www.contextualscience.org/act_training.

- ✔ The ACT special interest group within the British Association for Behavioural & Cognitive Psychotherapies, which regularly puts on excellent training events — www.babcp.com/Training/Events.aspx.

- ✔ The MSc in Applied Behavioural Analysis at Bangor University and the MSc in Behaviour Analysis and Therapy at the University of South Wales. These courses are designed to develop advanced theoretical and practical knowledge of the basic principles of behavioural analysis and the application of those principles within clinical and research settings — www.bangor.ac.uk/psychology/postgraduate-modules/C8BL/year1; http://courses.southwales.ac.uk/courses/841-msc-behaviour-analysis-and-therapy.

Websites

Check out these websites for additional online information about ACT:

- ✔ **www.contextualscience.org:** The website of the ACBS is the main source of information on ACT and RFT.

- ✔ **www.ACTMindfully.com.au:** ACT Mindfully is the website of Russ Harris, one of the best writers of accessible and fun books on ACT. The website is a great starting point for finding out more about ACT, how it works and how to do it. It also offers loads of freely download-able resources as well as online training. A highly recommended place to start.

- ✔ **www.uk-sba.org:** The website of the UK Society for Behaviour Analysis offers a forum for accreditation, professional development, network-ing and much more. Behaviour analysis is the scientific study of human beings' functional relationship with the environment and is the wider science within which ACT and RFT sit.

- ✔ **www.abainternational.org:** The Association for Behavior Analysis International (ABAI) is the foremost professional international organisa-tion representing and promoting behaviour analysis.

Index

About the Authors

Dr Freddy Jackson Brown, BSc, DClinPsych, is a Clinical Psychologist. He works in Bristol with children who have a range of disabilities and developmental needs. He has researched Acceptance and Commitment Therapy (ACT) and acceptance-based interventions that can be used in home, school and work settings. He has published over 30 research and professional articles in peer-reviewed journals and books. He is also the author of the ACT self-help book *Get the Life You Want: Finding Meaning and Purpose with Acceptance and Commitment Therapy* (Watkins).

Dr Duncan Gillard, BSc, DEdPsych, is a Senior Educational Psychologist. He completed his doctoral studies at Exeter University in Devon, UK. Duncan is an ACT practitioner and uses the ACT framework within his daily practice with children, young people, families and schools. He also provides training in ACT and has a particular interest in ACT and value-based living within the workplace.

Dedication

To Helen with love; you make everything possible. **FJB**

To the love of my life, Josie, and our two beautiful sons, Will and Toby. **DG**

Authors' Acknowledgements

From Freddy: A great many people have helped me along the way in life and to all of you I am grateful. To my parents, siblings and friends, thank you for being there through it all. And to Helen and Louis, an extra big thank you for your love, patience and support as this book was written.

I'd like to thank my co-author, Duncan Gillard. Your intellectual curiosity and strength are a marvel, and writing this book with you has been a pleasure.

Professionally, many different people have left their mark on me and supported my development. As an undergraduate it was Professor Derek Blackman and Dr Mecca Chiesa who first opened my eyes to a behaviour analytic view of the world, and for that I will be forever in your debt.

From Duncan: A huge thanks to Josie for her fathomless, unwavering support and patience throughout the writing of this book. You are an inspiration to me, my love. And thanks to my mum and dad for supporting me with so many things — I wouldn't know where to start!

I'd also really like to thank my friend Barry Farrimond and his wonderful family: Jojo, Akira and Koan. Though you may not know it, the time spent with you in between writing chapters helped me push on toward the completion of the book. I am so lucky to have you all in my life.

And thanks to Freddy. Over the last decade or so, you've been my supervisor, my colleague, my co-author and — most importantly — my friend. You're always an inspiration and I look forward to more (yes more) exciting projects with you.

From both of us: We would like to thank the developers of ACT and Relational Frame Theory: Steve Hayes, Dermot Barnes-Holmes and Kelly Wilson. You have been a great inspiration to us both.

We would also like to thank the philosopher and psychologist, BF Skinner, whom neither of us ever met, but whose writings encouraged us into this profession in the first place. It might seem a little odd to thank someone who is no longer alive, but his work has played such a role in both of our lives, professionally and beyond, that to not acknowledge this seems just wrong. Apart from the intellectual depth of his work, it was his vision for a fairer, more open and sustainable human society that has been such an inspiration. It is these same values of care, love and compassion that we see at the heart of ACT.

Thanks to Ben Kemble, Iona Everson and Michelle Hacker at Wiley for commissioning, supporting and cajoling us through the process of writing this book. We'd also like to say thank you to our technical editor, Dr Nic Hooper. Finally, thanks to Joe Munro, our illustrator, for doing such a great job in so little time.

Publisher's Acknowledgements

Commissioning Editor: Annie Knight

Project Manager: Michelle Hacker

Development Editor: Kate O'Leary

Copy Editor: Kerry Laundon

Technical Editor: Dr Nic Hooper

Production Editor: Kumar Chellappan

Cover Photos: ©marekuliasz/Stutterstock

Illustrations: Joe Munro

Take Dummies with you everywhere you go!

Whether you're excited about e-books, want more from the web, must have your mobile apps, or swept up in social media, Dummies makes everything easier.

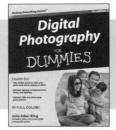

FOR DUMMIES®

A Wiley Brand

SELF-HELP

978-0-470-66541-1

978-1-119-99264-6

978-0-470-66086-7

LANGUAGES

978-0-470-68815-1

978-1-119-97959-3

978-0-470-69477-0

HISTORY

978-0-470-68792-5

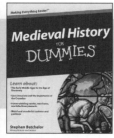

978-0-470-74783-4

978-0-470-97819-1

Laptops For Dummies 5th Edition
978-1-118-11533-6

Management For Dummies, 2nd Edition
978-0-470-97769-9

Nutrition For Dummies, 2nd Edition
978-0-470-97276-2

Office 2013 For Dummies
978-1-118-49715-9

Organic Gardening For Dummies
978-1-119-97706-3

Origami Kit For Dummies
978-0-470-75857-1

Overcoming Depression For Dummies
978-0-470-69430-5

Physics I For Dummies
978-0-470-90324-7

Project Management For Dummies
978-0-470-71119-4

Psychology Statistics For Dummies
978-1-119-95287-9

Renting Out Your Property For Dummies, 3rd Edition
978-1-119-97640-0

Rugby Union For Dummies, 3rd Edition
978-1-119-99092-5

Stargazing For Dummies
978-1-118-41156-8

Teaching English as a Foreign Language For Dummies
978-0-470-74576-2

Time Management For Dummies
978-0-470-77765-7

Training Your Brain For Dummies
978-0-470-97449-0

Voice and Speaking Skills For Dummies
978-1-119-94512-3

Wedding Planning For Dummies
978-1-118-69951-5

WordPress For Dummies, 5th Edition
978-1-118-38318-6

Think you can't learn it in a day? Think again!

The *In a Day* e-book series from *For Dummies* gives you quick and easy access to learn a new skill, brush up on a hobby, or enhance your personal or professional life — all in a day. Easy!

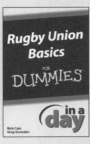

Available as PDF, eMobi and Kindle